# GR20 CORSICA

## THE HIGH LEVEL ROUTE

## About the Author

Paddy Dillon is a prolific walker and guidebook writer with over 90 guidebooks to his name, and contributions to 40 other titles. He has written extensively for many different outdoor publications and has appeared on radio and television.

Paddy uses a tablet computer to write his route descriptions while walking. His descriptions are therefore precise, having been written at the very point at which the reader uses them.

Paddy is an indefatigable long-distance walker who has walked all of Britain's National Trails and several major European trails. He lives on the fringes of the Lake District and has walked, and written about walking, in every county throughout the British Isles. He has led guided walks and walked throughout Europe, as well as in Nepal, Tibet, Korea, Africa and the Rocky Mountains of Canada and the US. Paddy is a member of the Outdoor Writers and Photographers Guild.

## Other Cicerone guides by the author

Glyndwr's Way
The Cleveland Way and the
   Yorkshire Wolds Way
The GR5 Trail
The Great Glen Way
The Irish Coast to Coast Walk
The Mountains of Ireland
The National Trails
The North York Moors
The Pennine Way
The Reivers Way
The South West Coast Path
The Teesdale Way
The Wales Coast Path
Trekking in Greenland
Trekking in Mallorca
Trekking in the Alps (contributing
   author)
Walking and Trekking in Iceland
Trekking through Mallorca

Walking in County Durham
Walking in Madeira
Walking in Mallorca (June Parker;
   updated by Paddy Dillon)
Walking in Menorca
Walking in Sardinia
Walking in the Isles of Scilly
Walking in the North Pennines
Walking on Guernsey
Walking on the Isle of Arran
Walking on Jersey
Walking on La Gomera and El
   Hierro
Walking on La Palma
Walking on Lanzarote and
   Fuerteventura
Walking on Malta
Walking on Tenerife
Walking the Galloway Hills

# GR20 CORSICA

## THE HIGH LEVEL ROUTE

### by Paddy Dillon

JUNIPER HOUSE, MURLEY MOSS,
OXENHOLME ROAD, KENDAL, CUMBRIA LA9 7RL
www.cicerone.co.uk

© Paddy Dillon 2016
Fourth edition 2016
ISBN: 978 1 85284 852 1
Reprinted 2018 (with updates)
Third edition 2014
Second edition 2012
First edition 2007

Printed in China on behalf of Latitude Press Ltd
A catalogue record for this book is available from the British Library.
All photographs are by the author unless otherwise stated.

 The routes of the GR®, PR® and GRP® paths in this guide
have been reproduced with the permission of the Fédération
Française de la Randonnée Pédestre holder of the exclusive
rights of the routes. The names GR®, PR® and GRP® are registered trademarks. ©
FFRP 2016 for all GR®, PR® and GRP® paths appearing in this work.

This guide includes the latest route changes, made in 2016, avoiding the
Cirque de la Solitude. The Cirque is no longer part of the GR20 and its
waymarks and safety aids have been removed. The route now crosses the
shoulder of Monte Cinto.

## Updates to this Guide

While every effort is made by our authors to ensure the accuracy of guidebooks as they go to print, changes can occur during the lifetime of an edition. Any updates that we know of for this guide will be on the Cicerone
website (www.cicerone.co.uk/852/updates), so please check before planning your trip. We also advise that you check information about such
things as transport, accommodation and shops locally. Even rights of way
can be altered over time. We are always grateful for information about any
discrepancies between a guidebook and the facts on the ground, sent by
email to updates@cicerone.co.uk or by post to Cicerone, Juniper House,
Murley Moss, Oxenholme Road, Kendal LA9 7Rl.

**Register your book:** To sign up to receive free updates, special offers
and GPX files where available, register your book at www.cicerone.co.uk.

*Front cover:* Descending from Bocca Crucetta (Stage 4)

# CONTENTS

# Mountain Safety

Every mountain walk has its dangers, and those described in this guidebook are no exception. All who walk or climb in the mountains should recognise this and take responsibility for themselves and their companions along the way. The author and publisher have made every effort to ensure that the information contained in this guide was correct when it went to press, but they cannot accept responsibility for any loss, injury or inconvenience sustained by any person using this book.

**International Distress Signal** *(emergency only)*
Six blasts on a whistle (and flashes with a torch after dark) spaced evenly for one minute, followed by a minute's pause. Repeat until an answer is received. The response is three signals per minute followed by a minute's pause.

**Helicopter Rescue**
The following signals are used to communicate with a helicopter:

Help needed:
raise both arms
above head to
form a 'Y'

Help not needed:
raise one arm
above head, extend
other arm downward

**Emergency telephone numbers**
General emergency, for all services, tel 112

Police (*Gendarmerie*) tel 17
Ambulance (*Samu*) tel 15
Fire Service (*Pompiers*) tel 18
Mountain Rescue (*PGHM – Peleton de Gendarmerie de Haute Montagne*) tel 04 95 61 13 95

**Weather reports**
(If telephoning from the UK the dialling code is 0033.)
Météo France, tel 08 99 71 02 20, www.meteofrance.com

**Note** Mountain rescue can be very expensive – be adequately insured.

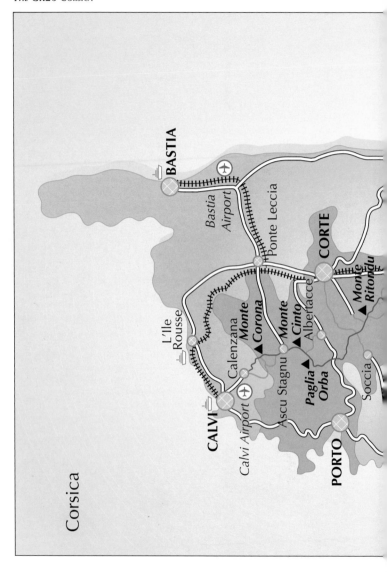

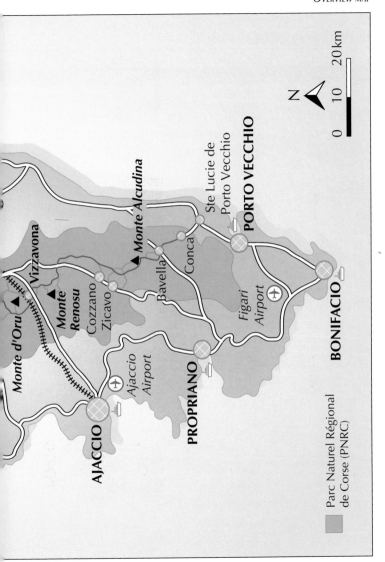

AJACCIO

PROPRIANO

BONIFACIO

PORTO VECCHIO

Monte d'Oru

Vizzavona

Monte Renosu

Monte Alcudina

Cozzano
Zicavo

Bavella

Conca

Ste Lucie de
Porto Vecchio

Ajaccio
Airport

Figari
Airport

Parc Naturel Régional
de Corse (PNRC)

N

0    10    20 km

# ROUTE SUMMARY TABLE

| Stage | Start | Finish |
|---|---|---|
| 1A (high-level) | Calenzana | Refuge d'Ortu di u Piobbu |
| 1B (low-level) | Calenzana | Refuge d'Ortu di u Piobbu |
| 2A (high-level) | Refuge d'Ortu di u Piobbu | Refuge de Carozzu |
| 2B (low-level) | Refuge d'Ortu di u Piobbu | Refuge de Carozzu |
| 3 | Refuge de Carozzu | Ascu Stagnu |
| 4 | Ascu Stagnu | Auberge U Vallone |
| 5 | Auberge U Vallone | Hôtel Castel di Vergio |
| 6 | Hôtel Castel di Vergio | Refuge de Manganu |
| 7 | Refuge de Manganu | Refuge de Petra Piana |
| 8A (low-level) | Refuge de Petra Piana | Refuge de l'Onda |
| 8B (high-level) | Refuge de Petra Piana | Refuge de l'Onda |
| 9A (low-level) | Refuge de l'Onda | Vizzavona |
| 9B (high-level) | Refuge de l'Onda | Vizzavona |
| 10 | Vizzavona | Bergeries d' E Capanelle |
| 11A (low-level) | Bergeries d' E Capanelle | Bocca di Verdi |
| 11B (high-level) | Bergeries d' E Capanelle | Bocca di Verdi |
| 12 | Bocca di Verdi | Refuge d'Usciolu |
| 13 | Refuge d'Usciolu | Refuge de Matalza |
| 14 | Refuge to Matalza | Refuge d'Asinau |
| Alternative 13/14 | Refuge d'Usciolu | Refuge d'Asinau |
| 15A (low-level) | Refuge d'Asinau | Village de Bavella |
| 15B (high-level) | Refuge d'Asinau | Village de Bavella |
| 16 | Village de Bavella | Conca |

| Distance | Total ascent | Total descent | Time | Page |
|---|---|---|---|---|
| 12km (7½ miles) | 1550m (5085ft) | 235m (770ft) | 7hrs | 48 |
| 20km (12½ miles) | 1610m (5280ft) | 295m (970ft) | 7hrs 45mins | 56 |
| 8km (5 miles) | 750m (2460ft) | 1050m (3445ft) | 6hrs 30mins | 67 |
| 12km (7½ miles) | 660m (2165ft) | 960m (3150ft) | 4hrs 30mins | 73 |
| 6km (3¾ miles) | 860m (2280ft) | 710m (2330ft) | 5hrs 30mins | 78 |
| 9km (5½ miles) | 1250m (4100ft) | 1230m (4035ft) | 8hrs | 84 |
| 15km (9½ miles) | 850m (2790ft) | 870m (2855ft) | 6hrs | 96 |
| 17km (10½ miles) | 670m (2200ft) | 475m (1560ft) | 5hrs 45mins | 106 |
| 10km (6 miles) | 980m (3220ft) | 740m (2430ft) | 7hrs | 123 |
| 11km (6¾ miles) | 500m (1640ft) | 910m (2985ft) | 5hrs | 137 |
| 8km (5 miles) | 390m (1280ft) | 800m (2625ft) | 4hrs 15mins | 142 |
| 11km (6¾ miles) | 670m (2200ft) | 1180m (3870ft) | 6hrs | 150 |
| 13km (8 miles) | 990m (3250ft) | 1500m (4920ft) | 7hrs 30mins | 155 |
| 16km (10 miles) | 1000m (3280ft) | 335m (1100ft) | 5hrs 30mins | 163 |
| 14km (8¾ miles) | 320m (1050ft) | 620m (2035ft) | 4hrs 30mins | 171 |
| 16km (10 miles) | 815m (2675ft) | 1110m (3640ft) | 7hrs 15mins | 177 |
| 16km (10 miles) | 1290m (4230ft) | 830m (2725ft) | 7hrs 15mins | 183 |
| 12km (7½ miles) | 340m (1115ft) | 640m (2100ft) | 4hrs 30mins | 194 |
| 11km (7 miles) | 665m (2180ft) | 545m (1790ft) | 4hrs 15mins | 208 |
| 17km (10½ miles) | 1010m (3315ft) | 1225m (4020ft) | 7hrs 15mins | 214 |
| 11km (6¾ miles) | 380m (1250ft) | 695m (2280ft) | 4hrs 45mins | 221 |
| 8km (5 miles) | 550m (1805ft) | 865m (2840ft) | 4hrs 15mins | 227 |
| 19km (12 miles) | 700m (2295ft) | 1670m (5480ft) | 7hrs | 233 |

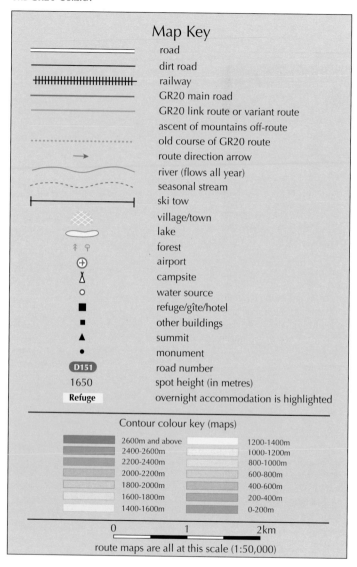

## Map Key

| | |
|---|---|
| | road |
| | dirt road |
| | railway |
| | GR20 main road |
| | GR20 link route or variant route |
| | ascent of mountains off-route |
| | old course of GR20 route |
| → | route direction arrow |
| | river (flows all year) |
| | seasonal stream |
| | ski tow |
| | village/town |
| | lake |
| | forest |
| ⊕ | airport |
| ⋀ | campsite |
| ○ | water source |
| ■ | refuge/gîte/hotel |
| ▪ | other buildings |
| ▲ | summit |
| ● | monument |
| D151 | road number |
| 1650 | spot height (in metres) |
| Refuge | overnight accommodation is highlighted |

### Contour colour key (maps)

| | | | |
|---|---|---|---|
| | 2600m and above | | 1200-1400m |
| | 2400-2600m | | 1000-1200m |
| | 2200-2400m | | 800-1000m |
| | 2000-2200m | | 600-800m |
| | 1800-2000m | | 400-600m |
| | 1600-1800m | | 200-400m |
| | 1400-1600m | | 0-200m |

0      1      2km

route maps are all at this scale (1:50,000)

# INTRODUCTION

Tents for hire, dotted around the Bergeries de Vaccaghja (Stage 6)

There is no doubt that the GR20, traversing the rugged mountains of Corsica, is one of the top trails of the world. Its reputation precedes it, and most who trek the route describe it afterwards as one of the toughest they have ever completed. Others find they are unable to complete it, having seriously underestimated its nature. The GR20 climbs high into the mountains and stays there for days on end, leading ordinary trekkers deep into the sort of terrain usually visited only by mountaineers. The scenery is awe-inspiring, with bare rock and sheer cliffs in some parts, contrasting with forests, lakes and alpine pastures in other places. Those who walk the route are only too eager to share their experiences with those who haven't, so that everyone who completes the GR20 is probably responsible for two or three more people trekking it. It has been estimated that as many as 30,000 people trek the route each year!

Most people would relish the opportunity to trek through wild mountains, feeling the roughness of the rocks with their fingers, enjoying the clarity of the views under a blazing Mediterranean sun, maybe enlivened with streaks of snow on the higher slopes. There is the perfumed scent of the *maquis*, and the chance to spot eagles in flight. You can do all this, provided you keep an eye on the weather, since Corsica is noted for severe summer thunderstorms, while in winter the mountains are truly alpine. There is the prospect of sleeping in rustic refuges, or even better, sleeping under canvas, peeping out to discover the mountains bathed in moonlight. On moonless nights, you can gaze awe-struck at the firmament speckled with millions of pinprick stars. You can enjoy all this and more provided you make careful plans and walk within your limits.

The GR20 is an experience, more than simply a trek, and those who try and rush the route may find they finish with certain regrets. While the 'classic' route can be covered in a fortnight, discerning trekkers will be happy to include variations – maybe climbing some of the nearby mountains, or visiting nearby villages. The main route allows little opportunity to meet ordinary Corsicans, but a detour into a village, or better still, a night or two spent with a Corsican family, will enhance the quality of the trek. Take the time to sample local foodstuffs, including the meat and cheese produced in the mountains, maybe washed down with a homemade wine, but always be aware of where your next fill up of water is available. Corsican food is generally simple and wholesome – ideal for a trek through the mountains, and all part of the joy of travel!

## GEOLOGY

Corsica is often referred to as 'the Granite Isle', and it is easy to dismiss the whole island simply as one enormous granite massif, but this would be wrong. Corsica is geologically divided into two parts by a line running very roughly from Île Rousse on the north coast, through Corte in the middle of the island, to Favone on the east coast.

Everything west of this line is referred to as 'Hercynian Corsica', named after a mountain-building era that occurred between 345 and 225 million years ago. The bedrock in this, the greater part of Corsica, is essentially a massive granite intrusion. It was pushed into the Earth's crust under immense pressure and temperature, so that the rock was in a molten state. As it cooled over a long period of time, coarse crystals formed, chiefly of quartz, feldspar and mica. Geologists sub-divide the granite according to its mineral composition, which varies from place to place, especially around the northwest of the island. Granophyres and quartz porphyries are common, and conspicuous linear dykes have been intruded into some rocks. The mountains that were raised during the Hercynian era are long gone, and the granite mountains of Corsica are merely their deepest roots.

Everything east of the dividing line is referred to as 'Alpine Corsica', simply because the rock types were pushed up during the later era of mountain building that was associated with the creation of the Alps. There are several rock types, including schists of uncertain age that have been folded and metamorphosed time and again. There are also layers of limestone and sedimentary rocks that were formed on the seabed, before buckling under immense pressure to form mountains. Fossils contained in these rocks reveal that they were formed in the Upper Carboniferous,

Liassic and Eocene periods – with respective ages from around 300, 150 and 50 million years ago.

The Ice Age, which ended only around 10,000 years ago, had a profound effect on the mountains of Corsica. The mountains were high enough to ensure that snow never melted from year to year, but increased in depth so that glaciers could form, grinding out deep corries and carving steep-sided valleys into the mountainsides. During a much wetter period than at present, powerful rivers scoured the valleys deeper, and spread fans of alluvial rubble further downstream, and around the coast. During harsh winters in the mountains, conditions are again reminiscent of the Ice Age, when the high corrie lakes freeze completely and deep snowdrifts are heaped up against the cliffs. By the time Man discovered Corsica, the island valleys were well wooded, although parts of the coast and the high mountains were bare rock, much as they are today.

Those who trek the GR20 may feel that they are completely bypassing anything of historical interest on Corsica. Transhumance, the seasonal movement of livestock to summer pastures in the mountains, followed by a retreat to the low ground before the onset of winter, has been practised in Corsica for thousands of years. The island has been invaded dozens of times by all kinds of armies, and native Corsicans have often fought to resist each successive attempt at colonisation. However, high in the mountains, there are few ancient monuments or proud fortifications, nor are there any museums to visit. The GR20 is essentially a tough mountain trek almost completely divorced from the history and culture of the island. History, by and large, was wrought elsewhere on the island, and the best you can do is at least be aware of some of the key events and turbulent times that Corsica has experienced.

| | |
|---|---|
| 7000BC | The first human settlers probably reached Corsica from Tuscany during the Palaeolithic era. They were hunter/gatherers who lived in caves and other natural shelters, using only basic stone tools and items of pottery. |
| 6600BC | 'Bonifacio Woman', a Neolithic woman whose skeleton was discovered near Bonifacio, is the earliest human being discovered on Corsica. Soon afterwards, people began the tradition of transhumance, involving the seasonal movement of animals to summer pastures in the mountains, retreating to the coast and lower valleys in the winter. As semi-nomads, shepherds and herdsmen built themselves temporary shelters. |
| 4000BC | The climax of the Megalithic era, during which huge stone monuments, menhirs and dolmens, were raised around the island. Human society was clearly well organised to enable people to build such structures, and the period of construction spanned several centuries. |

15

| | |
|---|---|
| **1500**BC | Invaders known as the Toréens, named after the stone towers they erected, landed at Porto Vecchio and gradually spread through Corsica. The earlier inhabitants, however, continued to raise their own stone monuments even into the Iron Age. |
| **565**BC | Greek refugees from Phocaea established a colony at Alalia, where Aléria now stands. They were traders who planted olives and vines, but were troubled by attacking Carthaginians and Etruscans. |
| **535**BC | The Greeks abandoned their colony, and the Etruscans who occupied the site were later displaced by the Carthaginians. |
| **259**BC | Roman soldiers were sent to Corsica to prevent the Carthaginians advancing through the Mediterranean. Native Corsicans joined forces with the Carthaginians to hold the Romans at bay, so the Roman conquest took 40 years to subdue the island. Roman power remained dominant for over 500 years, and while ports were constructed, little change took place in the interior. The Roman strategy was essentially to prevent any other power from occupying the island, which was conveniently close to Rome. |
| **303**AD | Christianity had been brought to Corsica, and the beheading of Santa Restituda gave the island its first Christian martyr. As the Roman empire began to wane, Vandals began to raid coastal settlements and were well established on the island in the middle of the 5th century. |
| **534**AD | Byzantine forces launched an invasion of Corsica and made it part of their empire. However, they in turn suffered a series of raids, notably from the Ostrogoths, and later from the Lombards. |
| **725**AD | The Lombards took control of Corsica, but by this time the Saracens were sending raiding parties to the island, harrying coastal settlements. |
| **754**AD | Pépin le Bref, King of the Franks, offered to give Corsica to the Pope after freeing it from Lombard control. The process took 20 years, and it was Pépin's son, Charlemagne, who finally handed the island to the Pope. However, the Saracens continued raiding the island and at times almost completely overran it. |
| **825**AD | Ugo della Colonna is reputed to have driven the Saracens from Corsica at the request of the Pope, but tales are legendary and it is difficult to separate the man from the myth. Seigneurial families, who were split by long-standing rivalries, dominated life on the island. The feudal system ensured that common folk were treated quite harshly, leading to some internal conflicts. |
| **1077** | The Pope appointed the Bishop of Pisa to administer Corsica, and for a time the island enjoyed a period of peace. |
| **1133** | The Genoese, who were rivals to the Pisans, successfully lobbied the Pope for a share of Corsica, and the island was divided between Pisa and Genoa. The Genoese gradually undermined Pisan control on the island. |

| | |
|---|---|
| **1284** | The Genoese finally defeated the Pisans at the Battle of Meloria, and began to erect considerable fortifications around Corsica. Resentment was rife, as many Corsicans were simply evicted from their properties and forced into servitude. The Pope handed Corsica and Sardinia to the Aragonese, but the Genoese refused to relinquish control, setting the scene for decades of conflict. |
| **1420** | An Aragonese force managed to take control of most of Corsica and a Viceroy ruled the island until 1434, when the Genoese beheaded him. |
| **1453** | The Genoese appointed a powerful financial body, the Office de St Georges, to administer Corsica. They installed a military regime, strengthened fortifications around the island, developed agriculture and raised taxes. |
| **1553** | Corsica was invaded by French troops, in which a colonel called Sampiero Corso, also known as 'The Fiery', and 'the Most Corsican of Corsicans', scored notable victories over the Genoese. Although Corsica was regarded then as a French possession, it was handed back to the Genoese under the Treaty of Cateau-Cambrésis. Sampiero Corso made another bid at conquest in 1564, but this was ultimately unsuccessful. The Genoese remained troubled by Saracen raids and therefore further strengthened the fortifications around the island. The lot of common Corsicans remained dire. |
| **1730** | When an old man refused to pay his taxes, increasing numbers of Corsicans joined him in refusing to pay theirs also, and this led to a rebellion against Genoese rule. In 1732, Austrian soldiers were dispatched to the island to restore order, and were soundly defeated at the Battle of Calenzana. The Genoese, however, quickly and brutally regained control. |
| **1736** | Obviously in need of a leader, many Corsicans flocked to support a German adventurer called Théodore de Neuhoff, who was proclaimed Théodore I, King of Corsica. Although he promised military support against the Genoese, it was not forthcoming, and Corsicans had to struggle on by themselves against their brutal colonisers. |
| **1738** | The Genoese accepted an offer of military assistance from the French. By 1741, the French considered that they had put down the rebellion and departed, only to return when trouble flared up again in 1748. |
| **1754** | Pascal Paoli, one of the most famous names in Corsican history, led a rebellion that briefly allowed a Corsican state to be established from 1755 to 1769, with its centre of control in the mountain citadel of Corte. Democracy, education and justice were central to Paoli's administration, but the Genoese again looked to France to regain control over the island. In the event, the French ended up taking control of Corsica away from both the Genoese and native Corsicans. |
| **1769** | The beginning of French rule in Corsica was followed closely by the French Revolution, which was wholeheartedly supported by Corsicans. Pascal Paoli enjoyed a brief period of favour with the French, and when he lost their favour, Corsicans proclaimed him 'Father of the Nation'. |

| | |
|---|---|
| 1794 | A British force attacked Calvi, where Nelson lost his eye, and an Anglo–Corsican state was proclaimed. Sir Gilbert Elliot was installed as viceroy, angering supporters of Paoli. Some Paoli supporters later joined forces with the French, so that the British eventually departed from Corsica. |
| 1796 | French rule was restored on the island, but there was widespread discontent, even though a famous son of Corsica, Napoleon Bonaparte, was crowned Emperor in 1804. It seems that Napoleon did little for his native island, and prevented native Corsicans from taking positions of control. |
| 1801 | Corsica found itself under military rule under General Morand, followed in 1811 by General César Berthier. |
| 1814 | British soldiers responded to an appeal from the inhabitants of Bastia, but were quickly withdrawn from Corsica following the abdication of Napoleon. |
| 1815 | Corsica's establishments and infrastructure were improved, with the construction of roads and a railway, schools and industry, but this did little to stem massive emigration from the island. In fact, Corsica's population was halved, and the island had a reputation as a place of crime and violence. |
| 1909 | A plan was proposed for the development of Corsica, but this suffered a setback due to the First World War. Thousands of Corsican soldiers enlisted in the army and died in battle, cutting further into the island's population. |
| 1940 | Mussolini had been interested in Corsica for some time, before helping to land some 90,000 Fascist and Nazi troops on the island. Many Corsicans waged a guerrilla war on the occupiers, coining the term 'Maquis' for the Resistance, after the impenetrable scrub covering much of the island. The Allies armed the guerrillas by dropping caches of weapons in remote parts on the island. At the end of the war, the Americans sprayed DDT on the island to rid it of malaria-carrying mosquitoes that had affected it for thousands of years. |
| 1962 | The 'events in Aléria', as they came to be known, started with *pieds-noirs* Algerians and a scandal in wine-making processes, and ended with a militant Corsican sit-in and the deaths of two policemen. Discontent had been brewing for some time around the island, and indeed, had its roots in centuries of domination and oppression. Corsican nationalism took on many forms, from street protests and political posturing, to crime and assassination, with bombing campaigns throughout the 1970s. Calls for autonomy have at least resulted in the Collectivité Territoriale de Corse having a distinct language and culture of its own, and a greater control over its affairs than any other region of France. |
| 1970 | Under the direction of Michel Fabrikant, surveys were made to determine the course of a mountainous route that would become the GR20. |

| 1972 | The Parc Naturel Régional de Corse (PNRC) was established, covering most of the high mountains and almost 40% of the island. The first refuges were established along the GR20. |
|------|------|
| 2001 | The French government gave Corsica limited autonomy, but this was later declared to be unconstitutional and was withdrawn. |
| 2003 | A plan for greater Corsican autonomy was put to the vote in a referendum, but was narrowly defeated by 51% to 49%. |
| 2013 | The Tour de France started in Corsica for the first time in its history. |
| 2014 | The GR20 was run non-stop in a record 32 hours by Guillaume Peretti. |
| 2015 | A landslide in the Cirque de la Solitude killed seven trekkers and resulted in the closure of that part of the route. |
| 2016 | All aids, including markers, were removed from the Cirque de la Solitude. The GR20 route now passes over the shoulder of Monte Cinto. |

A turbulent history indeed, and one that is set to run and run. It is a great pity that trekkers on the GR20 will barely be aware of any of it!

## GETTING TO CORSICA

Corsica can be reached by regular flights or ferries, while more adventurous travellers might consider an overland approach through Europe using long-distance trains or coaches. Getting to Corsica is considerably easier than getting around Corsica, so choose an entry point that has good connections with the GR20, and ensure that on completion of the trek, it will be possible to reach your exit point in good time. It is wise to build a couple of extra days into your itinerary in case of any ferry or flight delays, or in case inclement weather or fatigue cause alterations to your original carefully planned trekking schedule.

See Appendix E, Useful contacts, for a list of overland and air transport operators.

### By air

By far the easiest way to reach Corsica is to fly, and there are four airports on the island – Bastia www.bastia.aeroport.fr, Calvi www.calvi.aeroport.fr, Ajaccio www.2a.cci.fr/Aeroport-Napoleon-Bonaparte-Ajaccio.html, and Figari www.2a.cci.fr/Aeroport-Figari-Sud-Corse.html. All four airports are served by Air France www.airfrance.com and Air Corsica www.aircorsica.com, from mainland France, while Air Corsica also offer flights from London Stanstead. Other airlines with direct services from Britain to Corsica are available. Easyjet, www.easyjet.com, flies from London Gatwick to Bastia, Ajaccio and Figari, as well as from Manchester to Bastia. Flybe,

*Looking to the jagged peaks beside the Bocca a e Porte from the rocky shore of Lac de Capitellu (Link from Bocca a Soglia to Bergeries de Grotelle)*

www.flybe.com, flies from Birmingham and Southampton to Bastia. Charter flights are also available. A number of airlines fly direct to Corsica from a handful of European countries. Ryanair, www.ryanair.com, flies from France. Lufthansa, www.lufthansa.com, Germanwings, www.germanwings.com, and Air Berlin, www.airberlin.com, fly from Germany. When choosing a flight, it might be tempting to land at Calvi, because it is close to the start of the GR20 at Calenzana, but returning to Calvi from Conca takes a long time.

## By road and rail

Those travelling overland through France by car, coach or train will find that ports such as Nice or Marseille

provide the most straightforward ferry connections to Corsica. Check with Eurolines, www.eurolines.com, or Eurostar, www.eurostar.com, to find good coach or rail connections to the ports. Travelling overland to Nice or Marseille to catch an onward Air Corsica, www.aircorsica.com, flight to Corsica could also be considered.

## By sea

Ferries from ports such as Nice and Marseille serve the four main Corsican ports of Ajaccio, Bastia, Calvi and Porto Vecchio, but some ferries serve Île Rousse and Propriano. There are also ferries to Corsica from other ports in France and Italy. When linking overland travel with ferry timetables, be sure to check schedules and timetables carefully, with due regard to check-in times, to ensure a smooth transfer. The main ferry operators are Corsica Linea, www.corsicalinea.com, La Meridionale, www.lameridionale.fr, Moby Lines, www.mobylines.fr, and Corsica Ferries, www.corsica-ferries.fr.

## Taking or hiring a car

Taking a car to Corsica is not a particularly good idea, except for back-up purposes, and even then its use will be limited. Apart from the beginning and end of the GR20, the route is accessible at only seven other points for vehicles. Trekkers would take time to reach all those points, while the back-up driver would need to pursue other interests for the days between each meeting point. Cars can be hired at the airports and ferryports.

## GETTING AROUND CORSICA

### By train

Travel by train is remarkably simple. There is in effect one line between Ajaccio and Bastia, with a branch line running to Calvi. The junction is at Ponte Leccia, and the railway crosses the course of the GR20 at its midpoint at Vizzavona. The line is operated by Chemins de Fer de La Corse, www. cf-corse.fr. There is no harm picking up a timetable whether you plan to use the railway or not. Stations can be contacted as follows: Ajaccio 04 95 23 11 03, Bastia 04 95 32 80 61, Calvi 04 95 65 00 61, Corte 04 95 46 00 97, and Île Rousse 04 95 60 00 50.

Bear in mind that one timetable covers the peak summer period, while other timetables flank it, and yet another covers the winter period. Check the dates that timetables are valid, as they could change during the course of a trek along the GR20. On a daily basis, most trains operate from Monday to Friday, with variations on Saturday, and very few services on Sunday. Some small country halts are request stops, so use a hand signal to stop a train, or if already on the train, tell the conductor in good time to stop.

### By bus

If travelling by bus, it is essential to check and double-check timetables.

There are several bus operators, but some services operate only run in July and August, and there is no central authority issuing information. A useful website is www.corsicabus.org, which attempts to gather all services and timetables into a single place.

When you wish to catch a bus, be sure to turn up early and ask someone *exactly* where the departure point for the bus is located, as bus stops are rare. Bear in mind that some buses look very plain, and it may not be immediately obvious that they are being used for public transport. Most coaches are comfortable and air-conditioned, but some services are operated using more basic minibuses.

Buses usually leave on time, but delays are commonplace, so beware if you are trying to achieve a fairly tight connection somewhere along the way. Individual bus services and contact details are mentioned as appropriate throughout this guidebook. Some short shuttle-bus services are referred to as *navettes*, and this term is also used for complimentary transport offered by accommodation providers.

### By taxi

Taxis are available at all the airports and ports, in all the main towns, and in many villages and rural locations. The telephone numbers of certain taxi companies and individuals are given throughout this guidebook, since they may offer the only chance to reach or leave some of the places along or near the GR20. Fares may be metered or fixed, although you may be able to agree a price. Most drivers charge extra in the evenings and on Sundays, and there may be a small charge for your baggage too.

For short journeys, when you want to keep moving, a taxi is good value, but for a long transfer round the island, it will be very, very expensive. Bear in mind that on a long journey, you may have to contribute towards the driver's long journey home. A general rule of thumb is that a long taxi journey will cost ten times more than the bus fare.

## GETTING TO THE GR20

### From Calvi

Simply leave the airport and grab the first available taxi. Ask to be taken to Calenzana. One look at your pack and the driver will guess you are heading for the GR20. He may refer to the route with a word that sounds like *jairvan* – get used to the sound! If you have already arranged accommodation in Calenzana, leave it to the driver to take you there. The telephone numbers of some of the taxi drivers are given in the section about Calenzana.

If reaching Calvi by ferry, either take a taxi to Calenzana, or wait for the once-a-day bus in July and August, operated by Beaux Voyages, tel 04 95 65 11 35 or 04 95 65 08 26, www.corsicar.com. This bus only operates on schooldays for the rest of the year. Buses, taxis and trains all operate close to the Place de la Porteuse d'Eau, which is near the railway station in Calvi and only a short walk from the

Calvi has an airport and a ferryport close to the northern end of the GR20

port. If only trekking half of the GR20, north or south from Vizzavona, then it is easy to catch the train, tel Calvi 04 95 65 00 61, www.cf-corse.fr. Calvi tourist information office is nearby at Port de Plaisance, tel 04 95 65 16 67, www.portail-corse-balagne.fr.

### From Bastia
There are daily buses between the airport and Bastia, operated by the Société des Autobus Bastiais, tel 04 95 31 06 65, www.bastiabus. com. Alternatively, use Les Taxis de l'Aéroport, tel 04 95 36 04 65, www. corsica-taxis.com. Buses from Bastia to Calvi run daily from late June to early September, then weekdays for the rest of the year, and are operated by Beaux Voyages, tel 04 95 65 11 35 or 04 95 65 08 26, www. corsicar.com. Use Les Rapides Bleus Corsicatours, tel 04 95 31 03 79, www.rapides-bleus.com, to reach Ste Lucie de Porto Vecchio for Conca, if trekking the GR20 south to north. Buses run daily from mid-June to mid-September, but not on Sundays for the rest of the year. In July and August the bus also serves Bastia airport.

Trains run daily from Bastia to Calvi, Vizzavona and Ajaccio, tel Bastia 04 95 32 80 61, www.cf-corse. fr. A short taxi ride from the airport to nearby Casamozza might allow you to catch a bus or train that has already departed south from Bastia. If arriving by ferry to Bastia, a short walk straight inland from the ferry terminal leads to the bus terminus, behind the *mairie*,

and railway station. Bastia tourist information office is on the Place St Nicolas, tel 04 95 54 20 40, www. bastia-tourisme.com.

### From Ajaccio
There are daily buses between the airport and Ajaccio, operated by TCA, tel 04 95 23 29 41, http://capa-bus-tca. locbus.fr. Alternatively, use a taxi to get into town – there are several operators to choose from. Those arriving by ferry berth at the Gare Routière, which is a combined ferry and bus terminal. There are no direct buses from Ajaccio to Calvi or Bastia, so it may be best to catch a train, tel Ajaccio 04 95 23 11 03, www.cf-corse.fr. The railway station is only a few minutes' walk along the Quai l'Herminier.

Buses serve places on the southern half of the GR20. Use Autocars Santoni, tel 04 95 22 64 44 or 04 95 24 51 56, to reach Zicavo and Cozzano, daily in July and August, but not on Sundays through the rest of the year. Use Autocars Balesi Evasion, tel 04 95 70 15 55, www.balesievasion.com, to reach Bavella and Porto Vecchio, daily through July and August, then only on Monday and Friday through the rest of the year. Use Ricci Marcel Transports, tel 04 95 78 86 30, www. transports-voyageurs-ajaccio.fr, to reach Bavella, daily through July and August. Use Eurocorse Voyages, tel 04 95 21 06 30, www.eurocorse.com, to reach Porto Vecchio for onward travel to Conca, if trekking south to north, Monday to Saturday from July to mid-September. Ajaccio tourist information office is on Boulevard Roi Jérôme, tel 04 95 51 53 03, www.ajaccio-tourisme.com.

### From Figari or Porto Vecchio

Those who arrive at Figari airport can catch the airport bus, operated by Transports Rossi, tel 04 95 71 00 11, or use a taxi, tel 06 17 77 37 96, to reach Porto Vecchio. If arriving by ferry, it is a simple matter to walk into Porto Vecchio to catch a bus. Use Les Rapides Bleus Corsicatours, tel 04 95 20 20 20, www.rapides-bleus. com, to cover the distance from Porto Vecchio to Ste Lucie de Porto Vecchio, if heading for Conca to trek the GR20 from south to north. (To reach Conca, contact the Gîte de La Tonnelle, tel 04 95 71 46 55, www.gite-la-tonnelle.com, which operates a *navette* between Ste Lucie and Conca.) Stay on the bus to Bastia for onward connections by bus or train. Use Autocars Balesi Evasion, tel 04 95 70 15 55, www.balesievasion. com, to reach Bavella and Ajaccio, daily through July and August, then only on Monday and Friday through the rest of the year. Use Eurocorse Voyages, tel 04 95 21 06 30, www.eurocorse.com, to reach Ajaccio for onward connections by bus or train, Monday to Saturday from July to mid-September. Porto Vecchio tourist information office is on the Rue Général Leclerc, tel 04 95 70 09 58, www.ot-portovecchio.com.

### To and from the GR20

A handful of roads cross the GR20, and some of them offer transport links. Contact numbers for trains, buses and taxis are given at appropriate points along the course of the GR20 in this guidebook. Some nearby villages may also offer transport links, and where these are available they are noted in the guidebook. Note that there are very few buses running on Sundays, so check timetables carefully or contact the operators to confirm times and pick-up points.

## WHEN TO TREK

### May

Trekking the GR20 is not recommended until at least the beginning of June, although it is sometimes possible to start in the middle of May. Last minute travel arrangements can be made if you hear that the route is clear of snow, but those who plan well in advance are taking a big chance, and deep snow could affect the higher parts of the route. The presence of snow and ice on particular parts of the route is usually mentioned on the PNRC blog, randoblogpnrc. blogspot.co.uk. An ice axe and crampons might be required, as well as the skills to use them properly.

Trekking at this time means that the PNRC refuges, although open, will not be staffed and therefore will have no food supplies. The water supply may be disconnected and there may

*The picture on the left was taken towards the end of May and the GR20, up the gully, is heavily covered in snow; the one on the right was taken towards the end of July and the snow has gone*

be no fuel on the premises. Private *bergeries* may be locked and bolted. It will be necessary to carry most of your food, or it may be necessary to leave the route to obtain supplies. Bus services to and from the route will be fairly limited.

**June**

The PNRC refuges and private bergeries will all be fully staffed and in full operation. This used to be a quiet time to trek, but in recent years it has become very busy. The refuges will often be fully booked, and any hire tents pitched nearby might also be fully booked. Food supplies and cooked meals will be available at almost every overnight stop.

Bear in mind that some snow and ice will still be lurking in some of the more sunless gullies, and could pose problems early in the month. Days will be warm, but not too hot. Some bus services to and from the route might not be fully operational.

**July and August**

These are the peak summer months on the GR20. Expect large numbers of trekkers and expect the refuges and hire tents to be fully booked. All services are in full swing and it is easy to obtain food and drink along the way. Bear in mind that a few seasonal water sources dry up. Should it be necessary to leave or join the route at any point, the full range of summer bus services will be available.

This is also the hottest time of the year, with an increasing risk of afternoon thunderstorms. There have been devastating forest fires in the past around this time, closing parts of the route to trekkers.

## September

This used to be a quiet time of year, when the numbers of trekkers reduced, but in recent years it has remained quite busy. The refuges will probably be fully booked, as may the hire tents, but as the month progresses it might be possible to stay indoors without an advance booking. Some of the bergeries offering food and drink may close, and some of the bus services to and from the route will be withdrawn. It is usual for the PNRC refuges to remain fully staffed and supplied with food to the end of the month.

The days are cooler than the peak summer season, but remain warm and clear. After June, this is the best month to trek.

## October

The PNRC refuges remain open, but at some point they will be unstaffed, with no food supplies. While fuel might be available, it is best not to rely on it, and the water supply might be disconnected to avoid frost damage. Private bergeries will be locked and bolted, and any small food stores along the route will probably be closed, so it will be necessary to carry

food, or leave the route at intervals to obtain supplies. Very few bus services will be available, although the train through Vizzavona continues running.

Those who start the GR20 at the beginning of the month and aim to complete it by the middle of the month will experience cold nights and possibly frosts. After mid-October, snow could fall at any time. Snow obscures paths and waymarks, and when it accumulates on steep slopes, there is immediately a risk of avalanche. For ordinary trekkers, the route is closed throughout the winter, although ski-traverses are sometimes achieved.

### HOW TO TREK

## The main route

The most straightforward way to trek the GR20 is north to south, on the main red/white flashed waymarked trail from Calenzana to Conca, taking about two weeks to cover the distance. Be sure to build in a couple of spare days just in case they are needed. Note that whenever alternative routes are presented in this guide, the 'A' route is the main, or classic, route of the GR20.

## GR20 nord

It is possible to trek the northern section of the trail from Calenzana to Vizzavona in just over a week, maybe nine or ten days, and experience the most rugged highlights of the route. For those who are confident of their abilities, this is worth considering if time is limited.

### GR20 sud

Those who are wary of the level of difficulty involved on the higher parts could sample a week on the southern section from Vizzavona to Conca and reserve judgement on the northern section. This stretch also has its tough moments from time to time, so be warned!

### South to north

Although most people trek the GR20 from north to south, experiencing the toughest sections first, it is also possible to trek from south to north, thereby gradually building up to the most rugged and spectacular parts of the route. An increasing number of trekkers now cover part of the GR20, or all of it, in this direction.

### Alternatives

Note that there are sometimes high- and low-level alternatives along the way. This provides trekkers with a choice of route. Sometimes the main route is the low-level one, and sometimes the high-level route can be a bit easier than the low-level route. Alternative routes are fully described in this guidebook in exactly the same

*Those who follow only the classic course of the GR20 often regret not visiting villages or climbing mountains. This is the summit of Monte Renosu (Stage 11, high-level)*

detail as the main route. Note that whenever alternative routes are presented in this guide, the 'A' route is the main route and the 'B' route is the variant.

### Links

Trekkers who complete the whole of the GR20 sometimes regret that they didn't visit some of the villages off-route. This guidebook includes off-route links with a handful of villages, so that at least a little Corsican culture can be enjoyed. These links also allow trekkers to leave the route if time is limited, with onward transport services mentioned.

### Mountains

The hardiest enthusiasts could trek the whole of the GR20 and include a

handful of mountain peaks along the way. Some of the prominent peaks close to the route can be climbed with a little scrambling. Those trekking the GR20 and climbing a few extra peaks should allow about three weeks. Details of the more popular extra ascents are given in this guidebook, including some of the highest mountains in Corsica.

### Guided walking holidays

A number of companies offer guided treks along the GR20. Approach them with caution, as some operators require you to carry all your kit along the trail. Others may offer baggage transfers, but they may also require you to stay at places far off-route, missing some fine stretches of the GR20. In the north, some operators omit the high-level stages between Calenzana and the Refuge de Carozzu, passing through Bonifatu instead. At the southern end, they may not start and finish at Conca, but at Bavella. If you want to trek the full, classic GR20 as an organised trek, then be sure to question operators carefully to ensure that they are offering the sort of arrangements you really want.

### MAPS

The route of the GR20 is well marked throughout. While walking without maps can never be recommended, it is true to say that the waymarking is so good that trekkers might never need to refer to a map for directions.

However, this would mean walking in complete isolation from the surroundings, never knowing the names of nearby mountains and valleys, never knowing in advance the shape of the terrain, and never knowing of other route options. To walk without a map is to walk with no real knowledge of your surroundings.

The best maps of the route are produced by the IGN (Institut Géographique National) at a scale of 1:25,000. These maps have blue covers and belong to a series known as Top 25. Order these in advance of your visit from map suppliers such as Stanfords (12–14 Long Acre, London WC2E 9BR, tel 0207 836 1321), The Map Shop (15 High Street, Upton-upon-Severn WR8 0HJ, tel 01684 593146) or Cordee (3a De Montford Street, Leicester LE1 7HD, tel 0116 254 3579). Six sheets are needed to cover the entire route, as follows:
*   4149 OT Calvi
*   4250 OT Corte and Monte Cinto
*   4251 OT Monte d'Oro and Monte Rotondo
*   4252 OT Monte Renoso
*   4253 OT Petreto-Bicchisano and Zicavo
*   4253 ET Aiguilles de Bavella and Solenzara

The wonderfully compact Didier Richard map of the GR20, using IGN mapping at a scale of 1:50,000, covers the entire route on a single sheet and includes plenty of mountainous terrain off-route. The ISBN is 978-2-344-00043-4, and it is readily available at airport shops, tourist information offices and many other outlets around Corsica. The IGN Mini Corse map, which covers the whole of Corsica at a scale of 1:250,000, is handy to refer to if making long bus or train journeys around Corsica. IGN mapping at all scales can be viewed online at Géoportail, www.geoportail.gouv.fr.

The maps in this guidebook are basically diagrammatic, at a scale of 1:50,000. Transferring the route from these maps to one of the recommended walking maps should be fairly straightforward. The gradient profiles provide an immediate visual appreciation of all the ups and downs along the way.

## MOUNTAIN WEATHER

Mountain ranges have a habit of creating their own weather conditions. The mountains of Corsica boast several summits over 2000m (6560ft). In the summer months the sun beats down relentlessly on bare granite slopes, raising the temperature of the air and creating great up-draughts. This draws in cool, moist air from the Mediterranean, leading to condensation, cloud cover, rain and fearsome thunderstorms. The usual pattern is for the day to start sunny and clear, with cloud building up in the afternoon. Whether the cloud eventually results in rain or thunderstorms depends on the amount of build-up. The mountain ridges are very exposed in severe weather conditions and sudden lightning strikes have claimed trekkers' lives.

Even without thunderstorms the heat alone can be severe at times, causing problems of thirst, dehydration, sunburn and sunstroke. Seasonal streams dry up completely, so that a full day's ration of water needs to be carried. The recommended minimum is two litres, but three or four may be

*This picture was taken in November. When snow covers the markers, the route becomes very difficult to trace*

needed, so take careful note of the availability of water sources in the middle of the day, where these are available. At either side of the peak summer period trekkers can take advantage of cooler, clear conditions.

The onset of winter sees snow covering the paths, obliterating the trails and waymarks, making most slopes too dangerous to negotiate. Conditions may be truly Alpine. In general, consider the GR20 closed to ordinary trekkers from mid-October to the end of May, although much depends on the severity of the winter months. Bear in mind that it can snow in the mountains in summer, although this is very rare and any snow cover will be very short-lived.

Weather forecasts, known as *meteos*, should be obtained on a daily basis at the refuges along the way. Those trekking the GR20 early or later in the season could have difficulty obtaining forecasts. Either carry a small radio, or if a mobile signal is available, tel 08 99 71 02 20, or if internet is available, check www. meteofrance.com.

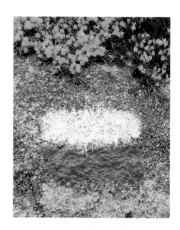

*The standard red and white flashes of paint marking the GR20 are being replaced by plaques*

## PATH CONDITIONS

In many places the GR20 is a narrow, stony, rocky mountain trail. Trekkers usually move in single file and give way to those coming in the opposite direction. However, some parts are well-trodden and well-marked, with multiple trodden paths. The standard form of waymarking quickly becomes

familiar. One red and one white stripe of paint, parallel to each other, are daubed at intervals on rocks, trees, boulders and other immovable objects. There are a few signposts, generally at the refuges, or at prominent intersections with other routes. Painted markers are slowly being replaced by small plaques fixed to rocks, posts, trees and buildings.

There are alternative routes and link routes from the GR20, and these are usually marked with yellow stripes of paint at intervals. The GR20 occasionally intersects with other long-distance routes crossing Corsica from coast to coast, and these are marked with orange stripes. Anyone walking for more than a few minutes without any sign of waymarking has probably gone off course, because the markers are usually abundant.

If the route in this guidebook is at variance with the waymarking, then it may well be that the route has been changed. This happens occasionally and it is best to follow the new markers, but if possible, ask someone else coming in the opposite direction what the extent of re-routing is.

Snow cover can linger well into the summer, but the amount of snow and the length of time it lies depend on many factors. Apart from the obvious risks of snow and ice being slippery underfoot, there is also the problem of painted waymark flashes being buried, so that trekkers find themselves unsure about the intricacies of route-finding in complex terrain. If there is too much snow cover, an ice axe and crampons become necessary. If using crampons, bear in mind that it will be necessary to put them on and off several times where the route crosses rocky areas bearing patches of snow and ice. Microspikes, while not as good as crampons, are better than nothing.

## MOUNTAIN RESCUE

Every year there is at least one casualty along the course of the GR20 and a number of accidents. On the whole, these incidents don't happen where you might expect them, but seem to be the result of a moment of carelessness or lack of concentration. Watch where you are putting your feet when you are trekking, as the ground is often rough and rocky or covered in stones and boulders. Trekkers scrambling up or down rock slabs and gullies should be careful how they move, and not make a move unless it can be reversed. Take special care if snow and ice lingers into the summer. If there is an unusual amount, an ice axe and crampons may be needed. Avoid getting into dangerous situations, as the terrain is unforgiving.

## LATEST NEWS

- Check randoblogpnrc.blogspot.co.uk before departure to see if there are any problems with any part of the GR20. Early in the season, it will mention any places where snow and ice linger. Late in the season, it will say when the refuges are unstaffed.
- Check http://corsica.forhikers.com/forum to gather the latest news and opinions as they are reported by other trekkers, or use the forum to ask questions about the GR20.
- Guide includes a major change, following the closure of the Cirque de la Solitude in 2015. A variant route over the shoulder of Monte Cinto was fully marked in 2015. In 2016 it was confirmed as the main (and only) course of the GR20.

*In 2016 all the chains were stripped from the Cirque de la Solitude, now not part of the official GR20 route*

In June 2015, a serious accident was caused when heavy rain caused a landslide in the Cirque de la Solitude. Seven trekkers were killed and several injured, resulting in the immediate closure and diversion of the route. An accident on this scale is very rare, and with hindsight it could have been avoided altogether. It reinforces the need to check the weather and avoid dangerous conditions. The chains, iron ladder and waymarks were completely removed from the Cirque de la Solitude in 2016, and the route now goes over the shoulder of Monte Cinto, described in Stage 4.

Any trekker suffering a serious fall or injury will have to be rescued. The international distress signal is given on the Mountain Safety page at the front of this guide. The mountain rescue service is generally free, but medical intervention can be costly. Some trekkers believe that insurance policies offered by the British Mountaineering Council (BMC) or Austrian Alpine Club (AAC) are best for routes such as the GR20. It is important, however, to read insurance policies carefully and ask questions if unsure about the level of cover being provided, or if unsure about specific exclusions that render such policies void.

Getting a message out in an emergency is not always easy. Mobile phones simply don't work along many parts of the GR20. When the refuges are staffed, most of them have radio contact with the outside world, and there are usually little helipads alongside. If it is possible to get a message out via one of the refuges, then help will be quickly forthcoming. Anyone using a VHF radio can call for assistance on the emergency *Canal E*, on 161.300 MHz.

Without a mobile phone signal, it might prove necessary to descend to a road and find a telephone, bearing in mind that delays can be crucial. The appropriate telephone numbers are police (*gendarmerie*) 17, ambulance (*samu*) 15, fire service (*pompiers*) 18, or the European emergency number 112. Any of these services can alert the mountain rescue, or PGHM (*Peleton de Gendarmerie de Haute Montagne*). The PGHM can be contacted directly at Corte, tel 04 95 61 13 95. However, try not to get into a situation in the first place where rescue is needed.

For less urgent health matters there is a pharmacy at Calenzana, and beyond that you would have to leave the GR20 and head for one of the larger villages or towns. If you need any regular medication, take plenty with you, or be prepared to leave the route. If a doctor or a trip to a hospital is required, European citizens should present their European Health Insurance Card, which may help to offset the cost of certain treatments.

## WHAT TO TAKE

Most trekkers on the GR20 carry far too much equipment. Think very carefully about the gear you plan to carry, and ruthlessly pare it to the bare minimum. The GR20 is a tough, steep and rocky trail that is generally followed in blazing sun, so it is unwise to carry a heavy load, which will sap your energy and slow you down.

Neither is there any need to carry much food, so long as you don't mind paying handsomely to buy food that has been carried up to the refuges. There is no need to carry heavy gear when lightweight gear is available. If you book all your overnights in the refuges, you can dispense with almost

## ESSENTIALS

- Good footwear – either lightweight boots or shoes, for those absolutely confident about wearing them, or heavier boots if you need them.
- Sock combination – try something like Bridgedales, with a dedicated Coolmax liner sock
- Clothing combination – polyester or polycotton, which is better than all-cotton for comfort, and dries quickly after washing
- Sun protection – those who burn easily should use light-coloured long sleeved/legged clothing and a sun hat
- Sunscreen – the sun can be very strong in the mountains and your skin can be burnt quite easily
- Waterproofs – a lightweight jacket is sufficient; trousers aren't necessary, but carry them if preferred
- Windproofs – a lightweight jacket is useful, but may be classed as optional, and your waterproof might suffice

33

- Rucksack – should be big enough to carry everything, and no more, and of course it should be comfortable
- Sleeping bag – a lightweight one is sufficient, as it will never get too cold in the summer months, and one is needed even if staying in refuges
- Tent – a lightweight one; it may not be used all the time and the weather in summer is often good
- Survival bag – just in case it is needed, and maybe for a bit of protection underneath your tent
- Sleeping mat – campsites are usually hard and stony, so use something like a Therm-a-rest mattress
- Water carrier – with a capacity of at least two litres, and preferably with a drinking hose
- Headtorch – there are plenty of tiny, high-power torches to choose from, and take a spare battery
- Wash kit – toothbrush, soap, towel, toilet paper, etc., and maybe a biodegradable travel wash for clothes
- First aid kit – a compact one for the usual cuts, sprains, blisters, burns, breaks, stings, pains, etc
- Money – take enough cash for the duration, as further supplies are only available off-route. Refuges don't usually take credit cards
- Maps – IGN maps of a scale and quality to see clearly what is happening along the route and off-route
- Ice axe and crampons – essential items if there is any chance of snow or ice cover early or late in the season.

## NON-ESSENTIALS

- Camera – for recording the sights and experiences of this remarkable journey, but keep it lightweight
- Stove and cookset – to cook outside refuges, but fuel may not always be available along the way
- Mobile phone – may be unusable for much of the time, and recharging opportunities are limited
- GPS – sometimes fail to pick up good signals, and recharging opportunities at refuges are limited
- Sunglasses – can be very useful in blazing sunshine, but are ultimately a matter of personal preference

- Trekking poles – can be very useful, especially a pair of them, but are a matter of personal preference
- Shoes/sandals – for comfort while strolling around in the evenings after completing each day's trek
- Slippers or flip flops – for use inside refuges, where outdoor footwear is banned
- Rope – only for the really insecure on the rocky parts, or if there is any chance of extensive snow cover
- Books – either field guides to Mediterranean flora and fauna, or the latest novel choice for the evenings.

all other backpacking gear and carry the lightest possible sleeping bag. Nor is there any great need to carry more than one complete change of clothing, since clothes can be washed and dried along the way. Keep your pack light and aim to enjoy the trek!

hostels, and even fewer hotels on or near the route.

See Appendix C for a stage-by-stage accommodation list.

*Inside the Refuge de Tighjettu (Stage 4), which is one of the more spacious refuges provided by the PNRC.*

## SERVICES ALONG THE ROUTE

Some say that the GR20 starts in Calenzana, passes through Vizzavona at the halfway stage, and ends in Conca. That is an over-simplification, and in fact a good half-dozen villages lie only two or three hours off the GR20. There are some good lodgings that lie even closer to the route, so don't imagine that the GR20 involves a complete commitment to a mountainous environment for a week at a time.

People looking for comfort should bear in mind that *basic* is *standard* along the main route, and camping spaces tend to be hard and dusty, with limited facilities. Anything above basic is the exception. There are a few *gîtes d'étape*, which are similar to

## Refuges

For trekkers staying strictly on the classic GR20, most services revolve around mountain refuges situated at intervals along the way. These are provided by the Parc Natural Régional de Corse (PNRC), www.pnr.corsica, and are open throughout the year, but are only staffed by a *gardien* and stocked with food from June until early October. Basic mixed-sex bunk accommodation and foam mattresses are provided, but you must bring your own sleeping bag as no covers of any sort are supplied. Electric lights are usually operated by solar-charged batteries. There is a kitchen/dining room with tables, pots and pans, knives and forks, crockery and gas cookers. Take slippers or flip flops for use inside the refuges as boots cannot be worn.

There is always a water supply, either inside or outside the building. Toilets and showers may be primitive and there will often be queues. Showers are solar-heated, but often run cold, while the toilets are sometimes the squat-type and occasionally out of use. You may need to provide your own toilet paper.

All the refuges provide at least a basic hot meal and stock basic supplies of food and drinks, but the choice varies from place to place. Those who will eat anything will not need to carry any food supplies beyond a snack for lunch. Although it is possible to trek the whole of the GR20 and stay indoors every night, bear in mind that beds at the PNRC refuges must be reserved and paid for in advance online, http://reserver.sitecresa.fr/centraleresa/parcnaturel. Anyone trekking without making bookings will be unlikely to find any beds available. Note that the site is in French and bookings are confirmed only when full payment is made. Print confirmations and present them on arrival at each refuge in turn. Tents may also be hired and paid for in advance. It is possible, but not essential, to book and pay for camping spaces in advance, if you are carrying a tent. Of course, advance booking ties trekkers to a fixed schedule, which can prove awkward if anything forces overnights to be re-arranged en route. The refuges hold between 16 and 48 people, but as many as 300 may descend on them in the peak season! There is a plan to gradually renovate and increase the capacity of the refuges over the next few years.

Refuges are non-smoking and dogs are not allowed indoors. Quiet is maintained from 2200 and trekkers are asked to vacate the buildings before 0900. However, some trekkers like to go to bed early and rise as early as 0300! Carry a tent and sleeping bag as back-up, and packing a stove and pans avoids queues in the refuge kitchens.

To stay in a refuge, present your booking confirmation to the gardien. If you want to camp, but haven't made a booking, explain this on arrival. If there is space free in the refuge, or in a hire tent, then it is possible to pay on the spot. If you are given a ticket for

*Simple summer farms, or bergeries, may sell food and drink to walkers, or allow overnight camping nearby (Stage 6)*

camping, or a label to fix to your tent, don't lose these or you may be asked to pay again. Evening meals should be ordered on arrival, and breakfast generally needs to be ordered the night before. Snack meals and drinks are usually sold throughout the day, and food items can also be purchased from whatever stock is held on the premises.

## Bergeries

Apart from the refuges, there are also privately owned *bergeries* along the way. These are working summer farms and some of them allow camping alongside, or provide hire tents. They also supply anything from basic food and drink to complete meals to passing trekkers. Some bergeries operate small cafés or bar restaurants. Camping and

eating at these places costs roughly the same as at the refuges.

## Camping

For those carrying a tent, camping is available near all the refuges and some of the bergeries, gîtes and hotels, but only very rarely in other places. It is generally forbidden to camp wild throughout the Parc Natural Régional de Corse (PNRC), no matter how tempting a site might look. Bear in mind that the ground reserved for camping is usually bare, hard, stony and dusty, so pack a sleeping mattress, such as a Therm-a-Rest or similar, and something to protect the groundsheet of your tent. Those who camp near the refuges have access to the toilets, showers and outside stoves and cooking areas, but they should check with individual gardiens to see if they can use the stoves, pans, crockery and utensils inside the refuges. Bergerie kitchens are generally off-limits. Even if not camping a lightweight tent is good insurance if anything prevents a refuge being reached.

## Luxury lodgings

There are a few hotels and gîtes d'étape on or near the GR20. Trekkers can indulge themselves at these places, enjoying comfortable rooms and hot showers, and eating in restaurants or dining rooms. It is possible to phone ahead and book accommodation at most of these places, and telephone numbers are given throughout this guidebook.

### Village life

Detours off-route for accommodation, food and drink in nearby villages are heartily recommended, as the course of the GR20 allows little interaction with native Corsicans. Information is provided about spurs and loops taking in a handful of fine little villages, listing their facilities and transport links.

### Back-up

For those wanting vehicle back-up for their trek, road access is possible at the start, finish, and at seven points in between: Calenzana, Ascu Stagnu, Hôtel Castel di Vergio, Vizzavona, Bergeries d' E Capanelle, Bocca di Verdi, Bassetta/Matalza, Village de Bavella and Conca. The back-up driver would need to find some other occupation for the days between supplying trekkers' needs, but there is plenty of interest around Corsica.

## FOOD, DRINK AND FUEL

The amount of food and drink, and what sort of supplies to carry, is entirely a matter of personal preference. Food and drink are available at every refuge along the way, but only when they are staffed from June to September. Most of the bergeries, as well as gîtes and hotels also stock food and drink, so there is no need to carry anything apart from a packed lunch and emergency rations each day. You can see where the next food is available along the route, whichever direction you choose to trek it,

*Always be aware of where your next water source is located, and guard against dehydration at all times.*

by consulting the tables in Appendix A and Appendix B.

Those who will eat anything, and who don't mind paying over the odds for food that has been carried on horseback to the refuges, or dropped from helicopters, can travel extremely lightweight. Fussy feeders, or those with special dietary requirements, may not find much to their taste, and may find appropriate supplies rather limited in some places. Fresh food is a rarity at remote refuges, and it will never be *haut cuisine*, although more imaginative meals may be obtained by moving off-route to a nearby village.

When cooked meals are available, as they are at almost every refuge, bergerie, gîte and hotel, be sure to order one as soon as possible. If breakfast is required, order it the night before, which seems to be essential even if it turns out to be nothing more than bread, jam and coffee. Prepared meals are of course expensive, partly because everything has been carried into the mountains, but if you don't feel like cooking or washing up, then they are good value. Picnic meals can be bought, or you can buy items to make your own.

Those who wish to carry food supplies should think lightweight, and choose freeze-dried and high-energy foods to keep their pack weight down. When given the chance to obtain more substantial fare, it makes sense to eat heavy foodstuffs on the spot and carry lighter items away. Carrying glass bottles can be dangerous and messy if they break. Drinks in plastic bottles or cans are safer, but the containers need to be disposed of at the refuges. Take careful note of re-supply points along the way. Remember that while supplies can be obtained at frequent intervals along the GR20, there is little or nothing available for long stretches outside the peak summer season.

Those who have special dietary requirements, or suffer from serious food allergies, would be well advised to have someone re-supply them at intervals along the trail, rather than run the risk of finding no suitable food available. Corsican food, or at least that which is generally available in remote refuges, tends to be based around pork products, pasta and cheese, with many foodstuffs containing plenty of sugar, nuts or salt. Packets and tins of food are likely to be unfamiliar brands, which is fine for those who like to experiment and sample new foodstuffs, but a nightmare for others! Vegetarians would struggle to find appropriate food at some points and vegans would struggle even more. Don't expect the refuge *gardiens* to provide alternative meals. Even if they do, it will be done with ill humour!

Water is available at all the refuges and bergeries along the route. It is spring water, straight from the mountainside, and considered safe to drink without boiling or treating, unless advised otherwise. Water from streams may be seasonal at best, and may need treating if used by animals or for bathing.

Bottled water is scarce in the mountains, but the two main Corsican brands are St Georges and Zilia. There is a bottled drink called Corsica Cola, for those who like a variation on a theme! Corsican beer, or *bièra Corsa*, on sale in the mountains includes Pietra, Serena, Torra and even a brand of chestnut beer, or *bière chataigne*. Wine is sometimes on sale, either from labelled or unlabelled bottles of varying quality.

Fuel can be a problem along the GR20. Those who fly to Corsica will not be allowed to carry fuel, so will need to buy it on arrival. The most common types are *alcool à bruler*, which is the nearest equivalent to methylated spirits, Camping Gaz and other types of gas canisters. If you are doing your own cooking, you will need a stove that uses alcohol or gas. When places sell out of a particular type of fuel, they may not restock immediately, in which case start asking in advance, so that you aren't left without fuel when your supply finally runs out. If that happens, it is possible to use the gas stoves outside the refuges, although there may be queues.

Lighting fires is forbidden along the GR20, as signs along the way will remind you.

---

### KEY POINTS ON FOOD SUPPLIES

- All the refuges sell meals and food supplies.
- Most bergeries, gîtes and hotels sell supplies.
- Supplies are very limited outside the summer.
- Order cooked meals as soon as you arrive.
- Order a prepared breakfast the night before.
- Supplies of fuel can be difficult to obtain.

---

### LANGUAGE

The Collectivité Territoriale de Corse has a distinct language and culture of its own, and a greater control over its affairs than any other region of France. The native island language is Corsican, which has its roots in the Tuscan dialect of Italy. However, French is spoken throughout Corsica and this is the language that visitors will use most. Many Corsicans are also fluent in Italian, but it is best to assume that English is not widely understood by the islanders.

Most placenames on maps and signposts, and in this guidebook, are in fact Corsican words, although often there is a variant French form, and there is a lot of variety in spellings in some locations. Corsicans use words like *bocca* where the French would use *col*. Corsicans often use the letter 'u' as the last vowel. The Corsican guttural compound 'ghj' is entirely unknown in French. These traits make it easier to distinguish between the two languages. (The Corsican name for the GR20, incidentally, is 'Fra li Monti', meaning 'Through the Mountains'.)

No one expects visitors to learn Corsican, but a few words of French are useful. You may start by greeting everyone you meet with a hearty *bonjour*, only to find out later that none of them speak French! In fact, trekkers from a dozen nationalities or more are likely to be met along the route, and English quickly becomes a common trail language. A knowledge of French, however basic, and a willingness to use the language is a distinct bonus when dealing with local people. While trekking the GR20, only a minimal amount of French is needed, but anyone travelling elsewhere around the island will require a wider vocabulary. See Appendix D for a basic selection of useful words and phrases.

---

### CURRENCY

Cash is king on the GR20, so be sure to have plenty of euros when you start the trek. Mountain refuges and bergeries along the way will only accept cash for accommodation, food and drink. In fact, they must accumulate countless thousands of euros between them each summer! Hotels may take credit cards, but payment by that method is only possible two or three times. There are no banks along the GR20, and money is available only by moving off-route to one of the larger towns.

In 2017, the standard price for a bed in the PNRC refuges was €14 per person, or €11 for two people in a hire tent, or €7 per person to camp near the refuges. Evening meals were around €13 to €20 and breakfasts €8. Private bergeries often match the refuge prices for camping and meals, but may be a little cheaper, or more expensive. Expect a demi pension rate in a gîte d'étape to be around €50 per person, while demi pension in a hotel could cost over €100 per person.

## USING THIS GUIDE

This book contains all the information needed to follow the GR20. The classic route from north to south is described from start to finish in 16 stages, and full details of high- and low-level alternative routes are given, as well as route descriptions for the ascent of nearby prominent peaks. It is therefore possible to pick and choose which sections to complete, and to compare and contrast any alternatives that are presented. You will probably use only half of the book, but you will have access to all of the options.

Information on the route is given near the start of the route description.

Distances are given in kilometres and miles, but for the most part these are irrelevant. What really counts is the nature of the terrain, the gradients on the ascents and descents, the conditions underfoot, and the amount of time it takes to cover each part. The total ascent and descent for each stage is presented in metres and feet. Route profiles show altitude on the vertical axis at 500m intervals and distance on the horizontal axis at 1km intervals. Conditions underfoot are noted in the actual route descriptions. The main features on the sketch maps are shown in bold type in the route descriptions, making it easier to monitor progress along the route.

Most trekkers measure their progress simply by time, and timings for various stages of the GR20 have been promoted so often that they might as well be carved in stone. In some instances, they are at least carved in wood on signs! As most trekkers are using the same times, they are given in more or less the same form in this book, in the route descriptions and in the summary tables in Appendices A and B. *Use these timings as a basic guide.*

Those who complete stages a little faster in the first couple of days are likely to complete all further stages faster. Trekkers who are a long way behind the given times should work out by how much, then apply that to their onward progress. Note that the times are walking times, *and take no account whatsoever of breaks for*

## ADVICE IN A NUTSHELL

- Don't start too early or too late in the year.
- Make sure you are fit and well prepared.
- Keep your pack weight as low as possible.
- Be sure to carry enough food and water.
- Walk slowly and steadily with care.
- Be aware of your options each day.
- Obtain a weather forecast each day.
- Consider using two trekking poles.
- Use a high-factor sunscreen and wear a hat.
- Learn at least a few words of French.

**and remember...**
- It is a tough trek but not a rock climb.
- The mountain refuges are always open.
- The refuges have well-equipped kitchens.
- Refuges must be pre-booked – http:// reserver.sitecresa.fr/centraleresa/ parcnaturel.
- Facilities outside the peak season are scarce.
- Snow can lie well into June and even July.
- Mobile phones only rarely get a good signal.
- Waymarking is usually very good.
- Many other trekkers are going your way.
- English is not widely spoken in Corsica.

*lunch, rests or taking pictures.* Over roughly two weeks most trekkers will cover a distance of about 200km (125 miles) and climb some 12,500m (41,000ft) in total.

The GR20 is a slow and often difficult trek, but one where the scenery is so magnificent that you wouldn't wish to be anywhere else. The best advice is to take it steadily. Don't rush the route or over-exert yourself. Aim to enjoy the experience and give the trek as long as it needs for a successful completion. The two tables in Appendix A and Appendix B will help you set your own pace, knowing where food and services are available along the route, whether you are trekking from Calenzana to Conca or Conca to Calenzana.

The French Foreign Legion, which is based in Corsica, generally takes a week to complete the GR20. The record for covering the distance non-stop is currently 31 hours 6 minutes, set in June 2016 by François D'Haene.

# PLANTS AND WILDLIFE ON CORSICA

Corsica is like most other long-established islands – it has a flora and fauna with a wealth of unique subspecies. It is unrealistic to think that you can trek the GR20 and also study the range of flora and fauna in any depth, but it is also amazing just how many things will gain your attention along the way. Be ready for surprises, such as finding a long line of pine processionary caterpillars shuffling through the forest.

*An uncommon wild olive tree might be spotted, while cultivated olives are seen at Calenzana and Conca*

The tangled *maquis* vegetation for which Corsica is renowned looks colourful and smells wonderful – a heady mix of perfume and herby aromas. The classic maquis species will be seen very little, however, because the route rises so quickly into the mountains and stays there for so long. The mountain scrub is largely composed of calycotome, or spiny broom, and a ground-hugging form of juniper – they are both

*Spiny broom, or calycotome, is a very common plant in the scrub cover on the high mountains*

as prickly as gorse. Bushy growths of alder are also present, indicating a little more moisture in the ground.

## TREES

Tree cover in mountain valleys is dominated by tall, straight laricio pines, maritime pines, birch and beech. There are a few localised patches of holm oak, mountain ash, sycamore and arbutus. While chestnuts may be one of the most important trees in Corsica, very few of them are seen in the mountains, but they are usually found by moving off-route to villages. Some areas of forest have been devastated in recent years by forest fires.

## FLOWERS

On the higher mountains there are interesting communities of plants. Violets and thyme can be abundant, and Alpine species include saxifrages and Alpine avens. As the snow melts in early summer, look out for delightful Corsican crocuses. Colourful orchids, big clumps of euphorbia and poisonous hellebores are also found. Corsican aconites grow only on the Plateau du Cuscione, alongside streams draining the closely cropped grasslands. Look out for curious parasitic plants. Mistletoe often thrives on laricio pines, while dense mats of dodder spread over spiny broom.

## WILDLIFE

Wild animals are rarely spotted in the mountains. There are herds of mouflon – wild, long-horned, short-haired sheep that graze on almost inaccessible ledges. Hundreds of them live on the island's mountains. Wild boar are shy and seldom seen – a more common sight is herds of feral pigs, ranging from black to piebald and pink. Pigs, cattle and goats graze at prodigious heights in the mountains and can be found even on high rocky ridges. Shepherds keep track of them by listening for the bongling bells on lead animals. Foxes are nuisances around campsites, so guard your food!

*The arbutus, or strawberry tree, is found in the lower valleys off-route and bears red fruit in the autumn*

*Pigs are turned loose to forage
for food through the summer and
are rounded up before winter*

*Cattle have been grazed high
in the mountains of Corsica
for thousands of years*

### Lizards and amphibians

Lizards can be spotted every day that
the sun shines brightly, and trekkers
may also catch a glimpse of the larger,
slow-moving salamander in woodland or near rivers, with its black body
speckled with yellow blobs to ward off
would-be predators. A curious newt-
like creature called the euprocte lives
and spawns in most streams on the
island, even high in the mountains.

### Fish

Fishermen are seen from time to time
on the larger streams or chancing their
arms at one of the lakes, generally

fishing for trout (including an endemic
Corsican variety) or eels.

### Birds

The lucky few may spot an eagle cir-
cling overhead, and other birds of
prey such as buzzards and peregrines
can be seen. Ravens are completely
at home in the mountain fastnesses,
as are Alpine choughs. Most trekkers
hear about the Corsican nuthatch,
which creeps head-first down tree
trunks in search of insects, but is rarely
seen. Most of the time, the birds seen
and heard are likely to be little pip-
its, with a delightful range of colours,

45

*Pots and pans outside a bergerie, where cows, goats and sheep are milked*

notes and songs, flitting across the mountainsides as you approach.

### Field guides

A couple of good field guides to birds and plants of the Mediterranean are useful for those prepared to carry the extra weight. There are specific guides to Corsican species, but only in French. Most bookshops on the island stock a selection and plenty of colourful books about the mountains.

# THE GR20

Towering peaks above Lac du Melo and Lac de Capitellu
(link route from Stage 7 to Bergeries to Grotelle)

# STAGE 1A

*Calenzana to*
*Refuge d'Ortu di u Piobbu (high-level)*

| | |
|---|---|
| **Start** | Calenzana |
| **Finish** | Refuge d'Ortu di u Piobbu |
| **Distance** | 12km (7½ miles) |
| **Total ascent** | 1550m (5085ft) |
| **Total descent** | 235m (770ft) |
| **Time** | 7hrs |
| **Terrain** | Mixed, including steep slopes of maquis, forest and rocky mountainsides. This is a tough day's trek because of the relentless ascent, and scrambling is required at times. Take it slow and steady, as some trekkers overtax themselves and finish the day exhausted and dehydrated. |
| **Maps** | IGN 4149 OT and 4250 OT |
| **Food and drink** | All necessary last-minute food supplies are available in Calenzana. There are a couple of streams on the ascent, but they dry up in the summer. The Refuge d'Ortu di u Piobbu serves meals and sells provisions. |
| **Shelter** | Shade is available in isolated stands of forest along the way. There is a drystone windbreak shelter on Bocca a u Salto. The higher parts are exposed in wind and rain. |

The first day on the GR20 is a shock to the system. Trekkers leave Calenzana with everything on their back, probably in hot weather, with a question mark over the availability of water along the way. Learn which plants in the maquis are the thorniest! Lizards scuttle for cover with every few footfalls. The ascent is unremitting – uphill all the way, climbing higher than anywhere in Britain, then climbing further, scrambling across a rocky mountainside. Carefully ration your water and hope that it will last. When the refuge is finally reached, take the accommodation and services as you find them, knowing that there is nowhere else within reach. This day is a fine introduction to the rigours and the delights of the GR20 – it's your baptism of fire!

## CALENZANA

*Calenzana is well worth exploring before starting a trek along the GR20*

Calenzana is often overlooked by those who are in a hurry to start the GR20. Try and spend at least a night there, if not a whole day, before starting the trek. Just outside the village is the Romanesque Chapelle di Santa Restituda, burial place of a revered Corsican martyr. Santa Restituda was beheaded for her Christian faith in the year 303AD, during the reign of the Roman Emperor Diocletian. Her marble sarcophagus is in the crypt of the chapel and was restored in 1951. The site has long been a place of pilgrimage, and although the chapel has been rebuilt and renovated many times, it contains some 11th-century stonework and 13th-century frescoes. The Festa di Santa Restituda takes place late in May alongside the old chapel, featuring a fairground with all the usual stalls and amusements, as well as food and drink.

The Baroque Église St Blaise stands in the middle of Calenzana, dating from 1691, although it took several years to complete. In 1732 the village rose up against the Genoese rulers of Corsica, who retaliated by sending in a force largely comprising Austrian soldiery. The villagers fought with whatever they could lay their hands on, from agricultural implements to beehives, killing some 500 troops. The soldiers were buried beside the church in a plot that became known as the Cimetière des Allemands. The church bell tower was planted there in 1862. There are other little chapels in the village, including an ancient brotherhood chapel at A Casazza, while U Pala was the ancient palace of the Bishops of Sagone.

Calenzana has a fairly small range of services, yet manages to cope admirably with large numbers of visitors and GR20 trekkers. There are a few accommodation options, a selection of bars and restaurants, shops selling food, drink and fuel, as well as a post office. A larger range of services, including banks with ATMs, is available in nearby Calvi.

**Accommodation** There is only a small range of accommodation in Calenzana. At the budget end, and the first place on the left at the entrance to the village, is the Gîte d'Étape Communal, tel 04 95 62 77 13 or 04 95 62 70 08. It has 8 small dormitories offering 30 beds, with space for camping alongside. The 13-room Hôtel Bel Horizon is in the middle of the village, opposite the church, tel 04 95 62 71 72. The Chambres d'Hôte L' Ombre du Clocher is located nearby on Chemin U Terraghiu, tel 04 95 31 17 12 or 06 20 18 80 08. Anyone looking for a wider range of accommodation could spend their first night at Calvi, which is a busy and attractive little port.

**Food and drink** There is a well-stocked Spar shop at the bottom end of Calenzana. Further up through the village is the little restaurant A Stazzona, closely followed by Le GR20 bar restaurant, which has obviously been named to catch the attention of trekkers! The Bar Picciu Glacier and Restaurant Pizzeria Prince Pierre are found before the church. L' Alivu and the Bar Restaurant Le Calenzana lie along a road to the left of the church, while Le Royal and L' Ecclesia are to the right of the church, opposite the bell tower. To sample local meat, cakes, honey or wine, simply follow little signs to the appropriate outlets. A Proxi grocery stands beside the post office, behind the town hall, or Hôtel de Ville. L' Atelier du Village stocks local produce further uphill. Eat a hearty meal and enjoy as much fresh produce as possible before leaving Calenzana.

**Transport** A bus service between Calvi and Calenzana is operated by Beaux Voyages, tel 04 95 65 11 35 or 04 95 65 08 26, www.corsicar.com. It runs once a day in July and August, then schooldays only for the rest of the year. There are no buses between Calvi Airport and Calvi, or from the airport to Calenzana, but taxis meet incoming flights. In Calvi, taxis are usually found on the Place de la Porteuse d'Eau, near the railway station. If there are no taxis at the airport or railway station, then phone Radio Taxis Calvais, tel 04 95 65 30 36. Those following the GR20 in reverse, who need to leave Calenzana at the end, should call Calenzana Taxis, tel 04 95 62 77 80 or 06 08 16 53 65. The village taxi stand is beside the Hôtel Bel Horizon, opposite the church.

Walk up through **Calenzana** from the gîte d'étape and campsite, passing the Spar shop at 255m (835ft). Follow the road up through the village to reach Le GR20 bar restaurant. It's possible to turn right and short-cut up the backstreet of A Torra to reach the Place Saint Antoine. However, stay on the main road to continue past the Bar Picciu Glacier and Pizzeria Prince Pierre to reach the Hôtel Bel Horizon and the Église St Blaise in the middle of the village, to follow the 'official' route.

Turn right along a narrow street signposted as the GR20, which soon climbs a broad flight of steps into a palm-shaded car park. Turn right beside the town hall, or Hôtel de Ville, down another flight of steps. Pass between the post office and Proxi grocery, climbing another flight of steps, as signposted for the GR20 and L' Atelier du Village. A narrow, winding path rises to a junction. Turn right at the Place Commune, then turn left to continue through the Place Saint Antoine along paved streets.

Pass the Oratoire St Antoine de Padoue and, as you do, offer a little prayer to the patron saint of lost things that you remembered to pack everything you needed for

*An hour after leaving Calenzana, the GR20 and the Tra Mare e Monti part company at a junction on the hillside*

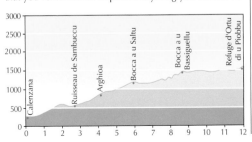

There is a view back to Calenzana, as well as to the neighbouring village of Moncale, while Calvi and Lumio are seen near the coast as the path climbs further.

the trek! Pass a signpost beside a stone-built well and follow a cobbled path up from the village. This runs through a deep groove overhung by trees, passing through a small gate. The path rises from the trees and reaches an area of bare granite at **Lavupargu**, turning right to follow a low drystone wall further uphill.

Dense growths of sticky leaved cistus press in on both sides as the path climbs up an eroded groove in the bedrock, and there are ruined drystone walls on either side. ◄ The slope is exposed to the sun and bears the charred remains of trees destroyed by a big fire in 1982. The area has seen smaller blazes in subsequent years.

Pass a stand of tall, charred laricio pines on the broom-covered slope, then later a water **source** spills on the left, before some charred chestnut trees. The path rises fairly gently, passing a couple more chestnut trees and a few pines, zigzagging up to a signpost at a junction of paths at 550m (1805ft). (There is a worn patch on the hillside, about an hour from Calenzana, where trekkers can't resist dropping their packs and taking a break.) The GR20 heads up to the left, marked by red and white paint flashes. The Tra Mare e Monti heads off to the right, marked by orange paint flashes.

At this point a choice must be made between the high-level

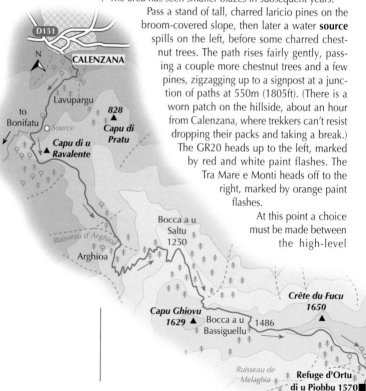

route and the low-level variant. See the next section, Stage 1B, for a description of the low-level variant.

Go left to follow the GR20 and zigzag up past a couple of monstrous boulders beneath the rocky peaks of **Capu di u Ravalente**. The path crosses a rocky gap at 625m (2050ft) where small boulders make good seats. If you haven't already learnt from painful experience, don't sit down on the maquis, which here is a mixture of cistus and spiny broom. Take a last look back to Calenzana before it passes from view.

The path is quite rugged as it descends a short way from the gap, passing beneath an overhanging rock with holm oaks growing in crevices. The surface is easier underfoot as the path contours along an old terrace high on the slope. Straggly barbed wire fencing runs alongside to the right, and the maquis is an exotic mix of aromatic species. The path rises to a few chestnut trees that draw moisture from a seasonal stream, the Ruisseau de Sambuccu, and it is clear that they have suffered a severe burning in the past. Bergeries can be seen on the valley sides, and the bongling bells of cattle or goats grazing in the maquis may be heard. ▶

The low-level track leading to Bonifatu can also be seen. Hopefully you won't be wishing you were on it at this late stage!

As it leaves the chestnut trees, the path is in an eroded rocky groove, but it levels out as it runs across the slope. The barbed wire fence is still visible on the right. Another stream called the **Ruisseau d'Arghioa** is crossed where tall laricio pines grow, and the path on either side of the watercourse is quite rocky. This is a fine place to fill up with water early in the summer, but it quickly dries away, leaving this whole stage waterless. Above the stream there is a pleasant grassy ledge at **Arghioa**, overlooking the valley from an altitude of 800m (2625ft). Those who reach this point within 1hr 30mins of leaving the GR20/TMM trail junction are doing fairly well.

A zigzag path leads up past young pines and heather scrub on a steep and stony slope. The path is well graded and well marked at all the crucial turnings, although there are a couple of other paths that lead away on either side. Note the clumps of

a di
gine

hellebores growing profusely in places. There is a rocky stretch where the path crosses a streambed at a higher level, then it swings right near a rocky pinnacle. There are more zigzags and a few tight squeezes where young pines and tall heather grow thickly between tall laricio pines on the higher slopes. Another series of zigzags leads above young pines and spiny broom scrub to reach a grassy gap, the **Bocca a u Saltu**, at 1250m (4100ft). Trekkers should reach this point 1hr 30mins after leaving Arghioa. There is a small drystone windbreak shelter to the left and the rocky spires of **Capu Ghiovu** to the right. Monte Corona is seen rising beyond the next gap.

*Impressive rock scenery on the slopes of Capu Ghiovu features some short stretches of scrambling*

Watch carefully as the GR20 markers lead away from the gap. The path runs downhill around the base of a cliff, then rises gently between tall laricio pines. A bouldery zigzag path climbs up to a rocky slope, then a series of short scrambles must be completed. Watch carefully for the markers, which always indicate the easiest course. The pitches are very short and there are plenty of holds, but those carrying a full pack on their first full day will find getting their balance right more of a problem. There is very little sense of exposure because of the tall trees alongside, and there is often good shade as the slope faces north. ▶

Looking around, it is often possible to spot long-horned mouflon grazing along some of the ledges.

There is another easy stretch of path and another bouldery ascent, then more scrambling on a more open slope of rock. A short cable marks the point where the route straddles a rock ridge and enters a gully, and there may be a drop of water here early in the summer. After more uphill scrambling, the path drops to pass beneath a spire of rock pierced with a hole, then crosses a bouldery slope. There are a couple of rocky notches to cross, with some grotesque outcrops of rock high above, and plenty of prostrate juniper and clumps of hellebore on the ground. An eroded groove leads up to another gap, the **Bocca a u Bassiguellu**, which has patches of grass and scrub at 1486m (4875ft). The scrambling from one bocca to the next should take 1hr 30mins, depending on how much caution is exercised.

Turn left to follow the path gently uphill past some tall pines. There is a sudden fine view of distant mountains, and their profiles will become familiar over the next few days. An easy, level stretch of path runs below the **Crête de Fucu**, where the juniper gives way to spiny broom. The refuge is visible across the valley. Young pines press in on either side and there are bouldery areas to cross. The path rises across slopes of broken rock, and is well wooded in places with birch and alder. There is a rugged little climb around the head of the valley, with a turn to the right and left, before the **Refuge d'Ortu di u Piobbu** is reached, within 1hr 30mins of leaving the Bocca a u Bassiguellu.

The PNRC **Refuge d'Ortu di u Piobbu** is perched at 1570m (5150ft), occupying the site of a former bergerie, on a tongue of sloping, open land surrounded by high mountains, overlooking a forested valley. It has two dormitories offering 32 beds, a kitchen/dining room and the gardien's quarters. Hot meals, food supplies and drinks are on sale. A toilet and shower stand away from the building. Hire tents and camping spaces are dotted around on the slope below the refuge. Although there is water in the refuge and a water trough near the refuge, the water is not suitable for drinking. Water should be drawn from a source signposted 200m beyond the refuge.

# STAGE 1B

*Calenzana to*
*Refuge d'Ortu di u Piobbu (low-level)*

| | |
|---|---|
| **Start** | Calenzana |
| **Finish** | Refuge d'Ortu di u Piobbu |
| **Distance** | 20km (12½ miles) |
| **Total ascent** | 1610m (5280ft) |
| **Total descent** | 295m (970ft) |
| **Time** | 7hrs 45mins |
| **Terrain** | Some short, steep slopes of maquis at first, followed by broad tracks and a road later. A long climb on rugged forest paths leads finally to the refuge. |
| **Maps** | IGN 4149 OT and 4250 OT |
| **Food and drink** | Water may be found in streams in the Forêt de Sambuccu, but water from la Figarella Rivière should be treated. The Auberge de la Forêt at Bonifatu provides accommodation, meals, and basic food supplies. Water is available near the hotel and may be found in a stream on the ascent to the Refuge d'Ortu di u Piobbu. The refuge serves meals and sells provisions. |
| **Shelter** | Shade is sparse for the first half of the day, then there is more tree cover beyond Bonifatu. |

If the first day's high-level trek along the main GR20 route seems daunting, then maybe ask why you are here in the first place! However, there can be good reasons for choosing to start with this low-level variant. Foul weather on the first day could lead to choosing this easier alternative. Searing heat could lead to choosing a route with more water and shade, and this low-level route enjoys good forest cover in its latter stages. Bear in mind that the distance is almost double that of the main GR20 route, and there is actually a little more ascent involved, even if the paths are easier. A cursory glance at the map reveals that it is actually easier to trek from Calenzana to the Refuge de Carozzu at the end of Stage 2 in a day, stealing a whole day's lead on the high-level trekkers, but this smacks of cheating!

Walk up through **Calenzana** from the gîte d'étape and campsite, passing the Spar shop at 255m (835ft). Follow the road up through the village to reach Le GR20 bar restaurant. It's possible to turn right and short-cut up the backstreet of A Torra to reach the Place Saint Antoine. However, stay on the main road to continue past the Bar Picciu Glacier and Pizzeria Prince Pierre to reach the Hôtel Bel Horizon and the Église St Blaise in the middle of the village, to follow the 'official' route.

Turn right along a narrow street signposted as the GR20, which soon climbs a broad flight of steps into a palm-shaded car park. Turn right beside the town hall, or Hôtel de Ville, down another flight of steps. Pass between the post office and Proxi grocery, climbing another flight of steps, as signposted for the GR20 and L' Atelier du Village. A narrow, winding path rises to a junction. Turn

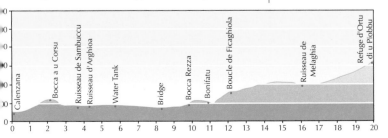

right at the Place Commune, then turn left to continue through the Place Saint Antoine along paved streets.

The Oratoire St Antoine de Padoue is passed by the GR20, and as St Anthony of Padua is the patron saint of lost things, maybe offer a little prayer in the hope that you remembered to pack everything you needed for the trek! Pass a signpost beside a stone-built well and follow a cobbled path up from the village. This runs through a deep groove overhung by trees, passing through a small gate. The path rises from the trees and reaches an area of bare granite at **Lavupargu**, turning right to follow a low drystone wall further uphill.

Dense growths of sticky leaved cistus press in on both sides as the path climbs up an eroded groove in the bedrock, and there are ruined drystone walls on either side. ◄ The slope is exposed to the sun and bears the charred remains of trees destroyed by a big

There is a view back to Calenzana, as well as to the neighbouring village of Moncale, while Calvi and Lumio are seen near the coast as the path climbs further.

map continues on page 62

D151

CALENZANA

N

Lavupargu

550    Source

Bocca a u Corsu

Capu di u Ravalente

Tra Mare e Monti

to Refuge d'Ortu di u Piobbu

Ruisseau de Sambuccu

Ruisseau d'Arghioa

Ruisseau de Curzolusu

Ruisseau de Vivariu

Tank

Forêt de Sambuccu

Route Forestière du Sambuccu

La Figarella Rivière

Punta Scaffa 693

to Calvi

D251

Dirt Road

Bocca Rezza

Bonifatu

Bridge

Source    continued

fire in 1982. The area has seen smaller blazes in subsequent years.

Pass a stand of tall, charred laricio pines on the broom-covered slope, then later a water **source** spills on the left, before some charred chestnut trees. The path rises fairly gently, passing a couple more chestnut trees and a few pines, zigzagging up to a signpost at a junction of paths at 550m (1805ft). (There is a worn patch on the hillside, about an hour from Calenzana, where trekkers can't resist dropping their packs and taking a break.) The GR20 heads up to the left, marked by red and white paint flashes. The Tra Mare e Monti heads off to the right, marked by orange paint flashes.

At this point a choice must be made between the high-level route and the low-level variant. See the previous section, Stage 1A, for a description of the high-level route.

Turn right along the low-level Tra Mare e Monti, following the path easily uphill beyond a solitary pine to reach a gap. This is the **Bocca a u Corsu** at 586m (1923ft), where grass and thistles spread in a circle beyond a marker post, with the more dense cistus at a distance. Enjoy the views of the surrounding mountains and the valley of la Figarella Rivière, where the route is heading next.

Follow the path downhill through the maquis, walking on bare rock or stones. The path is enclosed between low drystone walls, although they are only glimpsed from time to time. Follow a deep groove in the crumbling granite bedrock, where the maquis sometimes presses in on the path. An olive tree stands beside a huge boulder beside the **Ruisseau de Sambuccu**, which may offer a trickle of water early in the summer.

The way ahead is clear, taking advantage of an old cultivation terrace. A wall and fence are visible to the left from time to time. The arbutus scrub is still quite tall and dense, and must be brushed past in places. Zigzag a short way up to the left to cross the **Ruisseau d'Arghioa**, then follow the path gently uphill, emerging on a tight loop on a much broader track. This point, at 454m (1490ft), should be reached about 1hr 30mins after leaving the

There is a wide, flat, grassy area offering a good viewpoint over the valley. Any rifle shots that might be heard are probably from a firing range on the other side of la Figarella Rivière.

GR20/TMM trail junction. Trekkers on the high-level GR20 are directly uphill to the east.

Walk straight onwards, following the track gently uphill. The hillside is terraced and was once under cultivation, but now there are young pines and plenty of arbutus scrub. There are two fords paved with stone, and one of them offers a particularly attractive shady waterhole in times of flow. The track rises to a hairpin bend and a junction with another track beside a circular concrete water **tank**. ◄

Turn right at the track junction to follow a broad track, the **Route Forestière du Sambuccu**. There is a TMM signpost and the way is flashed with orange paint. Dense growths of arbutus rise on either side throughout the gradual descent. Walk straight onwards at a junction of tracks and cross a stream. The track runs fairly close to the broad and bouldery bed of **la Figarella Rivière.**

A curiously eroded outcrop, full of deeply weathered hollows, is passed just before a concrete **bridge** spans the river at 360m (1180ft). Trekkers should reach the bridge after following the track for 1hr 15mins. Take a break at the bridge and enjoy the mountains, which seem much closer now, and consider the flow of the river.

Rise from the river, but almost immediately turn left along a well-wooded path. This runs parallel to the river, heading upstream. It can be quite bouldery underfoot at times, and a bewildering mixture of vegetation grows alongside. In hot weather, some of the pools in the river look particularly inviting. The path is quite rugged in places, and a series of zigzags finally climbs up from the river, on a slope of arbutus trees. A road is reached at a memorial on a bend at **Bocca Rezza**, at 510m (1673ft), so watch for traffic when turning left.

The Maison Forestière du Bonifatu is visible, perched on a brow overlooking the river, with towering mountains all around. The road leads past the buildings and crosses a bridge over the Torrent le Terrible, where there is a shady picnic area and a water **source**. Stay high above a terraced car park to pass the **Auberge de la Forêt**. This point should be reached, at an altitude of 540m (1770ft),

*Cross a metal suspension bridge below the Auberge de la Forêt before the climb to the Refuge d'Ortu di u Piobbu*

about an hour after leaving the bridge over la Figarella Rivière.

The **Auberge de la Forêt**, tel 04 95 65 09 98, is a bar restaurant with a small 5-room hotel and 22-bed gîte d'étape, with camping spaces also available. Trekkers who have had enough and can't face a hot afternoon climbing could enjoy a good meal and a comfortable night here at Bonifatu instead. A limited range of food supplies are available for self-caterers. Although tour coaches regularly run to Bonifatu, there is no bus service. Radio Taxis Calvais, tel 04 95 65 30 36, offer a link with Calvi.

To continue, note that the Refuge d'Ortu di u Piobbu is 3hrs away, while the Refuge de Carozzu is 2hrs 30mins

The woods are
mixed pines and
holm oak, with
an understorey of
arbutus, tall heather,
broom and brambles.
Wildlife in the area
includes wild boar,
mouflon, the bearded
vulture and the
Corsican nuthatch.

away. Obviously, it would be possible to steal a whole day's lead on the high-level trekkers, but the route description assumes that you will be heading for the Refuge d'Ortu di u Piobbu, so walk down through the car park as signposted. Yellow paint flashes reveal a zigzag path down to the river. Cross a metal suspension **footbridge** and follow a woodland path to a junction. Turn right as signposted for the Boucle de Ficaghiola, following both yellow and red paint marks.

A bouldery path rises in tight, well-graded zigzags that are never very difficult despite the steepness of the slope. ◄

There are glimpses back down to Bonifatu, but for the most part the woods are dense. The path levels out among pines at 743m (2438ft) on the **Boucle de Ficaghiola**. Turn left, as flashed with yellow and signposted for the GR20. Keep zigzagging uphill, where there are fewer trees and more scrub as a rocky ridge is gained.

Watch for another path junction – the Boucle des Finocchi is signposted straight ahead in red, so turn right to follow another path flashed with yellow paint. Zigzag up the rugged ridge, then contour at roughly 1050m (3445ft) along the valley side. A gentle descent leads through scorched pines to a stony track. Turn left to follow the track, and there is soon an option to follow another yellow-flashed path running parallel, although both lines quickly lead to a ford in the bouldery streambed of the **Ruisseau de Melaghia**.

A signpost across the river appears to point into a heap of boulders, and gives an allowance of 1hr 30mins to reach the refuge. Yellow paint flashes indicate the way through the boulders and along a rough path flanked by tall heather and bracken. The trees in the forest are mostly laricio pines at this level, above the 1000m (3280ft) contour. The path crosses a streambed that carries water early in the season, then the terrain underfoot is rather easier.

The path rises up a steep slope clothed in tall pines, but it has been engineered in zigzags

A clear waymarked path cuts across the mountainside and leads into the valley of the Ruisseau de Melaghia

to ease the gradient. Looking up the slope, bare rock faces can be seen, and the path swings right and cuts across the foot of the cliffs. There is a pronounced swing to the left afterwards and the path zigzags up onto the rocky crest high above the valley. After passing through an area of

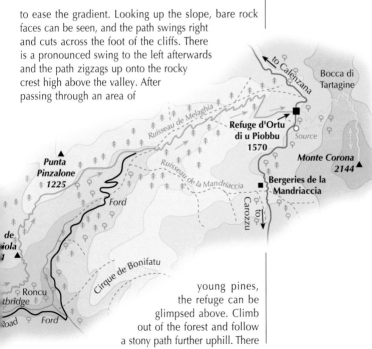

young pines, the refuge can be glimpsed above. Climb out of the forest and follow a stony path further uphill. There is spiny broom on the ground, and the path is flashed in yellow, leading directly to the **Refuge d'Ortu di u Piobbu**.

The PNRC **Refuge d'Ortu di u Piobbu** is perched at 1570m (5150ft), occupying the site of a former bergerie, on a tongue of sloping, open land surrounded by high mountains, overlooking a forested valley. It has two dormitories offering 32 beds, a kitchen/dining room and the gardien's quarters. Hot meals, food supplies and drinks are on sale. A toilet and shower stand away from the building. Hire tents and camping spaces are dotted around on the slope below the refuge. Although there is water in the refuge and a water trough near the refuge, the water is not suitable for drinking. Water should be drawn from a source signposted 200m beyond the refuge.

# EXCURSION

*Ascent of Monte Corona from*
*Refuge d'Ortu di u Piobbu*

| | |
|---|---|
| **Start/Finish** | Refuge d'Ortu di u Piobbu |
| **Distance** | 5km (3 miles) there-and-back |
| **Total ascent** | 575m (1885ft) |
| **Total descent** | 575m (1885ft) |
| **Time** | 2hrs 30mins there-and-back |
| **Terrain** | Wooded slopes give way to scrub-covered slopes, which can be rocky or stony in places, but are not particularly difficult. |
| **Maps** | IGN 4250 OT |
| **Food and drink** | There is no water on the ascent. The Refuge d'Ortu di u Piobbu serves meals and sells provisions. |
| **Shelter** | There is shade in the woods near the start, but the upper parts of the mountain are open and exposed to sun, wind and rain. |

Those who reach the Refuge d'Ortu di u Piobbu and are fighting fit might like to climb Monte Corona, on whose slopes the refuge stands. Alternatively, anyone who wants to enjoy a bit of a break at the refuge, yet still complete a short walk, could enjoy the ascent as a fine half-day route. The mountain can be climbed lightweight, which makes a big difference to progress. There is a waymarked zigzag ascent from the refuge to the Bocca di Tartagine, then a series of cairns lead up a rugged ridge to the stony summit, where views can be enjoyed. This is a fairly easy ascent and it might give trekkers a taste for more serious ascents further along the course of the GR20.

Walk straight uphill from the **Refuge d'Ortu di u Piobbu**, picking a way along narrow paths and aiming for the left-hand side of the birch woods higher up the slope. A

*Looking from the Refuge d'Ortu di u Piobbu to the rugged Capu a u Dente beyond the Bocca di Tartagine*

65

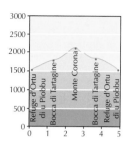

path marked with flashes of yellow paint enters the woods and zigzags uphill. There is a view back to the refuge from one rocky stretch. The zigzags swing more to the left, and on leaving the birch woods cross a slope of alder and juniper scrub, with stony patches in between. Next, reach the gap at the **Bocca di Tartagine**, at an altitude of 1852m (6076ft). There is a view across the Tartagine valley to Monte Padru, while Capu a u Dente raises its rocky towers to the left.

Turn right to leave the gap, following a rugged ridge southwards towards Monte Corona. There is a vague zigzag path marked by cairns, threading its way up a steep slope of alder scrub. Grapple with boulders and outcrops of rock at a higher level, and keep an eye peeled to spot more small cairns. On reaching a higher part of the ridge, there is a stony path away to the right that continues climbing. The summit of **Monte Corona** is a stony dome crowned with a cairn at 2144m (7034ft).

There are fine views of the surrounding mountains, and it is possible to pick out the course of the GR20 to the south, until Monte Cinto and Paglia Orba block the view. Calvi can be seen to the northwest, and there is also a bird's-eye view down to the refuge. Looking along the ridge, some might wonder if it is worth trekking straight towards the neighbouring peak of Capu Ladroncellu to rejoin the GR20. When heading back down the mountain to the refuge, be careful not to be drawn off-course to the left, which leads into an awkward area of alder scrub.

# STAGE 2A

*Refuge d'Ortu di u Piobbu to Refuge de Carozzu (high-level)*

| | |
|---|---|
| **Start** | Refuge d'Ortu di u Piobbu |
| **Finish** | Refuge de Carozzu |
| **Distance** | 8km (5 miles) |
| **Total ascent** | 750m (2460ft) |
| **Total descent** | 1050m (3445ft) |
| **Time** | 6hrs 30mins |
| **Terrain** | Rugged wooded slopes at the start and open mountainsides afterwards. The slopes can be steep and rocky, and a series of short scrambles must be completed on the higher parts. Paths leading downhill at the end of the day are steep and stony, running into woodlands. |
| **Maps** | IGN 4250 OT |
| **Food and drink** | Water is available on crossing the first two valleys, at the Ruisseau de la Mandriaccia and at a source near Leccia Rossa. The Refuge de Carozzu serves meals and sells provisions. |
| **Shelter** | The early and later parts of the day pass through woods that offer a certain amount of shade, but most of the route is across exposed rocky mountainsides. |

The high-level route from the Refuge d'Ortu di u Piobbu is a tough day's trek, especially after the exertions of the first day. It involves trekking round a rugged shoulder to reach a valley, then spending the morning climbing to the Bocca Piccaia at the head of the valley. The view from the gap is magnificent, providing the day is clear – full of spires and towers of rock. The route traverses round the flanks of the mountains, and although it starts easily it becomes quite difficult, with numerous short rocky ascents and descents. There is another chance to enjoy exceptional views before a long, steep and stony descent to the Refuge de Carozzu at the end of the day. (If this day sounds too tough, refer to the next section for a low-level alternative.)

*The GR20 picks its way between birch woods and sloping slabs as it climbs from the Ruisseau de la Mandriaccia*

Leave the **Refuge d'Ortu di u Piobbu** as signposted for Carozzu, entering a birch wood and crossing the stream used as a water **source** for the refuge. The path climbs steep and rocky terrain, and there are a couple of fine views back towards the refuge through gaps in the trees. After contouring more easily around a slope, reaching 1627m (5338ft), the path descends a steep and rugged slope where the slender birch trees are dwarfed by a few large laricio pines. Pass close to the **Bergeries de la Mandriaccia**, then

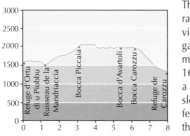

drop downhill to cross the **Ruisseau de la Mandriaccia** at 1510m (4955ft). This is usually a good source of water until midsummer, although it occurs early in the day, only an hour into the day, and some may prefer to wait until reaching the next source. ▶

Watch carefully for the paint flashes as the path climbs up a steep and bouldery slope covered in trees. The path leads up towards a sloping cliff and for the most part trekkers pick their way along the base of the cliff between the trees and the bare rock walls. There are more open views as the path climbs higher through the valley and the trees begin to thin out. Stay near the base of the cliff until the path climbs to cross a streambed at Leccia Rossa in an extensive area of alder scrub. This is a good source of water, until it dries up, and is reached around 1620m (5315ft). Take a drink and also drink in the surroundings, marvelling at the towers of rock on either side of the valley.

Climb uphill after crossing the stream, mostly scrambling on bare rocky stairways, watching for a painted indicator reading 'Source 200m GR'. A bouldery path leads down through the alder scrub to reach the small water **source**, but be sure not to be drawn off-course along an older waymarked route, which misses it. Watch carefully for more paint flashes as the path steers through the scrub, then scramble up the bouldery, rocky slopes of the valley. There is a series of zigzags, and early in the summer wonderful displays of Corsican crocuses. A final steep and bouldery slope leads to a gap at the head of the valley, called **Bocca Piccaia**, around 1950m (6400ft).

The rocky peaks of Punta Piccaia and Capu Ladroncellu flank the gap, but your attention is more likely to be focused on the awesome drop down into the Ladroncellu valley, which is surrounded by rugged mountains and filled with amazing pinnacles and towers of rock. If anyone ahead looked rooted to the spot as they reached this gap, you now understand why! Those who reach the gap 2hrs 30 mins after leaving the Ruisseau de la Mandriaccia are doing well.

The wooded valley is overrun by ants, so stopping or sitting for any length of time is not recommended.

Turn left to climb along the ridge, grappling with the rock in places and gradually rising towards **Capu Ladroncellu**. Don't climb to the summit, as the path heads off to the right before that point, cutting across slopes of broken rock and scree on the upper part of the mountain, around 2020m (6625ft). Juniper and spiny broom scrub bind the loose stones together. After passing an overhanging rock the path begins a sustained descent that can be steep and rocky in places, down to around 1900m (6235ft). After crossing a scree slope covered in juniper scrub, there is a short climb through an awkward arrangement of jammed boulders.

The path beyond the jammed boulders is a rocky roller coaster as it continues its traverse of the mountain. Trekkers have to grapple with the rock, and there must be at least 100m (300ft) of extra ascent and descent on this stretch, involving a few awkward moves. Even when the route reaches the **Bocca d'Avartoli**, there are still plenty of ups and downs. It is a particularly tiring part of the GR20. Watch carefully for the markers, as the path switches from side to side while traversing the gap. The altitude on the lowest part of the Bocca d'Avartoli is 1898m (6227ft), and it will probably take around an hour to reach the gap from the Bocca Piccaia.

The path seems to continue easily across the steep upper slopes of **Punta Ghialla**, but there is a short rock gully that has to be negotiated by scrambling up and down yet again. Corsican crocuses abound early in the summer as the path traverses the slope at the base of a cliff. The route drops down on the next gap, which is known as the **Bocca Carozzu**, or Bocca Inuminata, around 1865m (6120ft). Trekkers should reach the gap 45 mins after leaving the Bocca d'Avartoli. ◄

This is a last chance to look back across the pinnacles and towers of rock around the Ladroncellu valley to Bocca Piccaia, where this amazing scenery was first witnessed.

Turn left to leave the **Bocca Carozzu**, going down a steep scree path running through juniper and spiny broom scrub. Further downhill the route is rocky and bouldery as it weaves through alder scrub. As the path gradually swings right around a bend in the valley the refuge becomes visible, but it is still quite a long way below. Take care following the path, as there are some side-spurs that don't lead anywhere.

Pass birch and pines, then cross a bouldery streambed. The path becomes gentler as it descends through a birch wood, crossing another streambed, and although there are stony clearings along the way, the refuge remains concealed almost until it is reached. It will take around 1hr 15mins to complete the descent from the gap to the **Refuge de Carozzu**.

The PNRC **Refuge de Carozzu** is situated in an amazing location, at 1270m (4165ft) on the only flat bit of ground

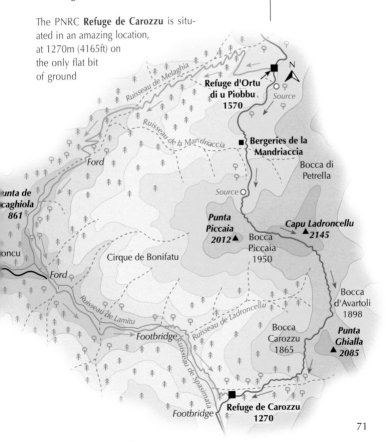

*A lone laricio pine grows from a rocky ridge, seen on the way down towards the Refuge de Carozzu*

in sight. It is hemmed in by tall mountains arranged around the Cirque de Bonifatu, yet features a view that extends down through the forested valley to the rugged little mountains near Calvi. A wooden terrace is positioned in front of the building so that weary wayfarers can rest and watch the sun go down at leisure, and marvel at the pines that cling to sheer rock all around. The building has a dormitory with 36 beds, a kitchen/dining room and the gardien's quarters. An architect's plan released in 2017 envisages the refuge being given an upper storey. Toilets, showers and water taps are located nearby. Meals, food and drink supplies are on sale. Hire tents and camping spaces are available in the woods behind the refuge, where abundant insect life flourishes, providing food for birds.

# STAGE 2B

*Refuge d'Ortu di u Piobbu to Refuge*
*de Carozzu (low-level)*

| | |
|---|---|
| **Start** | Refuge d'Ortu di u Piobbu |
| **Finish** | Refuge de Carozzu |
| **Distance** | 12km (7½ miles) |
| **Total ascent** | 660m (2165ft) |
| **Total descent** | 960m (3150ft) |
| **Time** | 4hrs 30mins |
| **Terrain** | Forested valleys with good paths and tracks. Generally easy trekking, although steep zigzags in places and some narrow, rocky paths. |
| **Maps** | IGN 4250 OT |
| **Food and drink** | Rivers in the valleys run throughout the year, although the water may need treating, and some tributaries may dry up. The Auberge de la Forêt is off-route at Bonifatu, providing accommodation, food and drink. The Refuge de Carozzu serves meals and sells provisions. |
| **Shelter** | Forest shade is available for most of the descent and ascent. |

The low-level variant between the Refuge d'Ortu di u Piobbu and the Refuge de Carozzu would suit those who have overexerted themselves on their first day on the high-level GR20. If the weather turns abysmal, some may prefer to take the lower route in order to keep moving, hoping for better weather later. The low-level route simply heads down a rocky crest and zigzags down rugged paths and tracks through a forested valley. After fording a river, the ascent to the Refuge de Carozzu is along a rough and narrow path, emerging suddenly into magnificent mountain surroundings at the end of the day. Anyone using this low-level route, as well as the low-level route on the first day are warned that without experiencing the high mountains, they are in for a shock soon afterwards!

Leave the **Refuge d'Ortu di u Piobbu** by walking down-hill, looking for yellow flashes of paint along a stony path

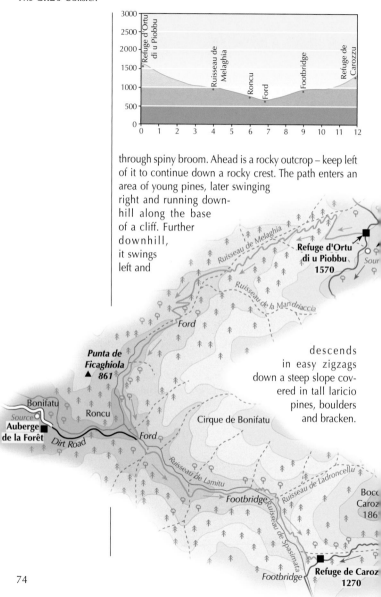

through spiny broom. Ahead is a rocky outcrop – keep left of it to continue down a rocky crest. The path enters an area of young pines, later swinging right and running downhill along the base of a cliff. Further downhill, it swings left and descends in easy zigzags down a steep slope covered in tall laricio pines, boulders and bracken.

The path crosses a streambed that carries water early in the season, then becomes more rugged and eventually runs through tall heather and boulders to reach a bouldery ford on the **Ruisseau de Melaghia**. The altitude here is around 1000m (3280ft).

After fording the river, a rugged forest track continues gently downhill, later signposted 'Carozzu par le Roncu'. Laricio pine gives way to maritime pine, holm oak and arbutus. ▶ The track zigzags down to the **Ruisseau de Melaghia** again. Cross at a flat concrete ford, or use boulders just upstream if the water is more than boot depth.

Continuing down the track, there are views of wooded valleys converging, and while waterfalls might be heard, it is difficult to see them through the foliage. The

There are a couple of points where, looking back up the valley, it is possible to spot the Refuge d'Ortu di u Piobbu, with Monte Corona rising above it.

*The path beside the Ruisseau de Lamitu is well wooded, but occasionally there are glimpses of the mountains*

75

track is surfaced in concrete where it has been cut from a cliff, and the cliff overhangs the track in places. There is another slab of concrete, then the rough and bouldery track lands beside a bouldery river below **Roncu**. Ford the river by hopping from boulder to boulder, although after heavy rain it could be a difficult crossing. The end of a **dirt road** on the other bank should be reached some 2hrs 30mins after leaving the Refuge d'Ortu di u Piobbu, and the altitude is around 620m (2035ft). ◀

Anyone needing a quick exit should note that the dirt road can be used to reach Bonifatu and the Auberge de la Forêt.

To continue with the trek, go past a signboard that indicates the path leading to the Refuge de Carozzu. Allow about 2hrs for the ascent to the refuge from this point. The path is quite rough and rocky at first, even though it has been specially constructed and fixed to a rocky ledge above the river. Avoid a right turn signposted for the Boucle de Candia. The **Ruisseau de Lamitu** can be seen, or at least heard, down to the left, as views are often obscured by pines, holm oak, arbutus and tall heather trees.

A streambed is crossed that carries water early in the summer, then later a larger streambed is crossed where water is more likely to be flowing. The path becomes much easier underfoot, almost level in places, then a rough stretch leads up to a suspension **footbridge** over the **Ruisseau de Spasimata**.

Take a break at this point, as the gorge is remarkably rugged and soaring peaks of pink granite rise all around. ◀ Tall laricio pines grace the slopes, and the peaks at the head of the valley may be streaked with snow early in the summer. Rock pools may prove irresistible on a hot day.

Photographers will find that good views are available from the middle of the bridge, but it wobbles too much to allow pictures to be taken easily.

After crossing the footbridge, a rugged path continues further up the valley side, with occasional glimpses of the rocky riverbed, its waterfalls, cascades and pleasant pools. Cross the bouldery **Ruisseau de Ladroncellu** and follow the rugged path further uphill. There are zigzags, tightly hemmed in by trees, cutting out views of the valley for a while, then the path leads across the base of awesome rock slabs to reach another inflowing river. Cross the river and follow the zigzag path uphill, passing a stone picnic table, dated 1938, on the way.

The path drifts away from the river and passes a stone hut with a corrugated iron roof. Signs forbid camping at this point, and those who get a shock seeing this rude hut are assured that it is not the refuge! The path zigzags further uphill through tall laricio pines and, by keeping left, a remarkable helipad construction is passed. Shortly afterwards, the **Refuge de Carozzu** appears quite suddenly in a clearing.

The PNRC **Refuge de Carozzu** is situated in an amazing location, at 1270m (4165ft) on the only flat bit of ground in sight. It is hemmed in by tall mountains arranged around the Cirque de Bonifatu, yet features a view that extends down through the forested valley to the rugged little mountains near Calvi. A wooden terrace is positioned in front of the building so that weary wayfarers can rest and watch the sun go down at leisure, and marvel at the pines that cling to sheer rock all around. The building has a dormitory with 36 beds, a kitchen/dining room and the gardien's quarters. An architect's plan released in 2017 envisages the refuge being given an upper storey. Toilets, showers and water taps are located nearby. Meals, food and drink supplies are on sale. Hire tents and camping spaces are available in the woods behind the refuge, where abundant insect life flourishes, providing food for birds.

# STAGE 3

*Refuge de Carozzu to
Ascu Stagnu*

| | |
|---|---|
| **Start** | Refuge de Carozzu |
| **Finish** | Ascu Stagnu |
| **Distance** | 6km (3¾ miles) |
| **Total ascent** | 860m (2280ft) |
| **Total descent** | 710m (2330ft) |
| **Time** | 5hrs 30mins |
| **Terrain** | The steep and bare Spasimata Slabs need special care, especially when wet, and should be avoided when icy. A long, steep and rugged ascent is followed by a long descent on rocky and stony slopes. |
| **Maps** | IGN 4250 OT |
| **Food and drink** | Water is available in rivers on the early part of the ascent, but there is none on the higher parts and barely a trickly on the descent. The hotel, refuge and a snack bar at Ascu Stagnu serve meals and sell provisions. |
| **Shelter** | Tall trees offer shade at the start and finish, but the highest parts cross open and exposed rocky mountainsides. |

This is a tough day and there are no easier alternatives. Only minutes after leaving the Refuge de Carozzu, there is a steep and rugged descent into a gorge. After crossing a suspension footbridge, trekkers pick their way up the Spasimata Slabs. Although cables have been fixed to the rock, most of the slabs are unprotected. Be warned that the slabs can be slippery when wet, and even a light frost will make them treacherous. A steep and rocky ascent, sometimes holding snow well into the summer, leads to a high rocky gap. After a traverse across the steep face of Muvrella to reach another gap, there is a bird's-eye view of the ski-station at Ascu Stagnu. The descent is very steep and rugged, taking longer to complete than some might imagine, but on reaching the ski-station there are abundant offers of food and drink, and a choice of accommodation.

Leave the **Refuge de Carozzu** as signposted for Asco and Bonifatu. After only a few paces, pass a remarkable helipad construction and turn left at a path junction as signposted 'Asco'. Birch trees give way to stately laricio pines, maritime pines and arbutus scrub. Cables protect part of the route, where inclined slabs of rock are crossed. A rugged stretch of path leads down to the **Ruisseau de Spasimata**, where a metal suspension **footbridge** spans the river. It is a very wobbly bridge, bearing a request that no more than two people cross at a time. The altitude is around 1220m (4000ft). The pool beneath the bridge is a popular bathing spot for weary wanderers in hot weather, and indeed, many motorists climb from the road-end at Bonifatu to reach it.

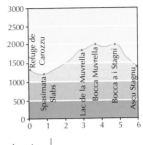

*Care is needed on the Spasimata Slabs, which can be slippery when wet and should be avoided when icy*

79

Find a safe stance and marvel at your surroundings – sheer rock walls and pinnacles rise all around, and a few isolated laricio pines appear to grow from solid rock on the cliffs.

A bouldery path climbs to the left, then the trees thin out and trekkers start crossing the sloping **Spasimata Slabs** high above the river. The first slabs are protected with a long chain and shorter cables. In dry conditions these aids are superfluous, but in wet weather the slabs can be greasy and the cables prove more useful. Do not cross the slabs if there is snow or ice present. ◄

There may be an inflowing watercourse and a little shade in hot weather, then more slabs have to be climbed, this time without the benefit of cables. Look out for unusual plants cowering in cracks, especially saxifrages. Later, there are more slabs, climbed with the aid of a long and shorter chain. Climb further, turning round a bend in the valley and enjoy a fine view of a waterfall down to the left. The path climbs into a wooded side-valley, steep and stony underfoot, with juniper scrub all around. Watch as the path suddenly switches to the right, climbing uphill beside a rocky rib. Also look out for a small, cool cave on the right, offering shade on a hot day.

The path roughly contours across the valley side, passing through alder scrub where slender mountain ash also grows. After crossing the valley, climb a path that is alternately rocky and stony. Watch for the markers and generally pass between the tree scrub and the rock walls to the left. Keep climbing until directed up

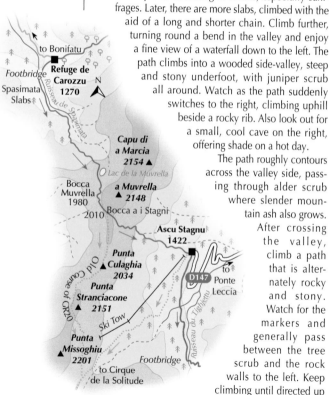

to Bonifatu

Footbridge

**Refuge de Carozzu 1270**

Spasimata Slabs ↑

N

*Ruisseau de Spasimata*

**Capu di a Marcia 2154 ▲**

*Lac de la Muvrella*

Bocca Muvrella 1980

**a Muvrella ▲ 2148**

Bocca a i Stagni

2010

**Ascu Stagnu 1422** ■

**Punta ▲ Culaghia 2034**

**Punta Stranciacone ▲ 2151**

Old Course of GR20

Ski Tow

D147

to Ponte Leccia

*Ruisseau du Tighjettu*

**Punta Missoghiu ▲ 2201**

Footbridge

to Cirque de la Solitude

onto a rocky ridge, then pass above a little rocky hollow containing **Lac de la Muvrella** at 1860m (6100ft). ▸ Big boulders around the lake offer shade and it might be a good place for a break before tackling the next part of the climb. Trekkers should reach the lake some 3hrs after leaving the Refuge de Carozzu.

The water is stagnant and should not be used for drinking.

Note that the next stretch can carry snow well into the summer. It is a north-facing gully full of boulders and broken rock. Zigzag up through the gully to reach the narrow, rocky gap of Bocca Muvrella at 1980m (6495ft). The towering peak of **a Muvrella** partly overhangs the gap, on the left-hand side, and trekkers can take a break to admire it, as well as the more distant view.

Turn right to leave the gap and scramble round a rocky corner, then turn sharp left and head downhill across the slope, scrambling on rock at times, as well as across slopes of juniper and alder scrub. Be sure to keep left at a path junction to reach another narrow gap, the **Bocca a i Stagni**, at 2003m (6572ft). Trekkers should reach this gap within an hour of leaving Lac de la Muvrella.

Cross the gap and go down a steep and stony path, watching carefully for markers, especially when there are rocky sections to be negotiated. The route shifts from side to side across the rocky valley, and although the complex of buildings at Ascu Stagnu are visible, they don't seem to move any closer! In fact, it takes about 1hr 30mins to complete the descent. In the lower part of the valley the buildings are lost from sight, and the path runs along the base of a sheer cliff, where there is usually good shade. A final bouldery slope covered in laricio pines leads down to a wide dirt road beside some chalets. Turn left, then right as indicated by paint flashes, to drop down to the buildings at **Ascu Stagnu**.

## ASCU STAGNU

Also known as Haut Asco, this ski-station is located at 1422m (4665ft), and it is difficult to imagine the winter ski season while the valley acts as a summer heat trap. Many trekkers who reach this point, especially those who have been struggling, yearn to take a day off. A few trekkers, sadly, will have had enough, feeling unable to face another day on the trail, and will be looking for a quick exit down the valley.

**Accommodation** There is a choice of accommodation. The most luxurious lodgings are at the Hôtel le Chalet, tel 04 95 47 81 08, which has 22 rooms. It also operates a gîte d'étape with a small 8-bed and a large 28-bed dormitory. The PNRC Refuge Ascu Stagnu offers 32 beds. Hire tents and camping spaces are available exclusively for GR20 trekkers around the foot of the ski-tows, and is organised at the refuge. Campers have access to the refuge toilets and showers, and can pay for meals at the hotel.

**Food and drink** Most trekkers will be happy to frequent the bar and restaurant at the Hôtel le Chalet, sampling good Corsican food and drink. Some may feel tempted to take a day off and indulge themselves further. A more limited choice of snack food and drinks is available at Snack l'Altore across the car park. When the time comes to leave, food supplies can be obtained either from the hotel bar, or from the 'GR20 Ravitaillement' operated by the Refuge Ascu Stagnu.

**Transport** Ascu Stagnu is at the end of the 30km (19 mile) long D147 that links with regular bus and rail services at Ponte Leccia. Two navette services run daily, from mid-May to mid-October, linking with trains at Ponte Leccia, operated by Corsica Giru Grisoni Autocars, tel 07 60 65 03 02 or 06 03 61 40 14. Outside the summer season, this service has to be booked. Using these buses also allows trekkers to enjoy a mini-break at the precariously stacked mountain settlement of Ascu, overlooking the dramatic Gorges de Ascu as well as being able to visit Ponte Leccia. If there are trekkers who wish to omit Monte Cinto, they can be taken to Calasima, from where it is possible to re-join the GR20 at the Auberge U Vallone. Talk to the driver if a connection is required with the bus serving Castel di Vergio. Check for notices or timetables at the Refuge Ascu Stagnu. Taxi Corse, tel 04 95 48 24 or 06 33 09 82 07 **www.taxi-corse.fr**, expect to have a vehicle on stand-by at Ascu Stagnu.

## PONTE LECCIA

Those who leave the GR20 at Ascu Stagnu can link with onward bus and rail services at Ponte Leccia, or spend the night in the village. The place is surprisingly busy, as most of the traffic around the northern half of Corsica passes through it at

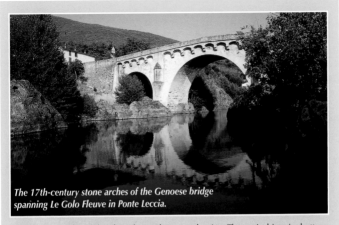

*The 17th-century stone arches of the Genoese bridge spanning Le Golo Fleuve in Ponte Leccia.*

some point, and people often change buses and trains. The main historical attraction is the graceful, 17th-century Genoese four-arched stone bridge from which the village takes its name, while the Domaine Vico vineyard is popular with visitors. There is a post office, a part-time bank with an ATM and two pharmacies. For tourist information tel 04 95 47 70 97.

**Accommodation** There are only two places to stay in Ponte Leccia. Hôtel Le Stuart, tel 04 95 47 61 11, is close to the Genoese bridge and has 18 rooms. The Hôtel Las Vegas, tel 04 95 47 61 59, has 8 rooms and is on the main road in the direction of Corte.

**Food and drink** Ponte Leccia straggles along main roads lined with a number of bars and restaurants, a few shops and two supermarkets.

**Transport** Buses linking Bastia and Calvi pass through Ponte Leccia daily from late June to early September, then weekdays for the rest of the year, operated by Beaux Voyages, tel 04 95 65 11 35 or 04 95 65 08 26, www.corsicar.com. Ponte Lecchia has daily train services linking Bastia, Calvi, Corte, Vizzavona and Ajaccio. Pick up a timetable from the station, or tel 04 95 32 80 61, 04 95 65 00 61 or 04 95 46 00 97, www.cf-corse.fr. Taxi Corse, tel 04 95 48 24 74 or 06 33 09 82 07, www.taxi-corse.fr, offers transfers to and from the GR20 and will also carry luggage by arrangement.

# STAGE 4

## Ascu Stagnu to
## Auberge U Vallone

| | |
|---|---|
| **Start** | Ascu Stagnu |
| **Finish** | Auberge U Vallone |
| **Distance** | 9km (5½ miles); addition for Monte Cinto: 2km (1¼ miles) return |
| **Total ascent** | 1250m (4100ft); Monte Cinto: 200m (655ft) |
| **Total descent** | 1230m (4035ft); Monte Cinto: 200m (655ft) |
| **Time** | 8hrs; Monte Cinto: 1hr 30mins |
| **Terrain** | A forested valley path gives way to scrambling on a steep and rocky slope. The higher parts of the valley feature steep and bouldery scree slopes, leading to a high ridge. Broken rock is traversed beside the ridge. The descent includes a steep scree slope and steep rock, requiring some scrambling. Rugged paths are used later. |
| **Maps** | IGN 4250 OT |
| **Food and drink** | Water can be obtained from a couple of streams on the ascent, but may be absent on the descent. The Refuge de Tighjettu and Auberge U Vallone serve meals and sell provisions. |
| **Shelter** | Some shade in the forest at first, but none on the open slopes of the mountain, which are exposed to sun, wind and rain, and can hold snow well into summer. Do not attempt this stage in bad weather. |

This was originally the variant after the Cirque de la Solitude was closed in June 2015 and is now the main route of the GR20. The route was previously marked with double yellow paint flashes, and in 2016 it was re-painted with red and white GR marks. The ascent is based on a long-standing route used to climb Monte Cinto. Once the initial climb is completed, the route runs close to a rocky ridge from Pointe des Éboulis to Bocca Crucetta, passing high above Lac du Cinto. This runs higher than any other part of the GR20, and would be challenging if there is snow or ice around. The route is well marked and should present little problem in mist, but rain could make the

## THE CLOSURE OF THE CIRQUE DE LA SOLITUDE AND SUBSEQUENT RE-ROUTING

Following the serious accident in June 2015, resulting in seven deaths, the Cirque de la Solitude was closed. A geologist's report concluded it was too dangerous to visit. A variant route was marked soon afterwards, and it was thoroughly checked for this guide. The Cirque de la Solitude is no longer part of the GR20, and the route that crosses the shoulder of Monte Cinto is now the main (and only) route.

Note that all the waymarks, chains and iron ladder have been removed from the Cirque de la Solitude. The geologist's report concluded that several tons of rubble remained poised to collapse without notice. Consequently, anyone attempting to traverse the Cirque would need to be equipped for rock-climbing, able to navigate complex terrain without markers, and be fully aware of the risk of sudden landslides or rock-falls. It is the author's opinion that the risks are too great, and that the Cirque de la Solitude should be avoided. The new route over the shoulder of Monte Cinto is a fine challenge in its own right, and is a much safer option than the Cirque. It might be the case that adventure companies might offer guided traverses of the Cirque, and trekkers might have the option of joining one of these.

Every so often, a trekker decides to chance passing through the Cirque de la Solitude, gets hopelessly lost and requires rescuing. Don't risk it. Check the Cicerone website for any further changes at www.cicerone. co.uk/852/updates.

*Crossing steep rock between Pointe des Éboulis and Bocca Crucetta*

rocks slippery, and there is no easy escape in the event of a storm. In clear weather, the mountain scenery is breathtaking. If time can be spared at Pointe des Éboulis, it is well worth the extra effort to visit the summit of Monte Cinto – the highest mountain in Corsica at 2706m (8878ft).

Cross the car park in front of the Hôtel le Chalet to leave **Ascu Stagnu** at 1422m (4665ft). A large signboard points the way and the path passes a wooden building hidden in the trees. Note the red and white paint flashes that mark the route, as well as the orange flashes that mark the way to the peak of Punta Minuta. A narrow path leads past laricio pines, roughly contouring across the slope. Pass a small water source, then cross a bouldery streambed and continue gently towards the **Ruisseau du Tighjettu**. Walk upstream roughly parallel to the river, leaving the shade of the pines and passing through juniper, alder and spiny broom scrub on rocky ground. Turn left as marked for 'Cinto' and cross a wooden **footbridge** over the Ruisseau du Tighjettu, at 1488m (4882ft). Pause to admire the fine array of peaks around the head of the valley.

The ascent becomes more difficult as it follows the paint marks in zigzags up a steep and rocky slope. Beware of any wet patches, where the rock can be greasy underfoot, and use a series of five chains for security. A long chain is followed by two shorter chains, then another long and another short chain. Those who start the ascent early in the day might find good shade on the slope before the sun strikes the rock. Watch carefully for the paint marks, which indicate crucial turns on rocky scrambles, or show the best way across awkward gullies. Easier stretches of path rise across scree slopes on the slopes below **Capu Borba**. The steep-sided valley is surrounded by towers of rock, including the ominous overhang of La Tour Penchée.

*The crest at Pointe des Éboulis, with Monte Cinto seen to the right*

The path is quite rough and stony, levelling out as it passes a rugged, stony hollow around 2150m (7050ft). ▸ Climb a scree slope, following the well-trodden and well-marked path, avoiding a left turn that leads to the tiny pool of **Lac d'Argentu**. Cross a rugged hump and pass several big boulders on a slight gap. Looking uphill, massive buttresses of rock rise skywards. The scree path occasionally reaches areas of broken rock where care is needed, and one part includes a chain.

*A small stream might be found nearby, if water is needed.*

Stay on the paint-marked route, avoiding other paths. After passing the base of a buttress, split by a dark gully, keep climbing and later go up another area of broken rock bearing a chain. The scree path finally reaches a high mountain crest at **Pointe des Éboulis**. At 2607m (8553ft), this is the highest point gained on the main route, where helpful signboards are bolted to rocks. At this point, reached 4hrs after leaving Ascu Stagnu, either turn left for an optional ascent of Monte Cinto, or turn right to continue the trek.

### Ascent of Monte Cinto

Turn left as signposted for Monte Cinto. The summit is clearly in view, but an older sign is soon reached, where the rugged path heads downhill, rather than following the rocky crest. White paint marks soon give way to red paint marks, and it is important to spot these to find the

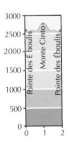

87

*On reaching the crest of the range, Monte Cinto is further along the ridge and is reached by easy scrambling*

best route. Trodden paths alternate with bare rock, with numerous short ascents and descents. When a summit is reached at 2651m (8698ft), a sign indicates that Monte Cinto lies further ahead.

Turn right downhill, which is soon confirmed by another sign. While going down a slope of huge boulders, watch carefully for a left turn, followed by scrambles and traverses across steep, rocky slopes. Eventually, turn left and scramble steeply up bare rock, which gives way to a pleasant and easy shoulder leading to the summit of **Monte Cinto** at 2706m (8878ft).

Take in the extensive views, with particular reference to the high mountains already passed, and those still to be passed, on the GR20. There might be a visitor book to record your ascent, and a number of ruined buildings are dotted around. Take particular care to retrace steps carefully to return to **Pointe des Éboulis**.

To continue the trek from Pointe des Éboulis, spot the signboard for Bocca Crucetta and Tighjettu, and follow the paint-marked path along the stony crest. As the path descends it crosses bouldery ground. Looking ahead, the rocky tower of Paglia Orba is seen beyond the nearby peaks of Punta Crucetta and Capu Falu, and those two peaks are separated by Bocca Crucetta. Broken rock is reached on the way to a gap, and the marked route drifts down to the left as it prepares to cut across the steep, broken, rocky flank of **Punta Crucetta**. Take this stretch slowly and carefully, and exercise extreme caution if the rock is wet and slippery. **Lac du Cinto** sits in a bouldery hollow, and it may be frozen well into the summer. A rocky scramble leads up to the gap of **Bocca Crucetta** at 2452m (8045ft), where helpful signboards point back and ahead. It should take less than an hour to reach this gap from Pointe des Éboulis.

An obvious, well-trodden path makes a broad loop as it descends a long scree slope, with a fine view through a valley dominated by the rocky buttresses and summit of Paglia Orba. Simply follow the path downhill and keep to the left of a bare hump of rock. Afterwards, take care where the scree rolls onto bare rock, then descend another short scree slope.

Ascu Stagnu 1422

to Ponte Leccia

D147

Ski Tow

Old route

Ruisseau du Tighjettu

Footbridge

Capu Borba 2305

Bocca Borba

La Tour Penchée

Lac d'Argentu

Pointe des Éboulis 2607

Monte Cinto 2706

Capu Larghia 2503

Punta Crucetta 2499

Lac du Cinto

2452 Bocca Crucétta

Ravin de Stranciacone

Old route

Ravin de Valle di Stagni

Capu Tighjettu 2273

Refuge de Tighjettu 1683

Auberge U Vallone 1440

Keep an eye on the paint marks, which show the way down a succession of bare rock outcrops. Juniper, thrift and parsley fern fill gaps in the rock, and short scrambles lead down a rocky cleft and a gully. Rather surprisingly, on a stony, level area, a small space has been cleared as a tent pitch.

Continue down bare rock and broken rock, passing a jammed boulder. Scramble down a rocky cleft and pass through an area of alder bushes and lush vegetation, around 2000m (6560ft). These are fed by damp patches and there might even be a stream trickling through a stony riverbed. This might be a handy water source, but don't rely on it. If the sun is setting, note that there are nearby places where tent pitches have been cleared, including one with an exceptional view down the valley. However, only use these if there is no hope of reaching the refuge far below.

Continue down slopes of bare rock and boulders into the **Ravin de Valle di Stagni**, briefly levelling out around 1800m (5905ft). More bare rock leads down to a stream where a little dam might be spotted. This impounds water for use at the Refuge de Tighjettu, and throughout the rest of the descent, which is much gentler, black plastic water pipes might be seen snaking across the slopes. Pass a little stone hut and continue to a signposted path junction beside a couple of tall laricio pines. This junction should be reached 2hrs 30mins after leaving Bocca Crucetta. At this point, either turn right to reach the **Refuge de**

**Tighjettu** with a very short ascent, or turn left to descend to the Auberge U Vallone in another 30mins.

The PNRC **Refuge de Tighjettu** isn't built in the usual stone bergerie style, but is a curious timber chalet construction, at 1683m (5255ft), partly supported on stilts. It enjoys a fine view down the valley and is couched on a rugged spur between the Ravin du Stranciacone and the Ravin de Valle di Stagni. The building has three dormitories with 36 beds and a large kitchen/dining area. The gardien's quarters are part of the building. Meals, food and drink are available. The showers are underneath the refuge, where there is a good sheltered space with a wash area, and there is a separate toilet block just downhill. Hire tents and small camping spaces are dotted around the steep slope below the refuge.

Follow a stony, bouldery path with red/white GR20 markers down through juniper and spiny broom scrub, or walk across bare rock, and cross the **Ravin de Valle di Stagni** at a cascade. Continue along the path, taking the time to look back at the refuge clinging to the steep and rocky slope. Cross the **Ravin du Stranciacone** and walk further down through the valley into an area of young pines. Keep to the marked path to reach the Bergeries de Ballone, also known as the **Auberge U Vallone**, at 1440m (4725ft).

The **Auberge U Vallone**, tel 06 12 03 44 65, operates a basic bar restaurant and offers meals, food and drink. Camping spaces are dotted around the area and there are also tents for hire. There is a shower, a toilet and a water source. Trekkers can sit at tables and chairs on a terrace and admire the surrounding mountains while eating and drinking, with the bongling bells of grazing cattle sounding nearby. Rock pools in the river are most welcome on hot days. There is an easy route leading away from the site, down through the valley to the little villages of Calasima, Pietra and Albertacce (see the Link from Auberge U Vallone to Albertacce for details).

# LINK ROUTE
## Auberge U Vallone to
## Albertacce

| | |
|---|---|
| **Start** | Auberge U Vallone |
| **Finish** | Albertacce |
| **Distance** | 13km (8 miles) |
| **Total ascent** | 60m (195ft) |
| **Total descent** | 625m (2050ft) |
| **Time** | 4hrs |
| **Terrain** | Forested slopes and rugged paths give way to easy road walking across open, scrubby slopes. Over half the route is on a tarmac road. |
| **Maps** | IGN 4250 OT |
| **Food and drink** | There are water sources at Calasima. Restaurants are available at Albertacce. |
| **Shelter** | There is initially shade in the forest, but much of the road crosses open, scrubby slopes. |

Trekkers occasionally leave the GR20 from the Auberge U Vallone. Some feel that they have seen the toughest four days of the route, and that the rest is going to be an anti-climax. They are wrong! Others, having suffered on the traverse near Monte Cinto, wish to see no more of the GR20, which is a pity. A rugged path leaves the bergerie to link with a dirt road through a forested valley, which quickly gives way to a tarmac road leading to Calasima – the highest village in Corsica. The road leads through another small village, Pietra, before zigzagging down to Albertacce. This route is used in reverse to supply the bergerie, and following the closure of the Cirque de la Solitude in 2015 it became busy with trekkers, who were offered a shuttle bus link between Ascu Stagnu and Calasima.

Leave the **Auberge U Vallone** and walk down a path flashed with yellow paint to find a ford across the stream. Follow the rough and stony path down past laricio pines to join a rugged track at a metal hut. Vehicles may be parked here and are used to supply the bergerie. Follow the

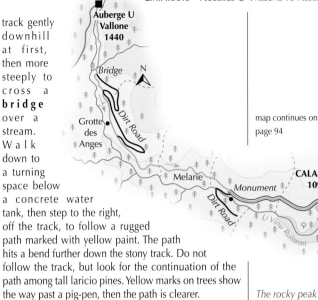

track gently downhill at first, then more steeply to cross a **bridge** over a stream. Walk down to a turning space below a concrete water tank, then step to the right, off the track, to follow a rugged path marked with yellow paint. The path hits a bend further down the stony track. Do not follow the track, but look for the continuation of the path among tall laricio pines. Yellow marks on trees show the way past a pig-pen, then the path is clearer.

map continues on page 94

There is a slight ascent, then a slight descent on a scrubby slope covered in huge boulders. A short detour along a cairned path, off to the right, reveals the **Grotte des Anges** – a cave beneath enormous wedged boulders.

*The rocky peak of Paglia Orba, seen from the Grotte des Anges, where there is a cave beneath huge boulders*

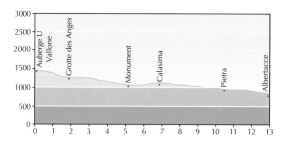

A monument stands to the right, in the shape of an aircraft propeller, commemorating three people killed while fighting a forest fire in 1979.

Re-join the track at another bend and follow it downhill. The track soon gives way to a tarmac road. ◀ Follow the road gently uphill beside mixed pines and chestnut trees to reach **Calasima** at 1095m (3593ft).

The little village of **Calasima** has a church, but no food, drink or accommodation. Following the closure of the Cirque de la Solitude in June 2015, two shuttle buses have operated daily in the summer, linking Calasima with Ponte Leccia and Ascu Stagnu. Trekkers wishing to use these buses between Ponte Leccia and Calasima must book in advance. Trekkers arriving at Calasima from Ascu Stagnu can follow the above route description in reverse to re-join the GR20.

The D318 leaves the village and crosses bridges over the Ruisseau de Sambuchellu and Ruisseau de Fiuminasca as it turns round a valley full of mixed woodland. Lose sight of the village while turning a rocky corner, then the road descends gently across a rocky, scrubby slope where there are very few

trees. Pass a fenced chestnut woodland where there may be pigs, then there is a slight ascent into the village of **Pietra**. Follow the road through the village and turn sharp right at a junction. Walk down the road in broad loops, passing houses, family tombs and little vegetable plots. Stay on the road all the way down to the main D84 in **Albertacce**, to reach the gîte d'étape, or shortcut straight down from the church to reach a couple of snack bars in the centre of the village.

## ALBERTACCE

The village of Albertacce straggles along the bendy main D84 around 860m (2820ft). It features a limited range of services, but offers enough to feed and accommodate trekkers until they can catch a bus. The Museu Archeologicu is the main attraction for most visitors. Local people have a Scandinavian ancestry in these parts.

**Accommodation** Hôtel a Sant Anna, tel 06 26 83 22 09, is a small 8-bedroom hotel.

**Food and drink** The Restaurant U Cintu, Restaurant Paglia Orba and Bar des Amis serve good Corsican fare. Blaring horns announce the arrival of visiting mobile shops.

**Transport** A bus service is operated by Autocars Cortenais, tel 04 95 46 02 12, 04 95 46 22 89 or 06 22 66 52 39, linking Albertacce with the Hôtel Castel di Vergio and Corte daily, from mid-May to mid-October. Taxi services in Albertacce are provided by Francois Luciani, tel 04 95 48 08 17, Françoise Luciani, tel 04 95 48 04 07, or contact Jean-Charles Antolini in Pietra, tel 04 95 48 01 97.

*The village of Albertacce offers a small choice of lodgings, restaurants and bars, as well as a summer bus service.*

# STAGE 5
*Auberge U Vallone to
Hôtel Castel di Vergio*

| | |
|---|---|
| **Start** | Auberge U Vallone |
| **Finish** | Hôtel Castel di Vergio |
| **Distance** | 15km (9½ miles) |
| **Total ascent** | 850m (2790ft) |
| **Total descent** | 870m (2855ft) |
| **Time** | 6hrs |
| **Terrain** | An easy walk through a forested valley gives way to a steep and rocky climb to Bocca di Foggiale and the Refuge de Ciottulu di I Mori. The descent through the valley of the Golo is steep, stony and rocky in places, but fairly easy to complete. An easy woodland walk ends the day. |
| **Maps** | IGN 4250 OT |
| **Food and drink** | Water can be taken from streams on the flanks of Paglia Orba. The Refuge de Ciottulu di I Mori serves meals and sells provisions. Water from the River Golo should probably be treated before drinking. A snack cabin is available at the Bergeries de Radule. The Hôtel Castel de Vergio offers meals and there is a small shop alongside. |
| **Shelter** | There is good shelter in the trees at the beginning and end of the day, and a break can be taken at the Refuge de Ciottulu di I Mori in the middle of the day. Even in poor weather, the valley of the Golo is more sheltered than the surrounding mountains. |

The first four stages of the GR20 are really quite tough, but that is all in the past. Ahead lies an easier day, and one that could be broken into two parts by climbing to the Refuge de Ciottulu di I Mori and staying overnight. However, it is possible to continue down from the refuge to the Hôtel Castel di Vergio and agree that the whole day isn't as tough as any of those earlier stages. There is a choice of accommodation options at the hotel, as well as abundant food and drink. On the other hand, those who decide to stay at the Refuge de Ciottulu di I Mori could also climb Paglia Orba, the third highest mountain in Corsica. (See the next section for an ascent route.)

Cross a little stream near the **Auberge U Vallone**, then follow a stony path through spiny broom and bracken scrub, passing clumps of hellebore and other flowers as the pine trees become more numerous. In some areas the pines drop abundant cones, but there are no saplings, while in other areas young trees grow into dense thickets, crowding each other out as they strive for the light. There is evidence of a former forest fire, but many of the tall laricio pines have survived. The path is fairly gentle and crosses huge boulders in the **Ravin de Paglia Orba**, where water usually flows. Looking up at the rugged buttresses of Paglia Orba, some trekkers might already be contemplating an ascent of the mountain.

The path continues to be fairly gentle, but it also begins to climb steadily as it makes its way through the pines and around a rocky shoulder to reach the next valley. Enjoy the shade of the pines at the entrance to this valley, as they quickly thin out and the path leads onto a more open slope of spiny broom and juniper scrub, where only a handful of laricio pines stand. The path becomes steep, stony and very worn as it climbs uphill, then it suddenly reaches a slope of bare rock. Watch carefully for paint flashes to follow the best line of ascent, and cross a stream at a series of cascades.

Looking up to the pinnacles and buttresses of Paglia Orba, mouflon might be spotted grazing on what appears to be bare rock. Looking down the valley, the barrage and artificial lake at Calacuccia are visible. There is less rock and more of a worn, stony path further uphill. One area is

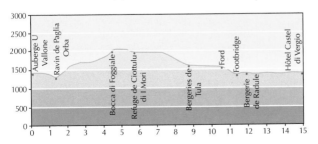

*A walker reaches the gap of the Bocca di Foggiale after a steep and rocky climb from the valley*

wet enough to support plenty of butterworts, and there is a tiny water source. The juniper, spiny broom and alder scrub is remarkably flowery in places. Keep climbing, grappling with rock where necessary or shuffling up the loose, stony, boulder-strewn path while following route markers. Cross an area of broken rock and swing to the right to rise above the **Bocca di Foggiale** at 1962m (6437ft).

The path cuts through patches of spiny broom on a reddish scree slope. Pass a cairn at 2050m (6725ft), then descend through patches of alder scrub with a view of the **Refuge de Ciottulu di I Mori** ahead. A few camping spaces, a helipad and water source are passed before reaching the refuge, and in early summer the grassy areas support plenty of Corsican crocuses. The refuge should be reached about 3hrs 15mins after leaving the Auberge U Vallone. Most trekkers take at least a short break here, while others consider the possibility of staying overnight, or even contemplate climbing **Paglia Orba**.

The PNRC **Refuge de Ciottulu di I Mori** is built in the bergerie style and situated at 1991m (6532ft), with a fine terrace overlooking the Golo valley and the mountains far beyond. There is a dormitory with 30 beds and a kitchen/dining room, while the gardien's quarters are at one end of the building. Hire tents and camping spaces are located alongside. Meals and supplies of food and drink can be purchased. A toilet and shower are located in a small building just below the refuge. A path leading towards Paglia Orba and Capu Tafunatu is signposted behind the refuge, where the source of the Golo, the longest river in Corsica, is located. (Those staying at the refuge to climb Paglia Orba should refer to the next section for details of the ascent.)

Continue along the path as signposted for the Refuge de Manganu, contouring along a stony path across a slope covered in spiny broom scrub, while the view down the valley stretches as far as distant Monte Alcudina. The path leads across a gentle gap and climbs a short way to a rounded summit at 1954m (6411ft), where the view westwards includes the sea around the Golfe de Porto. The path becomes more rugged as it begins to descend into the valley, passing through alder scrub and zigzagging down a slope covered in loose stones and spiny broom. There are fine views back to Paglia Orba, Capu Tafunatu and the Refuge de Ciottulu di I Mori at the head of the valley, while the ruined **Bergeries de Tula** are visible at the foot of the slope.

Swing to the right and follow the path downstream, keeping fairly close to the **Golo**. The path is stony, but

*The Golo can be forded at a point where there are broad, bare slabs of granite*

relatively easy, passing areas of juniper, spiny broom, alder scrub and a signpost. On hearing and seeing little waterfalls plunging into deep green pools, the thought of taking a dip and basking on the warm rocks might appeal. Reach a point where the valley bends to the left, and at this point cross the river easily on bare rock, just below a fine little waterfall and deep pool. Watch carefully for this crossing, which some trekkers miss. ◄

*If the river looks too dangerous to ford, continue downstream with care and cross a footbridge.*

After fording the river, views of Paglia Orba and Capu Tafunatu give way to the Monte Ritondu massif in the distance. Walk over rock slabs and cross bouldery slopes to continue downstream. Note the splendid laricio pines in this part of the valley. The Reserve Biologique Dirigée de la Forét Domaniale de Valduniellu has been established in this area to study the longevity of the pines. Some of them are over 300 years old and stand over 30m (100ft) tall. If the river was forded earlier, then *do not* cross the first **footbridge**, but continue down an old path, created by nudging boulders to one side across steep and rocky slopes. The paint flashes and a signpost reveal a zigzag path and the river is crossed at a second **footbridge**.

Blue paint flashes in this area indicate the Sentier de Radule, which runs concurrent with the GR20 for a while. A bouldery path leads across a steep slope covered in bracken and hellebore, and crosses rocky slabs to reach the **Bergerie de Radule**, about 1hr 30mins after leaving the Refuge de Ciottulu di I Mori. Pass between the buildings as marked.

The **Bergerie de Radule**, tel 06 14 39 41 87, which also styles itself 'GRadule', is a huddle of small stone buildings perched on a rocky ledge at 1370m (4495ft). Goats are milked on the premises and fresh brocciu is offered for sale. Below the buildings, a deep pool of water fills a rocky gorge, and beside that is a small camping area with a few hire tents and a shower. Food and drink are dispensed from a small snack cabin.

The GR20 crosses a small dam below a small waterfall. A path might be noticed rising to the right, marked with yellow flashes of paint, offering a route to the Col de Vergio. This provides fine views, but anyone following it would then have to walk down to the Hôtel Castel di Vergio.

The GR20 stays lower on the slope, passing through tangled birch woods dotted with stout laricio pines. Views are limited, but the path is

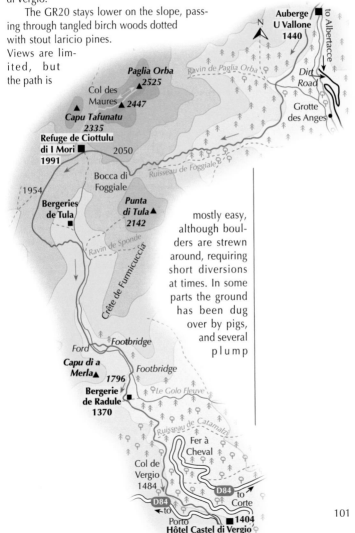

mostly easy, although boulders are strewn around, requiring short diversions at times. In some parts the ground has been dug over by pigs, and several plump

101

specimens may be seen before ending the day's trek. Avoid a path dropping down to the left, which leads to the **Fer à Cheval** on a nearby road bend. At another path junction, the Mare a Mare Nord, marked by orange paint flashes, crosses the GR20. Keep straight ahead and keep following the route markers to reach the main D184 at a bend. Turn left and the **Hôtel Castel di Vergio** is quickly reached, at 1404m (4606ft), some 1hr 15mins after leaving the Bergerie de Radule.

The **Hôtel Castel di Vergio**, tel 04 95 48 00 01, is a large, modern construction facing the foot of a ski tow, so it wins no prizes for prettiness.

The hotel offers 29 rooms for trekkers who are looking for more comfort at this stage, as well as a laundry. A separate building houses a 70-bed gîte d'étape, arranged in dormitories sleeping 6 to 10 people. One end of the building houses a small shop, while the other end of the building houses toilets, showers and a kitchen. A fenced-off area alongside is available for camping. Large pigs cannot enter the campsite, but small pigs and foxes can, so if carrying food or buying it from the shop, stow it at height. Anyone camping or staying in the gîte, who wishes to enjoy good Corsican meals in the hotel restaurant, should arrange this if they book in advance, or at the very latest on arrival. The hotel bar is open to everyone.

A bus service is operated by Autocars Cortenais, tel 04 95 46 02 12, 04 95 46 22 89 or 06 22 66 52 39, **www.autocars-cortenais-corse.fr**, linking the hotel with Albertacce and Corte daily, from mid-May to mid-October. Pack-carrying donkeys can be hired and taken onto the GR20 by arrangement with La Promenâne, tel 06 15 29 45 64, **www.randonnee-ane-corse.com**.

# EXCURSION

*Ascent of Paglia Orba from Refuge*
*de Ciotullu di I Mori*

| | |
|---|---|
| **Start/Finish** | Refuge de Ciotullu di I Mori |
| **Distance** | 3.5km (2 miles) there-and-back |
| **Total ascent** | 600m (1970ft) |
| **Total descent** | 600m (1970ft.) |
| **Time** | 3hrs there-and-back |
| **Terrain** | Easy paths at the start and near the summit, but bouldery in other places, with some quite difficult scrambling on steep rock. This is the most difficult scrambling in the whole book. |
| **Maps** | IGN 4250 OT |
| **Food and drink** | Carry water and food from the Refuge de Ciottulu di I Mori. |
| **Shelter** | Some shade in rock gullies, but the mountain is very exposed to wind and rain, in which conditions an ascent is not recommended. |

Paglia Orba, at 2525m (8284ft), is the third highest mountain in Corsica, and its profile displays very steep, bare rock in most views. The ascent is a considerable challenge for the ordinary trekker. Be warned at the outset that the scrambling required on this mountain, even by the easiest route, is a little more serious than that encountered on the toughest parts of the GR20. There are plenty of good holds for hands and feet, made possible because of the nature of the rock, which is a coarse puddingstone conglomerate, rather than the usual granite, but some moves are awkward and exposed. Don't try this ascent with a large pack, but take only the bare essentials, so as not to limit movement. The effort involved in reaching the summit, or even getting part way, is rewarded by awesome rock scenery at close quarters and splendid views of distant ranges of mountains. There is no harm in climbing part-way, then beating an honourable retreat to the refuge, but always ensure that it is possible to reverse your steps for the descent.

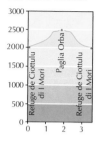

Start behind the **Refuge de Ciottulu di I Mori**, situated at 1991m (6532ft), where a path is signposted 'Paglia Orba' and 'Capu Tafunatu'. Even at the start, Paglia Orba looks unassailable to ordinary trekkers, and those who spot people already engaged in the ascent will realise that this is no ordinary route. The path is initially quite easy, rising gently across a scree slope and crossing the 'Source du Golo' – source of the longest river in Corsica. Enter a wild and rocky hollow, couched between Paglia Orba and Capu Tafunatu, with the rocky **Col des Maures** directly ahead. Watch out for a path branching off to the right, marked by small cairns, leading towards the rocky flanks of Paglia Orba. The scree becomes more and more bouldery, and scramblers are led into a leaning gully full of boulders, with a lumpy tower of rock watching over their progress.

*The route towards the rocky dome of Paglia Orba is signposted behind the Refuge de Ciottulu di I Mori*

Two or three cairned routes lead off to the left, so assess them in turn and choose one to your liking. Continue up a series of slabs and rocky paths, crossing more boulders, following the cairns as they lead ever upwards. As the path begins to swing to the right,

the scrambling appears easy, but on entering a steep rocky gully above some enormous jammed boulders, flanked by leaning towers of rock, the ascent suddenly looks quite intimidating. Look around to see the famous hole pierced through the neighbouring summit of Capu Tafunatu, which sometimes looks like a baleful blue eye. This eye watches unblinking while scramblers negotiate the hardest part of the ascent.

The cairns lead to the right-hand side of the gully. Scramble up some steep rocksteps that slant rather awkwardly downwards, making feet feel that they are insecurely planted. Stay well to the right where it isn't too exposed, but please ensure that you are capable of reversing all your moves later in the day. Approaching the top of the rocky gully, things become easier, and the cairns lead left to a rocky notch where there is an awesome view of the far side of the mountain. ▸

Look carefully for the cairns, which lead above the rocky notch, along a narrow and exposed ledge, then up an exposed little scramble where you simply cannot afford to slip. Above this, easier slabs and bouldery slopes lead to a summit. This is not the main summit of Paglia Orba, but a subsidiary summit at 2447m (8028ft).

The cairns lead down a slope of slabs and boulders, cutting well beneath a rocky gap, then a rather circuitous course leads back onto the main crest of the mountain. An amazingly easy path, brightly speckled with the yellow flowers of Alpine avens, leads along the crest towards the summit. Climb to the summit cairn on **Paglia Orba** at 2525m (8284ft) and enjoy the view, marvelling at how steeply the slopes fall in every direction except that used for the final ascent. It takes about 2hrs to reach the summit from the refuge.

From the top, look back towards Monte Cinto and the early stages of the GR20, and ahead to Monte Rotondu and the next stages of the route. Hopefully you will be able to retrace your steps to the refuge without too much difficulty. The descent can be accomplished in as little as an hour.

Scramblers may also notice that the eye of Capu Tafunatu is no longer watching them – maybe because the next move is too awkward and exposed to watch!

# STAGE 6

### Hôtel Castel di Vergio to
### Refuge de Manganu

| | |
|---|---|
| **Start** | Hôtel Castel di Vergio |
| **Finish** | Refuge de Manganu |
| **Distance** | 17km (10½ miles) |
| **Total ascent** | 670m (2200ft) |
| **Total descent** | 475m (1560ft) |
| **Time** | 5hrs 45mins |
| **Terrain** | A well-wooded walk around the head of a valley gives way to a relatively easy walk over the mountains and easy walking near Lac du Ninu. A more rugged path leads through a broad and bouldery valley, with some patchy woodland. Generally easy walking all day. |
| **Maps** | IGN 4251 OT |
| **Food and drink** | A water source lies off-route near Lac du Ninu. Snacks and drinks at the Bergerie de l'Inzecche. The Bergeries de Vaccaghja and Refuge de Manganu serve meals and sell provisions. |
| **Shelter** | The wooded slopes offer plenty of shade, but other parts of the route are more exposed. Patchy woodlands in the latter parts of the day offer a little shade. |

Despite its length, this is a relatively easy day. Indeed, considerable stretches are virtually level, such as the woodland walk at the start of the day and the path passing Lac du Ninu in the middle of the day. Even when there is an ascent to complete, up to the Bocca San Petru and on to the Bocca â Reta, the path features easy zigzags and gradients. For much of the day it is possible to stride out and walk in a manner that simply isn't possible on the rough and stony slopes of the earlier stages of the GR20. The scenery may not always be dramatic, but it is often charming and pleasant. This is a day to savour, without dashing ahead or over-exerting, to prepare for more hard trekking over the next few days on the way to Vizzavona.

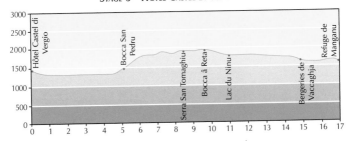

Walk a short way down the D184 from the **Hôtel Castel di Vergio**, and a sign on the right indicates the way to Lac du Ninu and the Refuge de Manganu. A forest path runs downhill, gradually levelling out as it swings to the right, contouring easily across the slopes. Tall laricio pines and young trees share the slopes with slender birch and a few stout beech trees. The path is well engineered and a joy to follow. Trekkers can stride out and strike a good rhythm after those earlier days watching every step on rocky mountainsides. There are views between the trees, back towards Paglia Orba and Monte Cinto, as well as down the forested valley and ahead to the mountain called u Tritore. The path weaves in and out on the slopes as it crosses the **Crête de Scupertu** and a few streambeds, some of which carry water early in the summer.

Watch carefully for a sudden right turn uphill. This turning is well marked and there is a signpost for San Petru. Another signpost points downhill for the Fontaine Caroline, but don't imagine that this is a useful water source, as it is actually a long way down the wooded slope beside the D184. The path initially looks as though it zigzags up a steep, stony slope exposed to the sun, but it quickly becomes a gently graded zigzag route in the shade of tall beech trees. ▶

Look out for pigs digging the ground while searching for beech mast.

The **Bocca San Pedru**, or Col St Pierre, is a grassy gap with fine views of the valleys on either side. There are views back to Capu Tafunatu, Paglia Orba and Monte Cinto. A tiny oratory stands on the gap at 1452m (4764ft), and this point should be reached about 1hr 30mins into the day.

Leading a donkey across the rocky slopes of u Tritore

Note how some isolated beech trees have been shaped by the westerly wind into grotesque shapes.

Turn left up a grassy ridge featuring low outcrops of rock. A zigzag mule track leads up the open slope and passes an electricity **pylon**. ◄

At a higher level, the path leaves the ridge and heads left across the slopes of **u Tritore**. The path is gently graded, passing beech trees and alder scrub. Watch out for a sudden right turn, where the path zigzags up onto a more open slope, crossing areas of rock and alder scrub. Follow the path close to the crest of the **Serra San Tomaghiu**, and take a peep through a couple of gaps at the valley on the southern side. The path leads through a rocky gap, zigzags downhill a short way, then climbs across the stony slopes of **Capu a u Tozzu**. It rises gently to the broad and grassy gap of **Bocca â Reta**, at 1883m (6178ft), where fine views of the mountains ahead can be enjoyed.

The path descends easily towards **Lac du Ninu**, which is a remarkably pleasant spot on a fine day. The blue lake is surrounded by short green turf grazed by cattle and horses, while the mountains in the distance lend grandeur to the scene, and may hold streaks of snow well into the summer. The lake is at an altitude of 1743m

(5718ft), is 11m (36ft) deep, and is frozen for almost half the year. It is the source of one of Corsica's finest rivers, the Tavignanu. The barren rock slopes of Punta Artica rise beyond.

Note that the path was diverted in 2015, from the southern to the northern side of the lake. Trekkers are asked not to follow the old route, but if water is desperately needed, there is a **source** on the southern shore, built into a small wayside shrine. The new route is very well marked, leading to the northern shore of **Lac du Ninu**, about 2hrs after leaving Bocca San Pedru. Look back to see Capu a u Tozzu reflected in the water.

The path runs level and easily past the lake, passing splendid, short-cropped mountain pasture dotted with little pools of water, known as pozzines. Remember that camping is forbidden, despite it looking like an ideal place to pitch a tent. The path gradually swings left, rising very gently into a broad valley. Follow the markers to reach a point where a notice invites a short detour left up to the **Bergerie de l'Inzecche**. Snacks and drinks are offered here, but if not stopping, simply turn right to continue.

Step across a small stream as marked and the path becomes rougher and stonier underfoot, with scrub alongside that features abundant Corsican crocuses in early summer. The path descends roughly parallel to the infant river **Tavignanu**, on a rugged, boulder-strewn slope. Spiny broom and juniper scrub give way to a patchy area of beech trees and beech scrub where a stream is forded. The trees and scrub become denser, but the path is reasonably clear, eventually leading across an open slope scattered with boulders. Turn a rocky corner and the **Bergeries de Vaccaghja** suddenly come into view, at 1600m (5250ft). Trekkers should reach this point about 1hr 15mins after leaving Lac du Ninu. It is a good place to take a break, even though the Refuge de Managanu can be seen ahead.

The **Bergeries de Vaccaghja**, tel 06 24 73 63 67, overlook the flat grassland of Pianu di Campotile, which is surrounded by mountains and used for grazing cattle

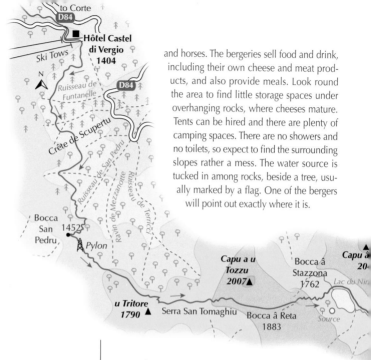

and horses. The bergeries sell food and drink, including their own cheese and meat products, and also provide meals. Look round the area to find little storage spaces under overhanging rocks, where cheeses mature. Tents can be hired and there are plenty of camping spaces. There are no showers and no toilets, so expect to find the surrounding slopes rather a mess. The water source is tucked in among rocks, beside a tree, usually marked by a flag. One of the bergers will point out exactly where it is.

On leaving the **Bergeries de Vaccaghja**, walk down a grassy, boulder-strewn slope and cross the level, grassy **Pianu di Campotile**. The Refuge de Manganu is visible ahead, but there is a climb up a short, steep, rocky slope to reach it, crossing the

*Trekkers on the Pianu de Campotile on the approach to Refuge de Manganu*

**Bocca d'Acqua Ciarnente** at 1568m (5144ft). The mountain rising to the left is the Punta di a Femina Morta. Cross a stream on its slopes, then cross a wooden footbridge on the right to reach the **Refuge de Manganu**, at 1601m (5253ft), about 45mins after leaving the bergeries.

The PNRC **Refuge de Manganu** is built in the bergerie style, featuring a dormitory with 31 beds and a kitchen/dining room. The gardien's quarters are in the same building, while the showers and new toilets are behind the refuge. Some trekkers prefer to take a dip in one of the pools in the nearby river, rather than take a shower. Hire tents and small camping spaces are located throughout the alder scrub behind the building. Meals can be ordered and stocks of food and drink can be bought. Stow any food safely at height, out of reach of predatory foxes! The terrace in front of the refuge looks back along the route of the GR20 to the Bergeries de Vaccaghja, with the mountains of Cimatella and Punta Artica dominating the scene.

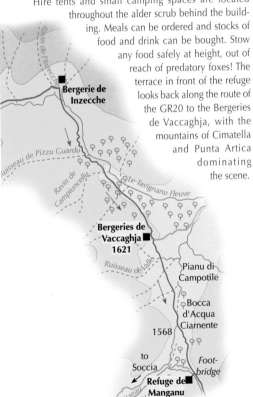

# LINK ROUTE
## Begeries de Vaccaghja to Corte

| | |
|---|---|
| **Start** | Bergeries de Vaccaghja |
| **Finish** | Corte |
| **Distance** | 21.5km (13½ miles) |
| **Total ascent** | 300m (985ft) |
| **Total descent** | 1420m (4660ft) |
| **Time** | 7hrs 30mins |
| **Terrain** | Mostly good paths and mostly gently downhill from open slopes into dense forest. However, there are patchy woodlands on open slopes as well as clearings in the forest. There are also some very rocky stretches involving short scrambles, and several short ascents. |
| **Maps** | IGN 4251 OT |
| **Food and drink** | Water might be available at the Bergerie de Tramizzole. The Refuge a Sega serves meals and sells provisions. There are water sources at the Ponte di u Russulinu and at a picnic site. There are plenty of restaurants, bars and shops around Corte. |
| **Shelter** | The higher slopes are largely open, with patchy woodlands. The greater part of the valley is covered in dense pine forest with occasional clearings. The forest thins out well before Corte is reached. |

Those who only intend covering the northern part of the GR20 may wonder where they should finish their trek. One option is to leave the route at the Bergeries de Vaccaghja, and walk down through the Tavignanu valley to Corte. On the map, this seems like a very long way, and some of it is indeed rough and rocky. However, there are also many stretches of easy path, and the gradient is mostly downhill, with a few short climbs along the way. If a break is needed, the Refuge a Sega is located halfway down the valley. There are splendid views at the top of the valley, but tall laricio pines dominate later. However, there are plenty of breaks in the forest, allowing views through a remarkably deep gorge, where the river flows between monstrous boulders. Occasional glimpses of Corte are noted towards the end, and the route finally leads towards the Citadel at the top end of town. A full range of services is available in what was once the island capital.

Leave the **Bergeries de Vaccaghja** by crossing the GR20, then look across a boulder-strewn slope to spot a couple of signs pointing the way to the Refuge a Sega. The path is fairly clear and is flashed with yellow paint marks. Pass some big boulders on the way down towards a beech wood. A bare granite ford is reached where the **Tavignanu** is usually a mere trickle, but there may be deep pools of water nearby. ▶ Cross the river and follow the path onwards through the wood, fording one or two little streams, depending on how wet or dry the ground is.

*If the river is in flood after heavy rain, use a footbridge visible upstream.*

Emerge from the woods and walk gently downhill, passing spiny broom, juniper and rock outcrops. The **Bergerie de Tramizzole** is reached at 1427m (4682ft), where small buildings enjoy a splendid view through the upper part of the valley. There might be an opportunity

*The Bergerie de Tramizzole is passed high in the Tavignanu valley*

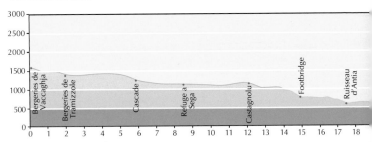

to get water here. The path continues into a dip, passing through a beech-wood, then climbing to a tall, square-built cairn on a slope of bare rock. Continue across an open slope, gradually rising to cross a grassy crest. Walk downhill and turn left at a prominent **beech** tree, reaching a signposted path junction.

The Mare a Mare Nord joins from the left, on its long coast-to-coast journey across Corsica, linking Moriani and Cargèse. Turn right as signposted for the Refuge a Sega, and descend into a broad, gentle hollow covered by spiny broom and juniper. Ford a stream and the path becomes rocky underfoot. There are plenty of pines, but also steep rocky slopes. Watch carefully for the yellow paint markers, as well as directional arrows painted on the rock. There are some narrow traverses and short scrambles near the **Tavignanu**, before the path climbs over a rocky crest. A rugged descent encounters an enormous fallen pine, which forms a stout wooden arch across the path.

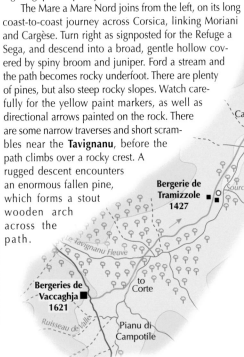

There is no way around this obstacle, so it is necessary to crouch and shuffle beneath it. Continue down into denser forest, reaching a wonderful

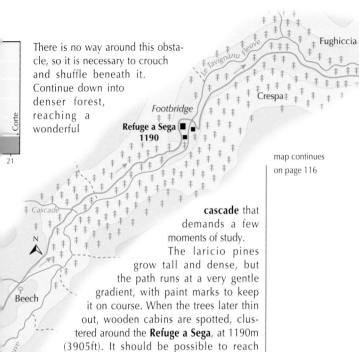

*Footbridge*

**Refuge a Sega 1190**

Fughiccia

Crespa

map continues
on page 116

**cascade** that demands a few moments of study.

The laricio pines grow tall and dense, but the path runs at a very gentle gradient, with paint marks to keep it on course. When the trees later thin out, wooden cabins are spotted, clustered around the **Refuge a Sega**, at 1190m (3905ft). It should be possible to reach the refuge 3hrs after leaving the Bergeries de Vaccaghja.

The PNRC **Refuge a Sega**, tel 09 88 99 35 57 or 06 10 71 77 26, is a large two-storey building with 36 beds and a huge kitchen/dining area. The toilets, showers and gardien's quarters are in the same building, which also includes a small 4-bed 'gîte'. A full meals service is available. Wooden huts are arranged near the refuge, with tents for hire and plenty of camping spaces. It is worth bearing in mind that this refuge tends to be fully staffed a month before the GR20 refuges, and remains staffed for a month longer (May to October).

Leave the Refuge a Sega as signposted for Corte and cross a footbridge over the **Tavignanu**. Pass a hut, climb quickly to a path junction and turn left. Tall laricio pines obscure the view, but the path is easy and leads roughly downstream, albeit well away from the river. Passing round the lower slopes of **Crespa**, the path becomes more rugged underfoot later. Watch carefully when the path

turns right to enter a side-valley at **Castagnolu**, as it might be possible to catch a distant glimpse of Corte far ahead. Ford a stream and walk back down into the main valley.

The path doesn't always descend, but occasionally climbs and even doubles back on itself for short stretches. When the path turns right to enter another side-valley, overhanging rock forms a shelter. Re-enter the main valley and continue down through it, passing through a rock cutting at one point. Later, descend to the **Tavignanu** and cross it using a **footbridge** – the Ponte di u Russulinu, at 760m (2495ft). If water is required, a few steps lead up to a **source**.

The path soon pulls away from the river as it negotiates steep, rocky and well-forested slopes. A memorial tablet might be spotted on the way round a rocky corner. The path has been built with considerable labour in places, stoutly buttressed against rock faces, and at one point climbing beneath overhanging rock as it turns another corner. As the path descends, a rocky **viewpoint** allows a glimpse of Corte, and after zigzagging further down, another rocky **viewpoint** allows another glimpse. The depth of the view, and the steepness of the valley sides is remarkable. The path is drawn deep into another side-valley,

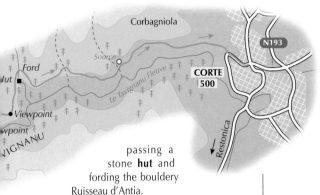

passing a stone **hut** and fording the bouldery Ruisseau d'Antia. Follow the path onwards as the forest begins to thin out, and cross another little side-valley. Later, an enclosed picnic site is reached where there is a notice, a small shrine and a water **source**. The path is quite rough, stony and rocky as it crosses the slopes of **Corbagniola**. Some parts are crudely boulder-paved or cross rock polished by constant use. Later, there are signposts as the path zigzags down, passing small animal pens. After going through a gate and passing olive trees, the path finally joins a road at the top end of **Corte**. Simply walk down the road and decide whether to stay high and visit the Citadel, around 500m (1640ft), or continue down into the centre of town to avail of all its services. Corte might be reached 4hrs 30mins after leaving the Refuge a Sega.

## CORTE

Corte sits squarely in the centre of Corsica, with its back to the mountains, overlooking a fertile valley. Whenever coastal settlements were attacked by invaders, Corte was generally able to hold out for at least a while longer. Corte has a long history and in 1735, after a period of strife, Corsican independence was declared in the town. However, power wasn't properly consolidated until Pascal Paoli achieved it from 1755 to 1769. He made Corte the island capital and established a university in the town. The main ports remained in Genoese hands, so he founded another port at Île Rousse. Paoli was honoured as 'Father of the Nation' and at one time was admired by fellow Corsican Napoleon Bonaparte. However, Napoleon later

*The mountain citadel town of Corte was once the capital of Corsica, and it remains a place of Corsican culture*

referred to him as 'traitor to the Republic'. The history of Corte is best appreciated by first visiting the Museu di a Corsica, tel 04 95 45 25 45, www.musee-corse.com, then continue exploring the Citadel. Corte tourist information office is also at the Citadel, tel 04 95 46 26 70, www.corte-tourisme. com.

**Accommodation** There is plenty of accommodation around Corte, but there are times when every bed is taken. A selection of hotels in the centre of town include the 63-room Hôtel de la Paix, tel 04 95 46 06 72, the 31-room Hôtel Sampiero Corso, tel 04 95 46 09 76, the 16-room Hôtel du Nord, tel 04 95 46 00 68, the 11-room Hôtel Duc de Padoue, tel 04 95 46 01 37, and the 8-room Hôtel Si Mea, tel 04 95 65 08 23. Hotels along the road into the Restonica valley include the 31-room Jardins de la Glacière, tel 04 95 45 27 00, the 27-room Hôtel Dominique Colonna, tel 04 95 45 25 65, and the 17-room Hôtel Arena Le Refuge, tel 04 95 46 09 13. At the budget end are the Gîte d'Étape U Tavignanu and its campsite, tel 04 95 46 16 85, Camping Restonica, tel 04 95 46 11 59, Camping Alivetu, tel 04 95 46 11 09, and Camping U Sognu, tel 04 95 46 09 07. Further up the road into the Restonica valley is Camping Tuani, tel 04 95 46 11 65.

**Food and drink** There are plenty of restaurants, cafés and bars to suit all tastes and pockets, as well as a range of shops, including a large supermarket with an impressive choice. Plenty of fine Coriscan food and drink is available.

**Transport** For such a large town, there are very few bus services. Autocars Cortenais, tel 04 95 46 22 89 or 06 19 83 26 18, **www.auto cars-cortenais-corse.fr**, links Corte with Albertacce and the Hôtel Castel di Vergio daily, from mid-May to mid-October. Autocars Cortenais also operates a navette service daily in July and August along the D623 Restonica valley road between Corte and the Bergeries de Grotelle. For local taxis contact Michel Salviani, tel 06 03 49 15 24 or Thérèse Feracci, tel 04 95 61 01 17. Trains operate daily from Corte to Vizzavona, Ajaccio, Ponte Leccia, Calvi and Bastia, tel 04 95 46 00 97, **www.cf-corse.fr**.

# LINK ROUTE
*Refuge de Manganu to Soccia*

| | |
|---|---|
| **Start** | Refuge de Manganu |
| **Finish** | Soccia |
| **Distance** | 10km (6¼ miles) |
| **Total ascent** | 60m (195ft) |
| **Total descent** | 930m (3050ft) |
| **Time** | 3hrs |
| **Terrain** | A rough and stony path leads down through a valley, becoming easier along the way, but ending quite steep and rugged. |
| **Maps** | IGN 4251 OT |
| **Food and drink** | There are water sources near Lavu a Crena. A café stands high above Soccia and the village has restaurants and bars. |
| **Shelter** | A pine forest offers some shade halfway through the day, but the valley itself is very sheltered throughout. |

Soccia is a quiet and pleasant village, originally huddled around a 15th-century church. Its stone houses now rise up the hillside and around the valley sides. Trekkers who are running out of time can leave the GR20 by walking from the Refuge de Manganu to Soccia. A day visit might also be considered, especially if a nasty weather forecast renders the higher parts of the GR20 unsafe to negotiate. A walk down to the village and back again takes all day, but there is a hotel for those who wish to stay overnight, as well as a marvellous restaurant. It is also worth walking halfway down the valley just to visit Lavu a Crena in a pine forest, and return to the Refuge de Manganu.

Leave the **Refuge de Manganu** by crossing the footbridge and turning left, as signposted for Lac du Ninu along the GR20. However, turn left again at a path junction in an area of juniper scrub, as signposted for Soccia – a path which is flashed with yellow paint. The narrow, rough and

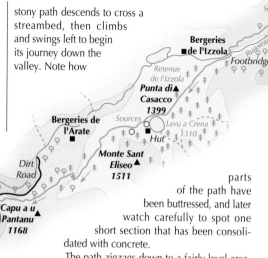

stony path descends to cross a
streambed, then climbs
and swings left to begin
its journey down the
valley. Note how parts
of the path have
been buttressed, and later
watch carefully to spot one
short section that has been consolidated with concrete.

The path zigzags down to a fairly level area,
then passes a bulbous mass of granite with a prominent beech tree growing alongside. Cross a rocky area
and note the little spring, the **Source de Zoicu**. The course
of the **Ruisseau de Zoicu** is fairly well wooded, but there
are few trees growing alongside the path. Another rugged
zigzag stretch leads down to a stout wooden **footbridge**
spanning the river. Cross over and turn right to continue
downstream, gradually pulling away from the course of the
river. There is a view of the tiny **Bergeries de l'Izzola** across
the valley before a forest of laricio pines is reached.

The path climbs gently among pines, where pigs may
have dug over the ground. A slight descent leads to **Lavu
a Crena**, at an altitude of 1310m (4298ft). ◀ The lake is
6.5m (21ft) deep, and is frozen for three or four months
in the winter. The charming grassy shore gives way to
reed-fringed waters with lily-pad islets. Look out for coots
on the water and Corsican nuthatches in the surrounding pines. It is worth walking round the shore, where the
view from the outflow stretches across a deep valley to
distant Monte d'Oru. There is a water **source** beside a
small stone hut.

According to local
lore, the lake was
created by the devil,
either from a blow
of his hammer or a
kick from his horse.

120

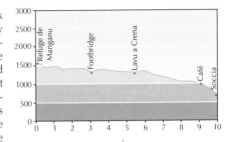

Look carefully for the continuation of the yellow-flashed path, which is not immediately obvious, although once it has climbed a little from the lake it is quite clear. It passes the Funtana di a Veduvella, where water spills onto the path, then later enjoys a view of the valley. Expect to see a lot of day walkers on this part of the path, which descends gradually through sparse pines and deep heather.

Keep right at a signposted path junction for Soccia – the other way goes to Ortu. The path runs almost level across the valley side, with chestnut trees being prominent, then later aligns itself to a gentle rocky ridge covered in deep heather and clumps of 'everlasting', where goats regularly graze. The path crosses a track, where there is an attractive view down to Soccia, but first pass a prominent tubular cross, following a road to a car park

*A view along the length of the Zoicu valley, which runs down towards Lavu a Crena and the village of Soccia*

121

and café. Donkey and pony rides are offered back to Lavu a Crena.

Follow the road round a bend, then go through a metal gate on the right. A clear, but steep and rather gritty path descends among scrub and chestnut trees. Keep a close eye on its course to land on a road end beside some houses at the top end of **Soccia**. Walk down the road in lazy loops, unless you later spot flights of steps short-cutting some of the bends. What few services exist in Soccia are either obvious from the road or are clearly signposted, and all are located within a few minutes of the church.

*The village of Soccia was originally huddled on a promontory close to its 15th-century church.*

## SOCCIA

Soccia has expanded from the promontory bearing its 15th-century church, up the hillside and down the valley, with lush gardens hung with grapevines. The church is open at certain times to allow visitors to view a fine triptych. Facilities in the village are few, but there is accommodation, food, drink and a post office. Most people who pass through the village are on their way to or from Lavu a Crena.

**Accommodation** The Hôtel U Paese, tel 04 95 28 31 92, has 22 rooms and is the only place offering lodgings in the village.

**Food and drink** The Hôtel U Paese has a restaurant. The Restaurant A Merendella is a wonderful garden restaurant in the old part of the village, and is one of the best within reach of the GR20. The Pane e Vinu restaurant only opens on summer weekends. The Bar Restaurant Chez Louis provides drinks, but rarely offers food, despite its name. There are no shops, beyond a house selling goats' cheese just above the hotel, but blaring horns announce the arrival of visiting mobile shops.

**Transport** There are no buses from Soccia. A taxi service is provided by Luc Canale, from nearby Sagone, tel 06 07 49 71 09 or 06 07 25 90 19. The nearest bus service is at Vico, where Autocars Ceccaldi, tel 04 95 21 38 06 or 06 09 96 15 37, **www.autocars-ceccaldi-ajaccio.fr**, links with Ajaccio all year round, except Sundays.

# STAGE 7

*Refuge de Manganu to*
*Refuge de Petra Piana*

| | |
|---|---|
| **Start** | Refuge de Manganu |
| **Finish** | Refuge de Petra Piana |
| **Distance** | 10km (6 miles) |
| **Total ascent** | 980m (3220ft) |
| **Total descent** | 740m (2430ft) |
| **Time** | 7hrs |
| **Terrain** | Steep and rocky mountainsides, with some rocky stretches and gullies requiring scrambling. This is one of the highest stretches of the main route and slopes can hold snow well into the summer. |
| **Maps** | IGN 4251 OT |
| **Food and drink** | Apart a river near the start, there is no reliable source of water. The Refuge de Petra Piana serves meals and sells provisions. |
| **Shelter** | There is hardly any tree cover on this section, and the mountain ridges are particularly exposed to sun, wind and rain. |

After yesterday's easy stage comes another tough day's trek along the GR20. The path climbs through a valley to reach one of the highest points on the main route. Views beyond the gap are magnificent, taking in the twin lakes of Lac de Capitellu and Lac du Melo. There are some awkward slabs, boulders, gullies and short scrambles to negotiate while traversing the high ridges to reach another high gap called Bocca Muzzella, also known as the Col de la Haute Route. After crossing the gap, simply go down a stony slope to the Refuge de Petra Piana. Be warned that all water for the day should be carried, as there is little along the way apart from seasonal streams. Also bear in mind that snow can lie late into the summer on the higher slopes. There are two gaps along the high ridge where it is possible to descend very steeply into the Restonica valley, where a road continues down to the town of Corte.

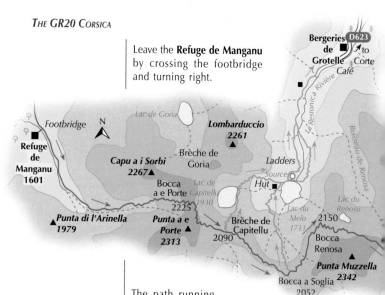

Leave the **Refuge de Manganu** by crossing the footbridge and turning right.

The path running upstream isn't too steep at the start of the day, although it is rough and stony. The ground is often wet enough to support butterworts. The path climbs a steep and bouldery slope to pass a fine waterfall. Climb over bare rock for a while to reach a fine, level, grassy patch. There is a good view around the head of the valley, displaying ominously spiky peaks of rock. There is another waterfall and more grassy areas with butterworts. Climb a little more to reach a wider area of grass at 1783m (5850ft).

A steep and rocky ascent well to the left of the stream leads further and further towards the rugged head of the valley. From here look down into narrow, rocky gorges containing small waterfalls and cascades, as well as at the jagged Crête de Rinella and the towering peaks and pinnacles of Capu a i Sorbi and Punta a

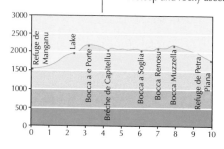

e Porte. The path levels out for a while in a narrow grassy area flanked by alder scrub, and a tiny lake is visible off to the right at 1969m (6460ft).

As the path begins to steepen again, it becomes quite stony and bouldery, and trekkers have to grapple with a heap of huge boulders, then pick a way across slabs of rock to reach a narrow rocky gap called **Bocca a e Porte**, at an altitude of 2225m (7300ft). This is one of the highest points reached on the main route of the GR20. It is possible for snow to lie well into the summer in gullies on both sides of the gap, which could require the use of an ice axe and crampons. The gap should be reached about 3hrs into the day

From here onwards, the attention of trekkers is often drawn to two deep blue lakes far below the rugged peaks. Lac de Capitellu and Lac du Melo lie in rocky hollows so steep and rugged that they look like craters. Monte Ritondu rises beyond, with Monte d'Oru also prominent. Quite a few people may be seen milling around the lakes, having climbed from a car park at the head of the Restonica valley.

Leave **Bocca a e Porte** and turn right to cut across the steep and rocky slopes of **Punta a e Porte**. Again, be warned that the slope can hold a considerable amount of snow into the summer, either on the open slopes or tucked away in gullies. Trekkers have to grapple with rocky slabs, boulders and awkward steep gullies as the route cuts across the mountainside. While scrambling down one gully, notice that the rock has been bolted, but there are no cables or chains to hang on to. A rocky notch, the **Brèche de Capitellu**, is reached at around 2090m (6855ft), between towering pinnacles on the ridge, about 30mins after leaving Bocca a e Porte. (Yellow paint marks indicate a way down to the

Monte Ritondu
2622

Lavu
Bellebone
2321

Manaccia
2496

Scafone

Refuge de
Petra Piana
1842

*Looking down on Lac de Capitellu and Lac du Melo from the rocky slopes below the Bocca a e Porte*

Bergeries de Grotelle, and this route is described in the next section.)

The GR20 cuts across to the southern side of the ridge, with views down into another deep and rugged valley. While traversing the slope, trekkers have to climb up and down, scrambling at times or following rough and stony paths. There is a stretch where it is possible to trek along the actual crest for a while, enjoying a view of Lac du Melo, then the route cuts off to the right again, regaining the crest further along. The route follows a good stretch of the crest, then as it gets rockier, shifts to the flanks again.

Watch carefully as the route swings sharply round to the left, crossing the ridge, then follow the path down through alder scrub to reach **Bocca a Soglia**, at 2052m (6732ft), about 45mins from the last major gap. There is a junction of paths just off the gap. (A sign and yellow paint marks indicate a way down to the Bergeries de Grotelle, and this route is described in the next section.)

The GR20 climbs a bouldery slope and is signposted for the Refuge de Petra Piana. The route involves clambering over huge boulders and pushing through dense alder scrub on the steep and rugged slopes of **Punta Muzzella**. The gradients are fairly gentle at first, but all of a sudden the path climbs steep and stony zigzags, verging on scrambling at times. This leads to the little gap of **Bocca Renosu**, at 2150m (7055ft), about 1hr 15mins after leaving Bocca a Soglia.

The path traverses a rocky, bouldery mountainside, but also passes through a delightful little grassy *pozzine* perched above the little **Lac du Renosu**, and within 30mins crosses **Bocca Muzzella**, which is more often called the Col de la Haute Route, at 2206m (7238ft). Take

*View of the little Lac du Renosu before crossing the Bocca Muzzella to descend to the Refuge de Petra Piana*

a break at this point and enjoy the view southwards, as most of the hard work is over and it's downhill all the way to the Refuge de Petra Piana. Looking northwards, Monte d'Oru and Monte Renosu are seen.

The path used for the descent slices across rough and stony slopes at **Stazzanelli**. Watch for the markers as they switch to the left across the mountain ridge. The path zig-zags rough and stony down through alder scrub, where the ground is wet enough to support butterworts, and lands on a level area where the **Refuge de Petra Piana** has been built, at 1842m (6043ft). Trekkers should reach the refuge an hour after leaving Bocca Muzzella.

The PNRC **Refuge de Petra Piana** is a fairly small wooden structure, built in the chalet style, having a dormitory with 25 beds and a little kitchen/dining room. There is a bit of extra space in the roofspace, but not much. The building sits on quite a small base and is held down with cables – be warned that it rocks a little bit in a strong wind! The gardien occupies a separate stone building nearby, where hot meals, food and drink can be bought. Another little building houses the toilet and shower. Water pours from the Funtana di Petra Piana. Hire tents and level camping spaces are available around the refuge, but it can be cold, windy and misty. The terrace looks along the length of the Manganellu valley to Monte d'Oru. Monte Ritondu is close to hand, although the summit cannot be seen. (If considering an ascent, see the section before Stage 8A for details.)

# LINK ROUTE

*Brèche de Capitellu or Bocca a
Soglia to Bergeries de Grotelle*

| | |
|---|---|
| **Start** | Brèche de Capitellu or Bocca a Soglia |
| **Finish** | Bergeries de Grotelle |
| **Distance** | 4km (2 miles) |
| **Total ascent** | 20m (65ft) |
| **Total descent** | 700m (2295ft) |
| **Time** | 2hrs 15mins |
| **Terrain** | Steep and rocky slopes, with a choice between a rough and rocky series of paths, or a route involving a chain and metal ladders. |
| **Maps** | IGN 4251 OT |
| **Food and drink** | A water source lies near the outflow from Lac du Melo. There are small snack bars and restaurants at the Bergeries de Grotelle. |
| **Shelter** | The higher parts of the route are exposed to the sun, wind and rain, but there is more shelter and tree cover in the valley. |

Those who follow the GR20 above Lac de Capitellu and Lac du Melo will be aware of the deep, rock-walled cleft of the Restonica valley dropping steeply beyond. There are nearly always crowds of people in view around the lakes and this should alert trekkers to the fact that there is a road nearby, even if it is hidden from sight. It is possible to leave the GR20, either to take a closer look at the lakes and enjoy food and drink at the Bergeries de Grotelle, or use a navette service to continue down to the ancient mountain citadel of Corte. There are two roughly parallel, steep and rocky routes available on this descent, with an option to switch from one to the other at the outflow from Lac du Melo.

There are two points at which trekkers can leave the GR20 for this descent – one is the **Brèche de Capitellu** at 2090m (6855ft) and the other is **Bocca a Soglia** at 2052m

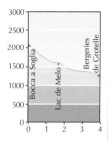

(6732ft). The first route passes both Lac de Capitellu and Lac du Melo, while the second route passes only Lac du Melo. Continuing downhill, there are two more options to consider – one described as *plus sportif* and the other as *facile*. (Think of them as 'sporty' and 'easy'!) Trekkers can switch from one route to the other at the outflow from Lac du Melo.

### Descent from the Brèche de Capitellu

Leave the GR20 at the rocky notch of **Brèche de Capitellu**, between towering pinnacles, around 2090m (6855ft). A route down a gully is clearly marked with 'Corte' fixed onto the rock, and abundant yellow flashes of paint. Scramble down jammed boulders to reach a gentle grassy hollow, then follow the paint flashes as they lead around a rocky lip holding **Lac de Capitellu** in place. Pause to admire the deep corrie lake, with its sheer granite headwall and rocky shore. The altitude is 1930m (6332ft), the water is 42m (138ft) deep, and it can be frozen for up to eight months in the year.

Continue steeply downhill, watching carefully for the yellow flashes that reveal easy scrambling routes down steep, bare rock, leading to stony, bouldery paths through alder scrub. The path passes close to a PNRC gardien's hut on the way to **Lac du Melo**. Keep to the left-hand side of the lake, following a path through alder scrub, to reach the outflow. The altitude is 1711m (5614ft), the water is 15.5m (51ft) deep, and it can be frozen for almost half the year.

Don't cross the outflow, but follow the yellow markers downstream, passing a small water **source**. When bare rock is reached, look for a short chain that helps on a steep part of the descent. (This

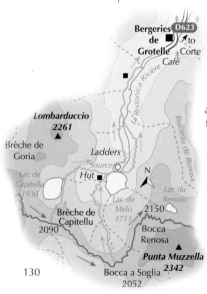

is described as *plus sportif* on a sign later, but there is no mention of this at the top of the route.) A zigzag path has been mortared in place, and this leads to a series of three short metal **ladders**, rather like fire escapes, that help on the next part of the descent.

Almost 30 steps are negotiated using the ladders, but it is still necessary to go down bare, unprotected rock slabs. Stony and bouldery paths are followed through alder scrub, then a clear path continues down through the valley. A small bergerie sells food and drink before the path reaches another bergerie operating as a snack

*The towering peak of Lombarduccio as seen from a level grassy space close to Lac du Melo*

bar at the **Bergeries de Grotelle** car park at 1370m (4495ft).

### Descent from Bocca a Soglia

**Bocca a Soglia** lies at 2052m (6732ft) on the GR20 and a sign nearby indicates a route down to Lac du Melo and the Bergeries de Grotelle. The path is clearly marked with yellow paint flashes, and is initially steep and bouldery, passing through alder scrub to reach wide and gentle slopes of grass. A small lake will be noticed off to the right, although this is soon lost to view. Watch carefully for the markers, which indicate a path roughly aligned to a small stream.

The route crosses from side to side, but also crosses grassy areas and expanses of bare granite. Once there is a clear view of Lac du Melo, be sure to cross the stream before it flows down through a sheer, rock-walled gorge. The route later swings left to traverse rock slabs, then drops straight downhill onto level ground. Cross a grassy area near a PNRC gardien's hut on the way to **Lac du Melo**. Keep to the left-hand side of the lake, following a path through alder scrub, to reach the outflow. The altitude is 1711m (5614ft), the water is 15.5m (51ft) deep, and it can be frozen for almost half the year.

Cross the outflow and follow yellow markers onwards, swinging left to continue the descent. (This is described as *facile* on a sign later, but there is no mention of this at the top of the route.) A rough and bouldery path is hemmed in between sloping slabs and alder scrub. It needs care all the way down to the floor of the valley, where a stream is crossed. Keep right to follow a clear path down through the valley. A small bergerie sells food and drink before the path reaches another bergerie operating as a snack bar at the **Bergeries de Grotelle** car park at 1370m (4495ft).

The **Bergeries de Grotelle** is like a small, secret mountain village, where most of the buildings are tucked away behind boulders and outcrops of rock. A couple of them offer snacks and drinks, or sell Corsican foodstuffs. The D623 through the spectacular Gorges de la Restonica runs 15km (9½ miles) down to Corte. A navette service is operated along the road daily in July and August by Autocars Cortenais, tel 06 20 17 17 55 or 06 19 83 26 18, **www.autocars-cortenais-corse.fr**. When this isn't running, one of the local taxis could be contacted – Michel Salviani, tel 06 03 49 15 24 or Thérèse Feracci, tel 04 95 61 01 17. It is possible to get a lift down to Corte by asking around the car park. (For details of what Corte offers, see the Link from Beregeries de Vaccaghja to Corte.)

# EXCURSION

*Ascent of Monte Ritondu from Refuge de Petra Piana*

| | |
|---|---|
| **Start/Finish** | Refuge de Petra Piana |
| **Distance** | 6km (3¾ miles) there-and-back |
| **Total ascent** | 850m (2790ft) |
| **Total descent** | 850m (2790ft) |
| **Time** | 4hrs 30mins there-and-back |
| **Terrain** | Rough and rocky slopes, quite steep in many places, requiring some scrambling. It is important to look carefully for small cairns marking the route. The ascent is not recommended in poor visibility. |
| **Maps** | IGN 4251 OT |
| **Food and drink** | Carry water and food from the Refuge de Petra Piana. |
| **Shelter** | The mountain slopes are very exposed to sun, wind and rain. There is a very basic hut on the summit. |

Monte Ritondu is the second highest mountain in Corsica, topped only by the mighty Monte Cinto. An ascent and descent is possible in a half day from the Refuge de Petra Piana, and this is an option some trekkers might want to consider, especially as the next stage of the GR20 is one of the easier stretches. Small cairns mark the usual line of ascent, but paths can be rather vague in places. Be aware that there are other cairned routes that could lead to confusion on the slopes. Make the ascent in clear weather and leave the mountain well alone in rain, mist or wind. The latter parts of the climb to the summit involve scrambling on steep slabs and boulders, and the higher slopes can hold snow well into the summer.

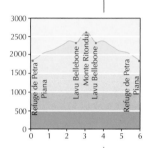

The **Refuge de Petra Piana** stands at 1842m (6043ft), which gives a fair leg-up onto Monte Ritondu. There might be a loose signboard reading 'Rotondu', but if it is missing, look for a stream just to the east of the refuge. Ford it, then climb through alder scrub and ford another stream. Look carefully, parallel to the stream, to spot a line of small cairns leading roughly northeast up a steep and rocky slope. Climb uphill a short way, and look to the left higher up the slope to see a grassy hollow in the mountainside containing a level area of short grass, around 1950m (6400ft). This is a sheltered *pozzine* where animals may be grazing.

Keep an eye open for more cairns as the path crosses over some boulders, then climb steeply up a blunt ridge on the mountainside. Height is gained in a combination of stony zigzags and very short rocky scrambles. There are fine views of Monte d'Oru, its close neighbour Punta Migliarello, and the high-level route of the GR20 along the crêtes, for trekkers interested in following that route. The Refuge de Petra Piana also looks quite interesting from this height – quite definitely a bird's-eye view.

The path slices across the mountainside to avoid rocky buttresses, then swings to the right to start climbing more steeply again. Scramble up a gully full of broken rock and boulders to reach a narrow gap at the top, around 2280m (7480ft). This gap should be reached an hour after leaving the refuge.

The view from the gap is startling, as Monte Ritondu is visible in all its glory, maybe streaked with snow as the high cirque can hold snow well into the summer. There are a couple of tiny lakes in the boulder-fields below, with attractive grassy areas nearby, but follow a cairned route off to the left, across and up a bouldery slope, to

*Walking high above the Refuge de Petra Piana on the way to climb the mighty Monte Ritondu*

*Seen at the beginning of June, ice covers Lavu Bellebone and Monte Ritondu holds considerable amounts of snow*

reach the larger **Lavu Bellebone**. This lake is frozen for most of the year, and is at an altitude of 2321m (7615ft). Spend a while admiring the lake and the rugged peaks and pinnacles clustered around the cirque, then focus attention on Monte Ritondu.

Pass round the shore of the lake, crossing the out-flowing stream, and study the steep and rugged slope rising above. There is a lot of scree and boulders, but look for cairns and pick a way up this slope to reach the gap called the Col du Fer de Lance, around 2490m (8170ft). The *lance* is the pinnacle of rock standing tall in the middle of the gap. Keep left of the lance, then start the final steep climb to the summit of Monte Ritondu. The slope is steep, bouldery and rocky, but can be climbed in a series of easy scrambles. Keep an eye peeled for the little cairns that steer trekkers along the best line up the slope. The summit of **Monte Ritondu**, at an altitude of 2622m (8602ft), should be reached about 2hrs 45mins after leaving the refuge. The basic Hellebronner Hut is available for shelter, wedged into a gap just below the summit.

The reward on reaching the summit is a wonderful view, taking in most of the major mountains running through the centre of Corsica. Spend a while trying to figure out the course of the GR20 around the prominent peaks of Monte Cinto and Paglia Orba, as well as ahead beyond Monte d'Oru and Monte Renosu. When ready to leave the summit, simply retrace steps carefully to return to the Refuge de Petra Piana, which might take only 1hr 45mins. Those who made the ascent early in the morning, and still feel fit, could continue along the GR20 to reach the Refuge de l'Onda. Others might prefer to have a relaxing afternoon rest.

## STAGE 8A
### *Refuge de Petra Piana to Refuge de l'Onda (low-level)*

| | |
|---|---|
| **Start** | Refuge de Petra Piana |
| **Finish** | Refuge de l'Onda |
| **Distance** | 11km (6¾ miles) |
| **Total ascent** | 500m (1640ft) |
| **Total descent** | 910m (2985ft) |
| **Time** | 5hrs |
| **Terrain** | Steep and rugged slopes at the start and finish, but relatively easy forest and woodland paths for most of the way. |
| **Maps** | IGN 4251 OT |
| **Food and drink** | The Bergeries de Gialgo sell cheese near the start. The Bergeries de Tolla provides food and drink low in the valley. Water can be drawn from rivers that flow all year. The Bergeries de l'Onda serves meals and sells provisions. |
| **Shelter** | Shade is available in the forest and woodland along the way. This stretch is particularly well sheltered. |

Here's a stage where trekkers can relax and take things easy for a change. This low-level route is actually the main GR20 route, and the high-level route over the 'crêtes' is the variant. There is a steep descent from the Refuge de Petra Piana, but this is followed by a gentle walk through a valley full of laricio pines, where trekkers can enjoy the shade and maybe even take a dip in the river. At the Bergeries de Tolla there is an opportunity to indulge in basic Corsican food and drink, and stock up on food supplies. An ascent through a valley full of beech trees demands a bit more effort on the way to the Refuge de l'Onda, especially for those who have eaten and drunk rather more than they should have at the Bergeries de Tolla!

Leave the **Refuge de Petra Piana** by walking beyond the Funtana de Petra Piana, where a sign points the way to the Refuge de l'Onda. There is a choice of routes at a junction, indicated as 'Par la vallée' or 'Par les crêtes'. The main route is down to the left into the valley, while the high-level variant is off to the right, cutting across a rugged slope. (See the next section for details of the high-level variant.)

The steep and rugged descent into the valley is along a stony path flanked by alder scrub. On reaching the **Bergeries de Gialgo**, turn left as

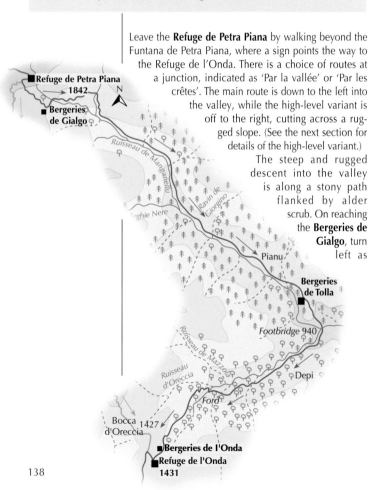

138

marked. Although early, it is possible to stop and buy cheese or fill up with water. The path continues its descent into the valley, cutting across the slope and crossing a couple of streambeds. After crossing the Ravin de Monte Ritondu, continue

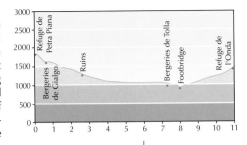

downstream to reach a more gently graded path running parallel to the **Ruisseau de Manganellu**. This is a bouldery river full of cascades and rock pools, where it is tempting to stop and take a dip.

The route passes small, ruined drystone buildings, and the path is built up with stone on one side and quite clear to follow. Small pines give way to large laricio pines further down the valley. Although the path is broad and stony for most of the way through the forest, there are a couple of rugged breaks in its course and some parts are narrow. On hot days there is plenty of shade in the forest and cool pools of water in the river. The path drifts away from the river from time to time, then does so rather more significantly to reach the **Bergeries de Tolla**. The bergeries are situated around 1000m (3280ft), and should be within 3hrs of leaving the Refuge de Petra Piana.

The **Bergeries de Tolla** are a huddle of low stone huts in a clearing surrounded by fences, with distant rocky peaks leading the eye towards Monte d'Oru. When the bergeries are occupied in the summer, food and drink are offered to passing walkers – either snacks with soft drinks or beer, or complete meals with wine, and there is an opportunity to stock up on food supplies. Some might feel like dropping their packs and staying for the night, but there is no accommodation, nor is camping allowed. Make the most of the opportunity to eat and drink at the bergeries, then continue walking. (Anyone

*The Bergeries de Tolla provide wholesome, simple meals in a clearing in the forested Manganellu valley*

who needs to leave the GR20 should refer to the section describing easy links with the villages of Tattone or Vizzavona, found after Stage 8B.)

Walk past the lowest of the fenced enclosures on leaving the **Bergeries de Tolla**, and continue through sparsely planted pines and tall heather. A stony path, braided in places, leads in just 15mins down to a **footbridge** called the Passerelle de Tolla, at 940m (3085ft). It spans the Ruisseau de Manganellu close to its confluence with the Ruisseau de Grottaccia. After heavy rain the water thunders through a rocky gorge, crashing over boulders. Climb a short way up a bouldery slope and reach a choice of signposted tracks.

The GR20 is marked off to the right above the Passerelle de Tolla. Don't be tempted to cross the footbridge over the Ruisseau de Grottaccia, but simply follow a stony track uphill roughly parallel to the river. Avoid the dirt road off to the left, which is the Route Forestière de Manganellu. ▸

The track drifts away from the river as it climbs, becoming narrower and rugged in places. Fallen branches and leaf mould, as well as the activity of pigs, conspire to obscure the way in places, so keep an eye peeled for the paint flashes.

The path drops down to a **ford** on the Ruisseau de Grottaccia, then zigzags up the other side and continues roughly upstream. There is one tall stand of laricio pines in the beech-wood, then a clearing where the Refuge de l'Onda can briefly be glimpsed at the head of the valley. The path wanders past more beech trees, then emerges on a rugged slope of bracken, juniper and spiny broom before reaching the **Bergeries de l'Onda**. Those who are camping should pitch their tent here, inside a fenced enclosure. Those intending to stay at the **Refuge de l'Onda** should check first with the gardien at the bergeries, before following the path further uphill. A short, steep, rugged path climbs to the refuge, at 1431m (4695ft), which is reached about 1hr 45mins after leaving the Passerelle de Tolla.

There are still laricio pines present, but beech trees dominate the valley. The ground beside the path might be furrowed where pigs have been rooting for beechmast.

*Looking down on the Refuge de l'Onda, where campers must stay down near the Bergeries de l'Onda*

The PNRC **Refuge de l'Onda** is built in the bergerie style and is surrounded by rocky mountains, with a view down through the valley from its terrace. Its position is best appreciated by those following the high-level variant over the 'crêtes'. It is one of the smaller refuges, so the little 16-bed dormitory is quickly filled to capacity, and there can be a lot of pressure on the little kitchen/dining room. A shower and toilet are located alongside in a small building. The campsite lies below the refuge, in a fenced enclosure next to the Bergeries de l'Onda, secure from pigs and cattle that graze the area. The campsite has its own toilet and shower block. The refuge gardien lives at the bergeries, where hot meals, food and drink can be bought.

# STAGE 8B
*Refuge de Petra Piana to Refuge de l'Onda (high-level)*

| | |
|---|---|
| **Start** | Refuge de Petra Piana |
| **Finish** | Refuge de l'Onda |
| **Distance** | 8km (5 miles) |
| **Total ascent** | 390m (1280ft) |
| **Total descent** | 800m (2625ft) |
| **Time** | 4hrs 15mins |
| **Terrain** | Although the route follows mountain ridges between the two refuges, gradients are mostly gentle and the mountain slopes are easy to negotiate. Some steep, rocky slopes require a bit of scrambling near the start and on the way to the Serra di Tenda. |
| **Maps** | IGN 4251 OT |
| **Food and drink** | There is no water on this stage. The Bergeries de l'Onda serve meals and sell provisions. |
| **Shelter** | The route along the mountain ridges is exposed to sun, wind and rain, and is not recommended in misty or wet conditions. |

This high-level route is actually an alternative to the main route of the GR20. The main route stays low in the valleys between the Refuge de Petra Piana and the Refuge de l'Onda. Trekkers who prefer to stay high will find that the route involves slightly less climbing and less distance, and can be completed in less time than the main route. Views are much more extensive, with Monte Ritondu and Monte d'Oru seen in all their glory. The drawback is that there is no opportunity to visit the Bergeries de Tolla deep in the valley, or to enjoy the food and drink offered there, nor is there a chance to enjoy a cool dip in the river. For those who enjoy the mountains and strive for the high places, however, this is the route to follow, which is fairly faithful to the crest of the mountains.

Leave the **Refuge de Petra Piana** by walking beyond the Funtana de Petra Piana, where a sign points the way to the Refuge de l'Onda. There is a choice of routes at a junction, indicated as 'Par la vallée' or 'Par les crêtes'. The main route is down to the left into the valley, while the high-level variant is off to the right, cutting across a rugged slope. (See the previous section for details of the low-level route.)

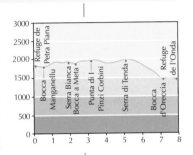

The high-level route is flashed with yellow paint and includes a bit of scrambling as it cuts across a steep and rocky slope covered in alder scrub. A gentler path continues to a gap called the **Bocca Manganellu**, and a sign is passed indicating a path off-route to the village of Guagno. Follow the path marked in yellow as it climbs uphill, and turn round from time to time to enjoy the mountain scenery behind. The Refuge de Petra Piana is in view, perched on its rocky ledge on the mountain-side. Rocky stairways and sharp arêtes are negotiated, then the path becomes quite easy as it slices across the higher, grassy slopes. Skirt the summit of **Punta Murace** at 1921m (6302ft) and reach a rounded summit on **Serra Bianca**, where there is a crude drystone windbreak shelter around 1970m (6465ft).

Look ahead along the crest to see other gentle summits. The one closest to hand is avoided as the path skirts around its eastern slopes. After climbing steadily up a stony ridge towards the two summits of **Punta di I Pinzi Corbini**, the path crosses only the first summit. As the route continues along a ridge of broken rock, the yellow markers shift to the left and narrowly miss the 2021m (6631ft) summit. A rather battered and broken path leads down a rocky slope to reach the Bocca a Meta at 1890m (6200ft).

Watch carefully for the yellow flashes as the path drifts left from the gap and starts cutting across steep and rocky slopes on the Serra di Tenda. The route includes short scrambles, and trekkers may have to grapple with the alder scrub where it presses in on the path. Swing gradually to the right and climb steeply uphill to reach a rocky notch on the crest of Serra di Tenda. While crossing this notch turn left and scramble only a short way to reach an easy path.

Follow the path parallel to the crest, narrowly missing the 1991m (6532ft) summit of **Serra di Tenda**. The high slopes are grassy, but also feature spiny broom and juniper. As the path starts to descend it becomes more and more rugged, passing boulders and low outcrops of rock. There is a fine view of Monte d'Oru, and the tiny shape of the Refuge de l'Onda is visible, tucked into a wooded hollow on its slopes. By the time the path leads down to the **Bocca d'Oreccia**, at an altitude of 1427m (4682ft), the refuge is out of sight and Monte d'Oru's slopes look lumpy and less interesting.

Follow a narrow path uphill from the gap to reach a minor ridge, then turn right to climb a short way along

*Walkers drop steeply downhill from the crêtes to the Bocca d'Oreccia on their way to the Refuge de l'Onda*

the crest. A narrow path on the left is signposted, and a gentle descent across a rugged slope leads quickly to the **Refuge de l'Onda** at 1431m (4695ft). Those who are camping must continue down to the **Bergeries de l'Onda**.

> The PNRC **Refuge de l'Onda** is built in the bergerie style and is surrounded by rocky mountains, with a view down through the valley from its terrace. Its position is best appreciated by those following the high-level variant over the 'crêtes'. It is one of the smaller refuges, so the little 16-bed dormitory is quickly filled to capacity, and there can be a lot of pressure on the little kitchen/dining room. A shower and toilet are located alongside in a small building. The campsite lies below the refuge, in a fenced enclosure next to the Bergeries de l'Onda, secure from pigs and cattle that graze the area.

The campsite has its own toilet and shower block. The refuge gardien lives at the bergeries, where hot meals, food and drink can be bought.

# LINK ROUTE

*Bergeries de Tolla to Tattone and Vizzavona*

| | |
|---|---|
| **Start** | Bergeries de Tolla |
| **Finish** | Tattone or Vizzavona |
| **Distance** | 9km (5½ miles) or 11.5km (7 miles) |
| **Total ascent** | 110m (360ft) or 210m (690ft) |
| **Total descent** | 310m (1015ft) or 350m (1180ft) |
| **Time** | 3hrs or 4hrs |
| **Terrain** | The forested riverside path can be easy or rugged in places, although a dirt road running parallel could be used instead. A tarmac road leads from Canaglia to Tattone, or a rugged forest path can be followed up through a valley to Vizzavona. |
| **Maps** | IGN 4251 OT |
| **Food and drink** | There is a small restaurant and a water source at Canaglia. Food and drink are available at Savaggio and Tattone. Restaurants and bars at Vizzavona. |
| **Shelter** | There is good shelter among the trees throughout the valleys. |

This is a simple link from the GR20 main route, near the Bergeries de Tolla, to the little village of Tattone. Those who find themselves running out of time, or lack the energy needed to cross over the mountains to Vizzavona, can bail out by completing a simple valley walk. The footbridge, the Passerelle de Tolla, is one of the lowest points on the GR20, and from there a riverside path and forest track lead to the hamlet of Canaglia. A simple road-walk continues onwards, either to a campsite at Savaggio, or to the little village of Tattone, in search of campsites and a gîte d'étape, as well as train services. It is also possible to follow a rugged path and easy tracks up through a forested valley from Pont de Mulinello to Vizzavona, re-joining the main GR20.

Walk past the lowest of the fenced enclosures on leaving the **Bergeries de Tolla**, and continue through sparsely planted pines and tall heather. A stony path, braided in places, leads in just 15mins down to a **footbridge** called the Passerelle de Tolla, at 940m (3085ft). It spans the Ruisseau de Manganellu close to its confluence with the Ruisseau de Grottaccia. After heavy rain the water thunders through a rocky gorge, crashing over boulders. Climb a short way up a bouldery slope and reach a choice of signposted tracks.

The GR20 is marked off to the right above the Passerelle de Tolla, so turn left to leave the route by following the riverside path downstream. (Note that there is a dirt road just a short way uphill, called the Route Forestière de Manganellu. If the easiest exit is needed, follow the dirt road.) The riverside path is flashed with orange paint and is a variant route of the coast-to-coast Mare a Mare Nord. Walk among tall laricio pines and cross a concrete bridge beside the slender **waterfall** of Cascade du Meli.

The broad but rough and rocky path descends alongside the rushing **Ruisseau de Manganellu**, where there are tall laricio pines, as well as an understorey of tall heather. On hot summer days almost every pool in the river will be full of bathers. The rugged path eventually leads onto bare rock close to the river, then links with an easier track. Follow this gently uphill past young pines, tall heather and even a solitary fig tree! The track joins the broader **Route Forestière de Manganellu**, then crosses a concrete bridge over a bouldery stream. Follow the track into **Canaglia**, to link with a tarmac road.

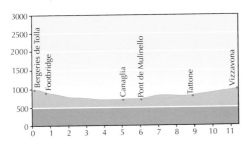

The little hamlet of **Canaglia** boasts a fine little bar-restaurant, the Osteria U Capitan Moru. There is a water source across the road. The nearest taxi is in Vivario, so anyone wishing to avoid the onward road-walk contact Taxi Alain, tel 04 95 47 23 17.

Follow the D23 away from **Canaglia**, overlooking a well-wooded valley and cross the **Pont de Mulinello** over a bouldery river. (See the 'Link Route to Vizzavona' below for a route to Vizzavona.) Continue along the road, which later climbs gently. Watch out for signs on the left, where there is a choice of two destinations – Savaggio or Tattone.

To reach Savaggio, turn left down a track, passing chestnut trees and tall pines. Cross a footbridge over a stream, then walk up a path flanked by bracken and stone walls. Turn right along the railway line to reach a tiny station/halt at **Savaggio.**

**Camping Savaggio**, tel 04 95 47 22 14 or 06 81 96 08 98, offers a choice of accommodation, from a campsite to a basic gîte d'étape. Food and drink are also available. As the site is next to the railway and timetables are posted, it is easy to catch a train, but give a clear signal to the driver as this is a request stop.

For Tattone, stay on the D23 road, which is flanked by trees, then watch out for a sign on the right which points along a track. Cross over the railway line at a little station at **Tattone** to reach the campsite.

Bar Camping Le Soleil, tel 04 95 47 21 16, is a camping and caravan site with a snack bar and pizzeria. It lies close to the railway station in Tattone, but if catching a train, give a clear signal to the driver as this is often treated as a request stop. Timetables can be studied at the station, or tel 04 95 46 00 97, **www.cf-corse.fr**. Anyone heading into the village of **Tattone**, which is on the nearby N193, can stay at the Refuge Chez Pierrot, which has 18 beds and offers

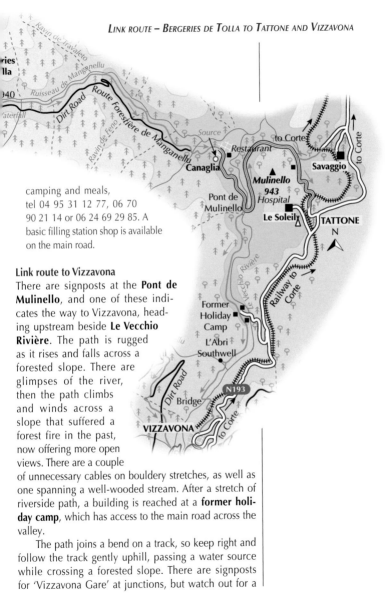

camping and meals, tel 04 95 31 12 77, 06 70 90 21 14 or 06 24 69 29 85. A basic filling station shop is available on the main road.

### Link route to Vizzavona

There are signposts at the **Pont de Mulinello**, and one of these indicates the way to Vizzavona, heading upstream beside **Le Vecchio Rivière**. The path is rugged as it rises and falls across a forested slope. There are glimpses of the river, then the path climbs and winds across a slope that suffered a forest fire in the past, now offering more open views. There are a couple of unnecessary cables on bouldery stretches, as well as one spanning a well-wooded stream. After a stretch of riverside path, a building is reached at a **former holiday camp**, which has access to the main road across the valley.

The path joins a bend on a track, so keep right and follow the track gently uphill, passing a water source while crossing a forested slope. There are signposts for 'Vizzavona Gare' at junctions, but watch out for a 'caveman' signpost pointing up to the right. This leads up to a nearby archaeological site – **L'Abri Southwell** – which was used as a summer dwelling by Neolithic hunters.

If not visiting this site, then keep left and later cross a footbridge. Climb to a forest track and turn left, following it as marked until it drops to cross a bridge over the river. Signposts indicate a path short-cutting uphill, later crossing the railway line. Simply turn right along a track to walk to the station at **Vizzavona**, at 920m (3020ft). (See end of Stage 9B for details of facilities at Vizzavona.)

# STAGE 9A

*Refuge de l'Onda to
Vizzavona (low-level)*

| | |
|---|---|
| **Start** | Refuge de l'Onda |
| **Finish** | Vizzavona |
| **Distance** | 11km (6¾ miles) |
| **Total ascent** | 670m (2200ft) |
| **Total descent** | 1180m (3870ft) |
| **Time** | 6hrs |
| **Terrain** | A steep and stony ascent to a gap is followed by a long descent through a valley. Although steep and rocky at first, gradients ease throughout the descent. The lower valley slopes are forested, where easier paths and tracks lead to Vizzavona. |
| **Maps** | IGN 4251 OT |
| **Food and drink** | Water is generally available from streams on the descent through the valley. There is a snack bar at the Cascade des Anglais. Vizzavona has restaurants, bars and small foodstores. A variant route to La Foce also has bar restaurants. |
| **Shelter** | There is little shelter in the early part of this stage. The mountain slopes are open and there is little shade from the sun, wind or rain. There is good forest cover towards the end. |

This stage of the GR20 looks relatively straightforward on the map, climbing uphill along a ridge after leaving the Refuge de l'Onda, then wandering down through a valley to reach the village of Vizzavona. It is a bit more difficult in practice, as the ascent is unremitting, and the descent through the valley is likely to take longer than imagined. However, take things at a steady pace, enjoying the views while relishing the prospect of abundant food and drink around Vizzavona, and it is a wonderful stage. Some trekkers might be interested to add a bit of height to the day's walk by climbing to the summit of Monte d'Oru. (See the next section, Stage 9B, for details of the high-level variant.)

Leave the **Refuge de l'Onda** by following the path sign-posted for Vizzavona, rising gently across a rugged slope to reach a blunt ridge. A boulder on the ridge also carries a sign for Vizzavona, so turn left there to start climbing. The stony path steepens and passes through alder scrub on the ridge. After climbing over boulders and passing outcrops of rock, there are widening views across the mountains. The gradient eases on a bare, stony shoulder, then climbs steeply again. There are good views of Monte d'Oru and Punta Migliarello ahead. The path is generally on the ridge, but later it swings off to the right and goes through a rocky notch. Cross boulders and bare rock and swing back onto the ridge, and almost immediately the path crosses the main crest near **Punta Muratello**, at an altitude of around 2100m (6890ft). This point should be reached 2hrs 30mins after leaving the Refuge de l'Onda.

Continue following the red and white flashes of the GR20 down a rough and stony path zigzagging down from the crest. The route cuts across a couple of bare slabs, then the markers suddenly swing round to the right. At this point there is the option of following yellow paint marks and small cairns

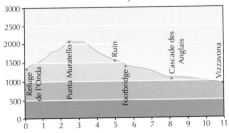

151

off to the left to climb Monte d'Oru. (See the next section, Stage 9B, for details of the high-level variant.)

Staying on the main route, however, the path zigzags downhill and is quite rocky in places, but any bare rock encountered is usually gently sloping, and there is no real scrambling to do. Between areas of bare rock there are patches of alder scrub to squeeze through. After crossing over a couple of seasonal streams, follow a bouldery path down past slender sycamore and rowan trees. The trail drifts to the left across more bare rock and crosses a larger stream.

The sycamore trees offer shade as the rugged path continues downhill. After crossing another stretch of bare rock to reach a tumbled ruined building, trekkers might like to detour a little to the right to look at a slender waterfall plunging into a deep and rocky gorge. Back on the trail, a bouldery path leads into denser woodlands dominated by beech trees. There is an open area where a small **footbridge** is crossed, called the Passerelle de Porteto, spanning a narrow gorge full of fine waterfalls.

Leaving the footbridge, the route seems to be a fairly easy woodland path, descending across gently sloping bare rock in little clearings. The river off to the left, the **l'Agnone Ruisseau**, is full of waterfalls and lovely rock pools. The woods are a mixture of laricio pines and beeches, and there may be pigs rooting around for food. It all seems very easy, but don't imagine it's going to be like this all the way to Vizzavona. In fact, there are some steep and bouldery sections to negotiate, but they are quite

■ **Bergeries de l'Onda**
■ **Refuge de l'Onda** 1431 ↑N

▲ **Punta Muratello** 2141

*L'Agnone Ruisseau*

*Ravin de Baccone*

*Footbridge*
**Bergeries de Porteto**

■ **Punta del Ceppo** ▲ *1632*

*Footbridge*
**Col de Vizzavona** 1163

*Cascade des Anglais*

N

*Bar*
**Hotel Monte d'Oro** ■ **La Foce** 1128

**VIZZA**

limited, and an easy path continues alongside the **Cascade des Anglais**. Perch on convenient rocky stances to admire the falls, and maybe enjoy a dip in one of the pools.

The path squeezes between some enormous boulders and a sign announces La Cascade Bar ahead. This wooden structure is tucked away behind a boulder almost as big as it, and isn't visible until the last possible moment. Take a break here for a snack and drink, at an altitude of 1092m (3582ft). It will probably take 2hrs 30mins to descend through the valley from the Punta Muratello to the bar. There is a choice at this point, depending on where the night's lodging is being sought.

*Walkers cross rock slabs on the way down towards l'Agnone Ruisseau, with Monte d'Oru towering above*

Either stay on the main route to reach Vizzavona, which is what most trekkers do, or short-cut to La Foce.

### Short-cut to La Foce

The short-cut simply involves following a clear track away from La Cascade Bar, keeping to the right among tall laricio pines and beech trees, passing adventurous aerial ropeways, to reach the main N193. A right turn leads quickly past La Halte du Prince and **A Muntagnera** to the **Hôtel Monte d'Oro**, only 15mins after leaving the bar. **La Foce** stands at 1150m (3770ft), and so has a distinct height advantage over nearby Vizzavona. (Refer to the section at the end of Stage 10 for the 'Link from La Foce to Bocca Palmento' to re-join the main GR20.)

## LA FOCE

**Accommodation** La Halte du Prince, adjacent to A Muntagnera, tel 04 95 46 31 02 or 06 09 95 63 06, has three chalets containing 4 to 6 beds each and one operating as a chambre d'hôte. There is also a small campsite with toilets, showers and hire tents. The Hôtel Monte d'Oro, tel 04 95 47 21 06, is a splendid old building with 23 rooms full of antique furniture and wooden panels, offering a high level of comfort. A separate gîte d'étape has 7 rooms with 4 beds in each. There is also a laundry.

**Food and drink** The Hôtel Monte d'Oro and neighbouring A Muntagnera offer extensive Corsican menus.

**Transport** The Hôtel Monte d'Oro operates a navette service to and from Vizzavona for its guests.

The main GR20 route to Vizzavona leaves La Cascade Bar and crosses a **footbridge** over the river. A broad forest path becomes narrower, then broadens again when it reaches a couple of wooden benches. Follow the track gently downhill and walk straight ahead at a junction of tracks to continue gently down in easy loops. The forest is very mixed in this area.

At a point where tracks cross each other, a signpost points left for Vizzavona. Follow the track down towards a bridge, but don't cross over it. Instead, turn right and follow a path downhill, as signposted again for Vizzavona. Cross a footbridge over a bouldery river. After the path makes a loop around a spur in beech-woods, turn left to cross another footbridge over the Ruisseau de Fulminato. A woodland track leads to **Vizzavona**, becoming surfaced with tarmac as it reaches the village. Turn left to walk down into the village to avail of all its facilities. The altitude is 920m (3020ft).

# STAGE 9B
*Refuge de l'Onda to Vizzavona (high-level)*

| | |
|---|---|
| **Start** | Refuge de l'Onda |
| **Finish** | Vizzavona |
| **Distance** | 13km (8 miles) |
| **Total ascent** | 990m (3250ft) |
| **Total descent** | 1500m (4920ft) |
| **Time** | 7hrs 30mins |
| **Terrain** | A steep and stony ascent to a gap is followed by a traverse across a rugged mountainside. There are rocky scrambles on the way to and from the summit of Monte d'Oru. The descent is long, often following a zigzag path that is steep and rocky in places. The lower slopes are forested, and easier paths and tracks lead to Vizzavona. The ascent is not recommended in misty, wet or windy conditions. |
| **Maps** | IGN 4251 OT |
| **Food and drink** | Water is generally available only on the descent from Monte d'Oru, down in the forest. Vizzavona has restaurants, bars and small foodstores. |
| **Shelter** | There is very little shelter on this stage. The mountain slopes are quite open, and there is little shade from the sun or shelter from wind and rain, although there is good forest cover towards the end. |

Monte d'Oru dominates the course of the GR20 for quite a few days, and trekkers have a good view of the mountain as they cross the gap between the Refuge de l'Onda and Vizzavona. The ridge leading to the summit looks fairly straightforward, but there are some very steep and rocky parts that involve scrambling. Beyond the rocky parts of the ridge there is more scrambling to the summit. The descent from the mountain is quite long, steep, rough and rocky in places, although there are easier forest paths and tracks on the lower slopes. For trekkers who wish to follow the GR20 only as far as Vizzavona, the ascent of Monte d'Oru is a splendid climax, with magnificent views on a clear day.

Leave the **Refuge de l'Onda** by following the path sign-posted for Vizzavona, rising gently across a rugged slope to reach a blunt ridge. A boulder on the ridge also carries a sign for Vizzavona, so turn left there to start climbing. The stony path steepens and passes through alder scrub on the ridge. After climbing over boulders and passing outcrops of rock, there are widening views across the mountains. The gradient eases on a bare, stony shoulder, then climbs steeply again. There are good views of Monte d'Oru and Punta Migliarello ahead. The path is generally on the ridge, but later it swings off to the right and goes through a rocky notch. Cross boulders and bare rock and swing back onto the ridge, and almost immediately the path crosses the main crest near **Punta Muratello**, at an altitude of around 2100m (6890ft). This point should be reached 2hrs 30mins after leaving the Refuge de l'Onda.

Continue following the red and white flashes of the GR20 down a rough and stony path zigzagging down from the crest. The route cuts across a couple of bare slabs, then the markers suddenly swing round to the right. At this point, head off to the left, following instead yellow paint marks and small cairns marking the way to Monte d'Oru.

The path contours across the mountainside, heading roughly eastwards. A short scramble and a stony path lead up to the crest

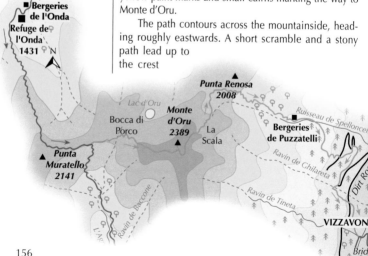

near **Bocca di Porco**, around 2160m (7085ft). Follow the stony path as it zigzags close to the crest, then scramble over a rocky part of the crest, watching carefully for

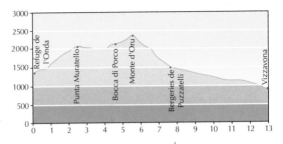

the small cairns and yellow marks. The rocky summit of Monte d'Oru towers above, while the little **Lac d'Oru** is visible far below. The route clings to the ridge, then yellow markers reveal that it cuts beneath an awesome rocky face, before leading up a shallow gully of upended rocks. A boulder painted with the words 'Muratello' and 'Oro' is reached. Packs can be left here while making a summit bid.

Climb a steep and bouldery slope, with the rocky peak of the mountain above. The markers and cairns lead to the left of the peak, where a final series of short scrambles leads to the rocky summit of **Monte d'Oru** at 2389m (7838ft). It takes around 1hr 30mins to reach the summit from the crest near Punta Muratello. The view stretches back along the GR20 to Monte Ritondu and Monte Cinto, as well as ahead to Monte Renosu and Monte Alcudina.

Double back along the last series of short scrambles to return down the bouldery slope to the painted boulder, then watch carefully for the yellow marks leading off to the left across stony and bouldery slopes on the eastern side of the mountain. The path zigzags a little, then reaches gentler grassy slopes dominated by a towering mass of rock. The path is funnelled into a bouldery, north-facing gully called **La Scala**. This can become a rather awkward trap if it is filled with snow, which can lie late into the summer. Unfortunately, there is no way to see if this is the case in advance.

*The final rocky peak of Monte d'Oru is accessed by a series of steep and rocky little scrambles*

On the descent of La Scala, it is generally best to keep to the right, near the foot of a cliff. Take care not to dislodge boulders on the way down. At the bottom, exit to the left, crossing boulders and walking through flowery alder scrub, where parsley fern is also common. Amazing pinnacles of rock tower high above and huge boulders litter the slopes below. The path zigzags down through alder scrub, crossing rocky areas where thrift grows, and a couple of seasonal streams, before entering an area of slender sycamore woodland. There are a couple of clearings in the trees, reached near the ruined **Bergeries de Puzzatelli**. Trekkers should reach this point, around 1500m (4920ft), about 1hr 30mins after leaving the summit of Monte d'Oru.

The path leads down a series of steep zigzags into denser forest dominated at first by laricio pines. Juniper and tall heather scrub grows in the clearings. Keep an eye peeled for the yellow markers, which lead across a bouldery stream called the **Ruisseau de Spelloncellu**. There are beech trees in this area, although as the path

*A patch of snow lingers through the middle of July, near La Scala, while flowers seem to burst from a barren scree slope*

leads away from the stream they give way to laricio and maritime pines. The path is quite broad, steep and stony in places, although it narrows and becomes a zigzag path leading down to a forest track.

Cross over this track and descend along another path to cut out a sweeping bend. Turn round a hairpin bend to rejoin the track, then walk down another path to join the track at a lower level. Pass a signpost that points back to Monte d'Oru. Turn right and follow the forest track gently downhill. There is a glimpse of Vizzavona just before leaving the track at a hairpin bend, where there is another signpost pointing back to Monte d'Oru.

Cross bouldery stepping stones near a seasonal waterfall and follow a forest path, turning left as signposted for Vizzavona. The path leads downhill and crosses another forest track. The woodlands are quite mixed and the ground cover is a rampant tangle of shrubs and flowers. At the next forest track, turn right to cross a bridge, then turn immediately left down another path signposted for Vizzavona. Once again trekkers find themselves following a path marked by the red and white flashes of the GR20. Cross a footbridge over a bouldery river. After the path makes a loop around a spur in beech-woods, turn left to cross another footbridge over the Ruisseau de Fulminato. A woodland track leads to **Vizzavona**, becoming surfaced with tarmac as it reaches the village. Turn left to walk down into the village and avail of its facilities. The altitude is 920m (3020ft).

## VIZZAVONA

There are all sorts of ways of looking at Vizzavona. For anyone trekking all the way along the GR20, it's roughly the middle of the route, and a fine place for a break to take stock of progress. For those trekking only the northern half of the route, this is the finishing point. Alternatively, some trekkers choose to cover only the southern half of the GR20 from Conca, finishing at Vizzavona. Some start here and head north to Calenzana, or finish here after walking from Conca.

As the village is on a regular rail route, Vizzavona is a place of comings and goings, or a place to halt and rest, maybe stocking up on food, enjoying a hearty meal, or morosely licking wounds and wondering what to do next. It can be very busy when full of GR20 trekkers and visiting day-walkers.

It is interesting to bear in mind that Vizzavona owes its origin to early 19th-century English aristocrats, who came in such numbers that the Grand Hôtel de la Forêt (now in ruins) had to be built to accommodate them in style. The idea for the provision of a railway dates from 1870, although it wasn't developed until 1878. The construction of the railway was a daunting project, requiring 43 important tunnels, 76 bridges and viaducts, as well as carefully engineered gradients, embankments and cuttings. Not only had natural obstacles to be overcome, but also the objections of landowners.

The line from Bastia to Corte opened in 1888. The link from Ponte Leccia to Calvi was opened in 1893. The line was extended from Corte to Vizzavona in 1894, and finally taken from Vizzavona through a 4km (2½ mile) tunnel to Ajaccio by 1898. It was at Vizzavona station that one of the most famous Corsican bandits, Antoine Bellacoscia, finally surrendered to the gendarmerie.

Those intending to take a break at Vizzavona might find themselves getting a bit restless after a few hours. If a short stroll appeals, then there are a couple of waymarked options. The Sentier des Cascades leads in an easy loop through the forest between Vizzavona and the Cascade des Anglais. Part of this loop is also followed by the GR20. The cascades were named after the English aristocrats who made them popular, seeking more adventurous tours away from the Côte d'Azur.

In the other direction the Sentier Archaéologique leads to an interesting cave structure formed beneath immense wedged boulders. With a bit of imagination, coupled with a perusal of the notes on an information board, it is possible to imagine Neolithic hunter-gatherers residing at the very heart of Corsica 7000 years ago. In the summer they would have lived here and sought game in the forests, then returned to the coasts for the winter months. The site was excavated by an Englishman called Charles Forsyth Major, and was named l'Abri Southwell after Edith Southwell, a friend who used to accompany him on his tours around Corsica. Trekkers who want a break from the GR20 altogether, and a chance to experience Corsican culture, should get a train to Corte for the day. This ancient citadel town was once the capital of Corsica, and remains a place of faded grandeur and power at the very heart of the island. Corte has a full range of services and is a stronghold of Corsican language and culture. (See the end of the 'Link from Bergeries de Vaccaghja to Corte' for details.)

**Accommodation** There is a range of accommodation in Vizzavona, with prices to suit all pockets. L'Alzarella, tel 04 95 31 13 19, is a campsite located near the railway, offering hire tents, toilets, showers and a kitchen. Just across the road from the station, the Bar Restaurant de la Gare, tel 04 95 47 22 20, operates a refuge with 30 beds. Just uphill from the station is the Hôtel Restaurant I Laricci, tel 04 95 47 21 12, offering 12 rooms in the hotel or 12 beds in a separate dormitory. There is also a laundry. Just above Vizzavona, off the main road in the direction of Corte, is the Casa Alta Chambres d'Hôte, tel 04 95 47 21 09, which has 5 rooms. Further along the road in the direction of Ajaccio is the luxury Hôtel U Castellu, tel 04 95 30 53 00, offering 10 rooms.

**Food and drink** Places to eat and drink in Vizzavona include the Hôtel I Laricci, the Restaurant du Chef de Gare beside the station and Bar Restaurant de la Gare opposite the station. The Hôtel U Castellu, up on the main road, also has a restaurant. All these places offer extensive Corsican menus, and between them provide the widest choice of food and drink since leaving Calenzana. There is also a small alimentation in the station building and an épicerie at the campsite. If starting a trek north or south along the GR20 from Vizzavona, it shouldn't be necessary to carry much food away, as many places provide meals or sell basic foodstuffs.

**Transport** The railway runs daily and has immense appeal simply for its own sake. It links Vizzavona with Ajaccio, Corte, Ponte Leccia, Bastia and Calvi. Timetables can be obtained from the station, or tel 04 95 46 00 97, **www.cf-corse.fr**.

*The Hôtel I Laricci is one of the few hotels on the GR20, and it also operates a more basic dortoir.*

# STAGE 10

*Vizzavona to
Bergeries d' E Capanelle*

| | |
|---|---|
| **Start** | Vizzavona |
| **Finish** | Bergeries d' E Capanelle |
| **Distance** | 16km (10 miles) |
| **Total ascent** | 1000m (3280ft) |
| **Total descent** | 335m (1100ft) |
| **Time** | 5hrs 30mins |
| **Terrain** | A forested ascent from Vizzavona is accomplished on well-graded paths. Other paths rise or fall gently, or simply contour across rugged forested slopes. Paths become more rugged towards the end. |
| **Maps** | IGN 4252 OT |
| **Food and drink** | There is a water source near Bocca Palmento and a couple of streams along the way. The Bergeries – both U Renosu and U Fugone – serve meals and sell provisions. |
| **Shelter** | There is fairly good tree cover for most of the day, but some parts cross open slopes. |

After the rigours of the northern part of the GR20, the southern stretch looks and feels gentler. Make no mistake, it is still tough trekking, but anyone who has come this far should have no problem finishing. Aim to leave Vizzavona well nourished, after a good rest. There is a long climb up a forested slope from the village, but gradients are easy. Stony paths cut across rugged slopes, and there are wonderful views ahead of Monte Renosu and its neighbouring peaks. There is a bit of a sting in the tail later, when the path climbs a steep and rugged woodland slope to cross over to the Bergeries d' E Capanelle, but afterwards it is possible to relax and enjoy good food and drink. Those who stay at La Foce can use a variant route to re-join the main GR20 at Bocca Palmento. (See the next section for details.)

On leaving **Vizzavona** follow the minor road uphill from the Hotel I Laricci. Turn left as signposted for the GR20

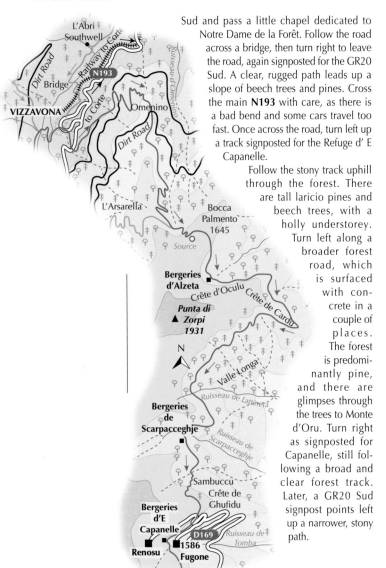

Sud and pass a little chapel dedicated to Notre Dame de la Forêt. Follow the road across a bridge, then turn right to leave the road, again signposted for the GR20 Sud. A clear, rugged path leads up a slope of beech trees and pines. Cross the main **N193** with care, as there is a bad bend and some cars travel too fast. Once across the road, turn left up a track signposted for the Refuge d' E Capanelle.

Follow the stony track uphill through the forest. There are tall laricio pines and beech trees, with a holly understorey. Turn left along a broader forest road, which is surfaced with concrete in a couple of places. The forest is predominantly pine, and there are glimpses through the trees to Monte d'Oru. Turn right as signposted for Capanelle, still following a broad and clear forest track. Later, a GR20 Sud signpost points left up a narrower, stony path.

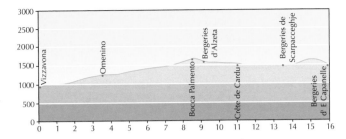

The path zigzags up the slope of pines and is flanked by bracken and tall heather. It becomes narrower and passes a couple of large boulders. A clearing is reached, where the trees have been cut away to accommodate an overhead pylon line at 1200m (3935ft) at **Omenino**, then the route crosses a forest track where signs indicate the GR20 Nord and GR20 Sud. There is another good view of Monte d'Oru at this point.

As the path continues further uphill through the forest, the pines give way to beech trees, and the way rises gently or contours around a slope, leading almost to a stream. The path is evenly graded and can be covered quite quickly. Zigzags lead back towards the stream a couple more times, then the path leaves the woods and continues up a more open slope, passing patches of alder scrub. There is another fine view of Monte d'Oru. Watch out for the path crossing the Fontaine de Palmento, a good **source** for replenishing water.

The path climbs a little further to cross the **Bocca Palmento**, at 1645m (5400ft), where it is worth taking a break. The gap features broad, gentle, stony slopes liberally strewn with tiny saxifrages. Take the opportunity to look back to Monte d'Oru and Monte Ritondu, or ahead through the valley of the Fiumorbu to the distant sea. Trekkers should reach Bocca Palmento about 2hrs 45mins after leaving Vizzavona.

The path swings to the right as it descends from the gap, and is quite rough and stony as it cuts across a slope of juniper to reach a patchy woodland of beech and alder. It then passes the picturesque **Bergeries d'Alzeta**,

*The attractive Bergeries d'Alzeta crouch at the foot of an immensely tall beech tree below the Bocca Palmento*

where there are often pigs foraging for food. Cross a stream just beyond the bergeries and continue following the path, roughly contouring across a slope covered in patchy beech-woods. There is an open area sparsely clad with pines as the path turns around the ridge of the **Crête d'Oculu**.

Continue through beech-woods again then, on reaching another area sparsely clad in pines on the **Crête de Cardu**, stop and admire the view. All of a sudden, Monte Renosu and neighbouring peaks are well

displayed across the forested **Valle Longa**. Walkers should reach this point, at 1515m (4970ft), about an hour after leaving Bocca Palmento. A signpost points off-route to the village of Ghisoni.

Although the path continues to contour around the forested slopes, it is quite rough and stony underfoot. There are some blasted laricio pines at first, but later more beech trees appear where the path crosses a stream. Water is drawn off through a black plastic pipe, but even if the streambed is dry, there is water available at a bouldery cascade further along the path at the **Ruisseau de Lattineta**. This is a good place to enjoy the shade among bigger beech trees.

As the path continues around another crest, it again passes pines on the rugged slope where the ground is drier. Notice that the beeches re-establish themselves towards the next stream, where the route crosses the **Ruisseau de Scarpacceghje**. The path passes the **Bergeries de Scarpacceghje**, where a variety of interesting plants grow.

*Much of the GR20 is forested around Valle Longa, but there are glimpses of the mountains through the trees*

167

Pass more laricio pines while swinging round into the next valley, and cross the Ruisseau de Giargalozeo. A signpost for the GR20 Sud points uphill to the right. Climb up a bouldery slope covered in beech trees, which is fairly short, but can be difficult underfoot. There is good shade, and in fact it is so shady that hardly anything grows on the ground, which is littered with leaf mould, fallen branches, toppled trees and stones.

Zigzags ease the gradient a little, then the path becomes easier and drifts more to the left. After it swings to the right on the shoulder of the **Crête de Ghufidu**, it hits a hairpin bend on a road at 1630m (5350ft). Walk gently uphill a short way along the road, then head off to the left as signposted for the Bergeries d' E Capanelle.

Follow a rugged path gently downhill on a slope sparsely covered in beech trees. By following the markers exactly, the Refuge d' E Capanelle is reached before swinging left down to the **Gîte d'Étape U Fugone**. The temptation, of course, is to short-cut straight down to U Fugone, at 1586m (5303ft). Trekkers should reach it 1hr 45 mins after leaving Crête de Cardu.

## BERGERIES D' E CAPANELLE

These bergeries have been transformed over the years. Originally they were nothing more than a huddle of stone huts, and a few of these remain. The area was developed as a ski-station, accessed by a lengthy zigzag extension of the D169 road. There is a choice of accommodation, as well as an opportunity to enjoy an ascent of nearby Monte Renosu. However, some trekkers decide to make the most of the good paths in this area, pressing onwards to reach Bocca di Verdi.

**Accommodation** The PNRC Refuge d' E Capanelle is very small and basic, built in the bergerie style with a 16-bed dormitory and kitchen. It was re-roofed in 2017. Unlike other PNRC refuges, it cannot be booked in advance, but an overnight costs less, payable at the nearby gîte, and free camping is permitted. The Gîte d'Étape U Fugone, also known as the Gîte de Capanelle, tel 04 95 57 01 81, has 62 beds spread around 12 dormitories, as well as three chalets with 6 to 10 beds each. Hire tents are also available. Trekkers staying in the refuge or camping nearby can pay for showers.

**Food and drink** U Fugone has a busy bar restaurant offering good Corsican food and drink. A small épicerie is available for those who wish to cook their own meals, but the choice is rather limited.

## LINK ROUTE
*La Foce to
Bocca Palmento*

| | |
|---|---|
| **Start** | Hôtel Monte d'Oro |
| **Finish** | Bocca Palmento |
| **Distance** | 5km (3 miles) |
| **Total ascent** | 460m (1510ft) |
| **Total descent** | 60m (195ft) |
| **Time** | 1hr 30mins |
| **Terrain** | Gentle woodland paths and forest tracks are followed by a steep zigzag path climbing from the woods onto open scrubby slopes. |
| **Maps** | IGN 4252 OT |
| **Food and drink** | There is a water source near Bocca Palmento. |
| **Shelter** | The woodlands offer good shade and shelter. |

Trekkers who choose to stay at La Foce, near the Col de Vizzavona, can re-join the GR20 without having to descend to Vizzavona. They can avoid the hustle and bustle of the village, and keep more of a sense of remoteness about the route, without losing an opportunity to obtain food, drink and accommodation. A signposted and waymarked variant is available from La Foce to a point where it re-joins the GR20 below Bocca Palmento. The variant uses forest tracks and a zigzag path up a slope covered in beech trees, offering a saving of 2km (1¼ miles) and 270m (885ft) of ascent over the main route.

Leave the **Hôtel Monte d'Oro** or the chalets and campsite at **A Muntagnera**, and walk to a building in-between them. This is set back from the road and bears the words 'Ponts et Chaussées'. Walk round the left-hand side to find a clear track signposted 'Sentier Femme Perdue', which leads into beech-woods behind A Muntagnera. (There is a short-cut onto the track from the chalets and campsite.) The track rises and falls very gently, then narrows as it rises to a path junction. Left is signposted for Vizzavona, so keep right to zigzag up to a forest track. Walk along the track, which is later signposted 'GR20', and avoid the path signposted 'Sentier'. The track is flashed with both blue and yellow paint at intervals, and it drops gently past tall pines to ford the cobbly bed of the **Ruisseau de Fulminato**.

Continue along the track, but watch for a sharp turn to the right up a more rugged stony track. Follow this, taking note of the blue and yellow paint flashes at any junctions along the way. The woods are mostly pine, but when they become mostly beech, a GR20 signpost indicates a sharp right turn. Follow the rough and stony path up to a bouldery junction of paths. Turn left, as signposted for the Bocca Palmento.

There is only one obvious zigzag path climbing uphill at **l'Arsarella**, sometimes easy underfoot, but sometimes rough and stony. Mixed beech and pines give way at a higher level to pines, then to beech. Eventually, emerge from the trees to cross a small rocky outcrop and enjoy a splendid view of Monte d'Oru across the valley. The path leads back into the beech-woods and almost immediately joins the main course of the GR20 on a hairpin bend.

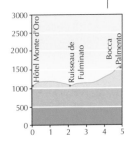

Keep right, in effect straight ahead, to follow the GR20 uphill, out of the woods, zigzagging up a more open slope, passing patches of alder scrub. There is another fine view of Monte d'Oru. Watch out for the path crossing the Fontaine de Palmento, a good **source** for replenishing water.

The path climbs a little further to cross the **Bocca Palmento**, at 1645m (5400ft), where it is worth taking a break. The gap features broad, gentle, stony slopes liberally strewn with tiny saxifrages. Take the opportunity to look back to Monte d'Oru and Monte Ritondu, or ahead through the valley of the Fiumorbu to the distant sea. Continue to the Bergeries d' E Capanelle as described in the previous section, Stage 10.

# STAGE 11A

*Bergeries d' E Capanelle to Bocca di Verdi (low-level)*

| | |
|---|---|
| **Start** | Bergeries d' E Capanelle |
| **Finish** | Bocca di Verdi |
| **Distance** | 14km (8¾ miles) |
| **Total ascent** | 320m (1050ft) |
| **Total descent** | 620m (2035ft) |
| **Time** | 4hrs 30mins |
| **Terrain** | The route traverses forested slopes for most of the day. Although there are some steep and rugged ascents and descents, these are quite short, and most of the time the gradients are gentle, and the paths and tracks followed are fairly easy. |
| **Maps** | IGN 4252 OT |
| **Food and drink** | Water can be obtained from streams along the way. The Casetta di Ghjalcone serves meals and sells provisions. The Relais San Petru di Verdi operates a bar restaurant and sells provisions. |
| **Shelter** | Trees provide good shade and shelter throughout the day. |

This is one of the easier stages of the GR20, and although the first part is actually quite rugged, it is quickly completed. For the most part the route rises and falls gently, and basically contours across forested mountainsides.

There is good shade, as well as water in a number of streams, with food and drink on offer during and at the end of the day. An alternative high-level route is also available, crossing Monte Renosu (see the next section for details). It is also possible, after reaching Bocca di Verdi, to continue along the GR20 and endure a stiff climb to the Refuge de Prati. So, ponder over the alternatives and decide whether to stop at Bocca di Verdi or climb to the Refuge de Prati. Either way, it is likely that the next stop will almost certainly be the Refuge d'Usciolu.

Leave the Gîte d'Étape U Fugone and turn left after passing the first two ski-lift pylons. A sign points left at a small bergerie building, indicating the course of the GR20. Climb a short, rocky slope and turn round a corner, noting

*View of the mountains from the Bergeries d' E Traghjete, shortly after leaving the Bergeries d' E Capanelle*

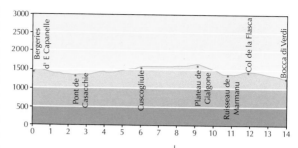

that beech and alder scrub gives way to laricio pines and juniper. There are glimpses of high mountains on the way down a rugged path, then there are much better mountain views near the **Bergeries d' E Traghjete**.

Swing left to follow the path as it zigzags down stony slopes between the pines. It is quite bouldery in places, with a water source just to the left and cascades down to the right. Clumps of hellebore grow in profusion among lush undergrowth. After landing on the D169 road at the bottom, turn right and cross a bridge over the river. This bridge, the **Pont de Casacchie** at 1344m (4409ft), is reached about 30mins after leaving the Bergeries d' E Capanelle.

Head off to the right, away from the road, as signposted for Bocca di Verdi. A broad track narrows as beech trees give way to pines on a steep and rugged slope. ▶

The path climbs up a rocky slope for a short way, below the **Rocher d'Accella**, then crosses a slope covered in pines to reach a cut filled with beech trees.

Keep climbing gradually, turning sharply to the right around a ridge at Serconaccie where pine trees grow. As the stony path continues onwards, the pines gradually give way to beech while approaching the **Ruisseau de Cannareccia**. There are good views of the mountains in more open areas, then there is more forest cover as the route crosses a couple of bouldery streams at **Cuscogliule**.

The path continues rising gently on a rough and bouldery slope covered in beech trees, although in a couple of places pines grow on more arid ridges. Take a sharp right turn around one of these ridges, then cross a couple of open slopes covered in scrub and young pines. There is a denser cover of beech trees as the route crosses

There is a view between the trees, across to the mountains, taking in Punta Kyrie Eleison.

173

*The GR20 cuts straight across an open slope on its way to the Plateau de Gialgone*

the **Ruisseau de Lischetto**. The path contours across a slope of spiny broom and crosses the foot of some rock slabs, then there is a mixture of dense beech-woods with some more open spaces. Pigs might be noticed rooting for food.

Turn right around the **Crête de Pietra Scopina**. Cross another broad area of spiny broom to reach a point where signboards announce the **Plateau de Gialgone**. This is a bouldery area of scrub with a few tall beech trees, reached some 2hrs 30mins from Pont de Casacchie, at an altitude of 1591m (5220ft). The **Casetta di Ghjalcone** lies nearby.

**Casetta di Ghjalcone**, tel 06 16 56 10 81, opened in 2015, offering food and drink at the point where the low-level GR20 and high-level variant over Monte Renosu meet. The little stone-built bergerie has wooden huts alongside with a toilet and shower. Horses and donkeys, some of which are used to supply the place, graze nearby. The ground is rugged, but camping spots are available.

The GR20 zigzags down an open slope then passes a mixture of beech and pine trees, becoming rather more rugged by the time it reaches the **Ruisseau de Marmanu**. Cross the river using a footbridge, at 1390m (4560ft), then turn left to follow a rugged path through flowing

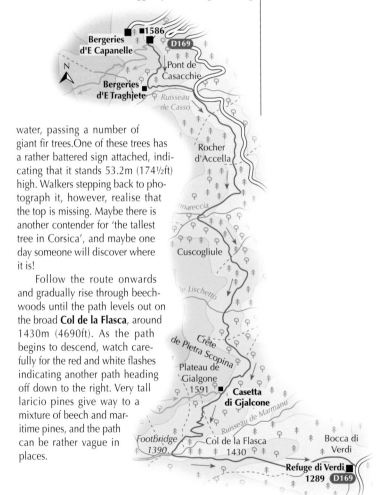

water, passing a number of giant fir trees. One of these trees has a rather battered sign attached, indicating that it stands 53.2m (174½ft) high. Walkers stepping back to photograph it, however, realise that the top is missing. Maybe there is another contender for 'the tallest tree in Corsica', and maybe one day someone will discover where it is!

Follow the route onwards and gradually rise through beechwoods until the path levels out on the broad **Col de la Flasca**, around 1430m (4690ft). As the path begins to descend, watch carefully for the red and white flashes indicating another path heading off down to the right. Very tall laricio pines give way to a mixture of beech and maritime pines, and the path can be rather vague in places.

Later, the path broadens to a stony track and passes a big boulder, continuing rough and stony down through a plantation of young pines. There is a river running roughly parallel, and although a couple of tracks head off to the right, don't follow them and don't cross the river. On reaching a car park and picnic site, follow a broad, firm track gently uphill. This reaches the Relais San Petru di Verdi, situated on the gap of **Bocca di Verdi** at 1289m (4229ft). It takes about 1hr 30mins to reach from the Plateau de Gialgone.

The **Relais San Petru di Verdi**, tel 04 95 24 46 82, is more generally known as the Refuge di Verdi. It has a bar restaurant serving meals, snacks and drinks, which can be enjoyed out on a terrace. Basic food supplies can be bought to take away. Walkers who start to feel comfortable can stay at a refuge alongside – a small wooden chalet with 26 beds, showers and toilets. There are camping spaces, as well as tents for hire. Water is available from a fountain near the road. The D69 road crosses Bocca di Verdi, but there are no bus services. Walkers who need to leave the route could ask around a nearby car park to try to secure a lift down to Cozzano or Zicavo, which have a bus service. Those with plenty of energy can continue through the afternoon to reach the Refuge de Prati high in the mountains.

# STAGE 11B

*Bergeries d' E Capanelle to Bocca
di Verdi (high-level)*

| | |
|---|---|
| **Start** | Bergeries d' E Capanelle |
| **Finish** | Bocca di Verdi |
| **Distance** | 16km (10 miles) |
| **Total ascent** | 815m (2675ft) |
| **Total descent** | 1110m (3640ft) |
| **Time** | 7hrs 15mins |
| **Terrain** | The ascent of Monte Renosu is relatively easy in clear, calm weather, although the ridge beyond is rough and rocky. There is a long, steep, stony descent to level grasslands at I Pozzi. Remaining paths are well graded, and cross open slopes or run through woods to reach Bocca di Verdi. |
| **Maps** | IGN 4252 OT |
| **Food and drink** | Water is absent on the mountain, but can be obtained from streams in the valleys. The Casetta di Ghjalcone serves meals and sells provisions. The Relais San Petru di Verdi operates a bar restaurant and sells provisions. |
| **Shelter** | There is very little shelter on the mountain, but there is good tree cover towards the end of the day's walk. |

The GR20 main route from the Bergeries d' E Capanelle to Bocca di Verdi is fairly easy, but some walkers might prefer more of a challenge. A path marked by cairns allows an ascent of Monte Renosu, and this is offered as a high-level route. One option is to climb the mountain simply for its own sake, walking with a lightweight pack from the Bergeries d' E Capanelle to the summit and back. Alternatively take everything, climb the mountain and descend the far side to I Pozzi, then walk to the Plateau de Gialgone to continue along the GR20 to Bocca di Verdi. This is a surprisingly easy ascent, compared to other mountain climbs on or near the route, but the descent is quite rugged and needs more care. There are delightful *pozzines*, or waterholes, to study at I Pozzi.

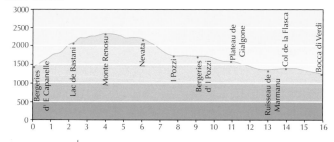

*Monte Renosu reflects in the Lac du Bastani and holds snow well into the summer*

Leave the Gîte d'Étape U Fugone and follow a zigzag path uphill, weaving between the pylons of the ski tow. The GR20 main route heads off to the left at a small bergerie building, while the path climbing uphill is signposted for Lac de Bastani and Monte Renosu. Follow the zigzag path all the way to the top pylon of the ski tow. After enjoying a view of Monte Renosu from this point, continue along a clear, cairned path up a blunt ridge. The route passes boulders and continues through alder scrub, and there is a big protuberance of rock off to the right. This rock is prominent even from the start of the climb.

Continue up the ridge, then cross a little stream near a level grassy area before climbing again. The path is rather vague as it climbs up a gently sloping, grassy, bouldery valley, but follow it faithfully and suddenly reach a point overlooking

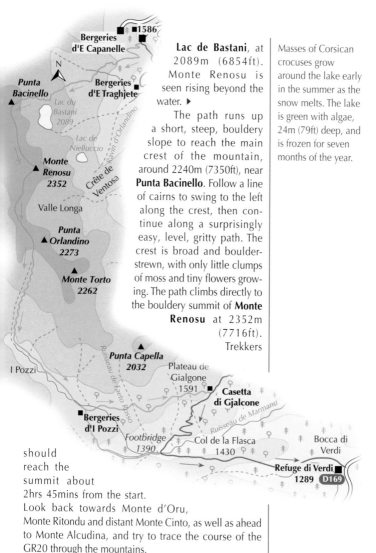

**Lac de Bastani**, at 2089m (6854ft). Monte Renosu is seen rising beyond the water. ▶

The path runs up a short, steep, bouldery slope to reach the main crest of the mountain, around 2240m (7350ft), near **Punta Bacinello**. Follow a line of cairns to swing to the left along the crest, then continue along a surprisingly easy, level, gritty path. The crest is broad and boulder-strewn, with only little clumps of moss and tiny flowers growing. The path climbs directly to the bouldery summit of **Monte Renosu** at 2352m (7716ft). Trekkers

should reach the summit about 2hrs 45mins from the start. Look back towards Monte d'Oru, Monte Ritondu and distant Monte Cinto, as well as ahead to Monte Alcudina, and try to trace the course of the GR20 through the mountains.

Trekkers climbing the mountain only for its own sake can retrace their steps back to the Bergeries d'

Masses of Corsican crocuses grow around the lake early in the summer as the snow melts. The lake is green with algae, 24m (79ft) deep, and is frozen for seven months of the year.

E Capanelle. The rest of this route description leads to Bocca di Verdi.

Continue along the cairned path to leave the summit, walking down a slope of boulders and gritty inclines to reach a narrow, rocky, complex gap near the Punta di Valle Longa. Follow the cairned route carefully, by-passing rocky obstacles and completing simple scrambles. ◀

The rocky ridge ends quite suddenly on a gap at 2244m (7362ft). The cairned path leads up a broad and stony slope, littered with boulders, in the direction of **Punta Orlandino**. Don't climb to the summit, but drift off to the right instead, then swing right again to walk down into a grassy, stony hollow on the mountainside at Nevata. A seasonal stream flows down to I Pozzi, and it is necessary to step over the streambed to continue.

Look very carefully for a sparse line of small cairns while walking down a steep and rugged slope. There are patches of juniper and spiny broom, broken rock and alder scrub, all to be negotiated with care. Keep looking ahead for those elusive little cairns and don't venture onto precarious rocky edges. Even when the path reaches the lower ground, pick a way carefully through the alder scrub, where the narrow path is almost totally obscured. On emerging, swing left to follow the path down through the valley.

Things become much easier while walking beside the closely cropped grasslands of **I Pozzi**, just below the 1800m (5900ft) contour. The valley floor is level and the bongling bells of grazing cattle break the silence as feet make hardly any sound on the velvet turf. Complex waterholes, or *pozzines*, drain the valley floor, and little streams sometimes rush along or flow more sluggishly. Leave the grasslands to continue through more rugged scrub further down the valley, and cross a stream using a boulder as a stepping stone. Paint marks and cairns on boulders indicate the path to follow through the spiny broom to reach the **Bergeries d' I Pozzi**.

Beyond the bergeries, the paint-marked route heads off to the right, but walkers should follow another cairned path off to the left. Watch carefully for the line of the path,

*There is a fine view off to the right down to the little Lac de Vitalaca.*

*Distant walkers explore the delightfully lush and grassy pozzines (waterholes) around I Pozzi*

which is vague in places, and cross a wooded stream further along. ▶ Follow the path across the rugged slopes to cross another stream, the Ruisseau de Faeto Rosso, and cross the slopes beyond. Note the blasted beech trees on the slope of boulders, spiny broom and juniper scrub. The stony path leads down to signboards on the **Plateau de Gialgone** at 1591m (5220ft). It will probably take about 3hrs to reach this point after leaving the summit of Monte Renosu. Rejoin the main GR20 and turn right to follow it as signposted for Bocca di Verdi, or visit the nearby **Casetta di Ghjalcone**.

This can be followed downstream to join the GR20 at a footbridge, but misses the Casetta di Ghjalcone.

**Casetta di Ghjalcone**, tel 06 16 56 10 81, opened in 2015, offering food and drink at the point where the low-level GR20 and high-level variant over Monte Renosu meet. The little stone-built bergerie has wooden huts alongside with a toilet and shower. Horses and donkeys, some of which are used to supply the place, graze nearby. The ground is rugged, but camping spots are available.

The GR20 zigzags down an open slope then passes a mixture of beech and pine trees, becoming rather more rugged by the time it reaches the **Ruisseau de Marmanu**. Cross the river using a footbridge, at 1390m (4560ft), then turn left to follow a rugged path through flowing water, passing a number of giant fir trees. One of these trees has a rather battered sign attached, indicating that it stands 53.2m (174½ft) high. Walkers stepping back to photograph it, however, realise that the top is missing. Maybe there is another contender for 'the tallest tree in Corsica', and maybe one day someone will discover where it is!

Follow the route onwards and gradually rise through beech-woods until the path levels out on the broad **Col de la Flasca**, around 1430m (4690ft). As the path begins to descend, watch carefully for the red and white flashes indicating another path heading off down to the right. Very tall laricio pines give way to a mixture of beech and maritime pines, and the path can be rather vague in places.

Later, the path broadens to a stony track and passes a big boulder, continuing rough and stony down through a plantation of young pines. There is a river running roughly parallel, and although a couple of tracks head off to the right, don't follow them and don't cross the river. On reaching a car park and picnic site, follow a broad, firm track gently uphill. This reaches the Relais San Petru di Verdi, situated on the gap of **Bocca di Verdi** at 1289m (4229ft). It takes about 1hr 30mins to reach from the Plateau de Gialgone.

The **Relais San Petru di Verdi**, tel 04 95 24 46 82, is more generally known as the Refuge di Verdi. It has a bar restaurant serving meals, snacks and drinks, which can be enjoyed out on a terrace. Basic food supplies can be bought to take away. Walkers who start to feel comfortable can stay at a refuge alongside – a small wooden chalet with 26 beds, showers and toilets. There are camping spaces, as well as tents for hire. Water is available from a fountain near the road. The D69 road crosses Bocca di Verdi, but there are no bus services. Walkers who need to leave the route could ask around a nearby car park to try to secure a lift down to Cozzano or Zicavo, which have a bus service. Those with plenty of energy can continue through the afternoon to reach the Refuge de Prati high in the mountains.

# STAGE 12
### *Bocca di Verdi to*
### *Refuge d'Usciolu*

| | |
|---|---|
| **Start** | Bocca di Verdi |
| **Finish** | Refuge d'Usciolu |
| **Distance** | 16km (10 miles) |
| **Total ascent** | 1290m (4230ft) |
| **Total descent** | 830m (2725ft) |
| **Time** | 7hrs 15mins |
| **Terrain** | A forested climb gives way to steep, open mountainside. The route drifts from side to side along a ridge. It can be steep and rocky in some places but quite easy in others. There is forest around Bocca di Laparo, followed by a climb onto open mountainsides again. |
| **Maps** | IGN 4252 OT |
| **Food and drink** | The Refuge de Prati and Refuge d'Usciolu serve meals and sell provisions. Water might be available at Bocca di Laparo. |
| **Shelter** | The Refuge de Prati is passed shortly after crossing the ridge. Apart from forest cover at the start and around Bocca di Laparo, there is very little shade or shelter from sun, wind or rain. |

This stage starts with a climb from Bocca di Verdi to Bocca d'Oru. Those who took the option to reach the Refuge de Prati the previous day can rejoice as almost half the climbing is done. What follows is essentially a ridge walk – not exactly along the ridge, but along a path switching from side to side. The ridge is rocky in some places and progress can be slow, but in other places there is a good path and easy gradients, where progress is faster. Water is absent along the ridge, so fill up at the Refuge de Prati, although there might be water available at Bocca di Laparo. In hot weather plenty of water is necessary, as there is little shade from the sun, apart from a couple of forested areas. Views are excellent, overlooking forested valleys and taking in distant ranges of mountains. The proximity of the sea is a reminder that the GR20 is in its closing stages, but there is plenty of exciting terrain to traverse before reaching Conca. Forest fires damaged a number of places on this stage of the GR20 during 2017.

Cross the D69 to leave **Bocca di Verdi**, as signposted for the Refuge de Prati. Swing right and follow a stony track uphill. Mixed woodlands quickly give way to pine forest. Cross a track and continue uphill as marked, then keep left up a narrower, slightly steeper track. When the track narrows to a path, it passes a rather unreliable water source as the pines begin to thin out. There are views of jagged peaks on the ridge as an interesting hollow in the mountainside is reached. There is a surprising amount of shrubby vegetation in this sheltered place, with clumps of euphorbia being particularly abundant. A gritty path passes through the shrubs and sparse tree cover, crossing streambeds.

The path leads into denser birch-woods, although there is a view back to the higher mountains first. Zigzag up a bouldery slope between beech trees and emerge in a pleasant clearing dominated by a towering mass of rock. Looking to the right of the rock, the high gap that needs to be reached is visible on the ridge. Zigzag up a bouldery slope covered in juniper, spiny broom and a wealth of colourful flowers.

The path finally levels out as it crosses the broad and stony gap called **Bocca d'Oru**, where there are only a few low clumps of vegetation. A cairn and a sign stand at this point, around 1840m (6035ft), which should be reached around 1hr 45mins after leaving Bocca di Verdi. ▶

There is a view of the fertile coastal plain and the sea near Ghisonaccia, looking surprisingly close. Monte Renosu, Monte d'Oru and Monte Ritondu are also visible.

Bocca di Verdi

**Refuge di Verdi 1289**

*Dirt Road*

**D69**

Pont de Ghiraldino

*to Zicavo*

*Le Taravo Fleuve*

*Ruisseau d'Orziolo*

*Punta Bocca d'Oru 1934* ▲

Bocca d'Oru 1840

*Punta del Prato 1954* ▲

**Refuge de Prati 1820**

map continues on page 189

▲1988

*Punta Cappella 2041* ▲

*Ruisseau de Nursoli*

*Punta di Campitello* ▲ 1937

*Rocher de la Penta* ▲1675

*Punta di Latoncello 1722*

Bocca di Rapari 1614

*Punta di Campolongo* ▲ 1695

continued 1594

Follow a path that climbs very gently through spiny broom, passing patches of short grass favoured by grazing cattle. The main crest of the ridge is off to the right, while to the left are granite tors. A short descent on a stony path through alder scrub leads to the **Refuge de Prati**. It is only a 15min walk from the Bocca d'Oru, and stands at an altitude of 1820m (5970ft), being only 85m (280ft) below the summit of Punta del Prato.

Following a lightning strike in 1997, the PNRC **Refuge de Prati** was rebuilt in its original bergerie style and appears quite modern inside. There is one large dormitory with 32 beds, a large kitchen/dining room and the

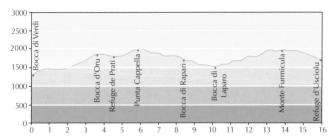

gardien's quarters. A terrace looks out towards the sea and along the high ridge. Water is available to one side of the building, and there is a toilet and shower in a little building just downhill. A grassy slope is used for camping and bears hire tents. Meals, food and drink supplies are on sale. Trekkers might notice a plaque

*Horses are frequently used to re-supply the Refuge de Prati from the road crossing Bocca di Verdi*

fixed to a nearby rock, recording the landing of arms by parachute during World War II, enabling Corsicans to fight Nazi and fascist occupation forces.

Leave the refuge as signposted for Bocca di Laparo and Usciolu. The path is narrow and easy, crossing grassy areas at first, giving way to alder scrub as it climbs steep and bouldery slopes to gain a point on the ridge at 1988m (6522ft). ▶

*There are fine views back to the refuge, as well as beyond to Monte Renosu, Monte d'Oru and Monte Ritondu.*

Watch carefully as the marked route drops off to the left of the crest, crossing sloping slabs that need special care when wet. Follow the line indicated by the markers, which lead first across the slabs, then reveal a zig-zag rocky climb back onto the crest. Turn left to continue along the crest, then drift left of the crest, skirting close to the summit of **Punta Cappella** around 2000m (6560ft). The slope is littered with huge boulders and alder scrub. It takes about an hour to reach this point from the Refuge de Prati, as the terrain is so awkward.

When the path descends from Punta Cappella it is much easier underfoot. There are grassy patches and juniper scrub, then a gap where there are some large

*Cloud drifts across the gap of Bocca di Laparo, with Punta Cappella seen far beyond*

outcrops of rock. Slip to the right, across the crest, then walk down across bare rock and follow a rather worn and stony path further downhill. There are good views down the forested valley to the villages of Palneca and Cozzano, but trekkers are more likely to be watching where they plant their feet.

Pick a way across the rugged slopes of **Punta di Campitello** and cross a notch in a spur ridge. Continue down another worn and stony path as marked, taking care when crossing a slope of big boulders, then cross another rocky notch and aim to regain the main crest of the ridge. This involves following rough and bouldery paths, then passing jagged outcrops on a gap. An easier path crosses a gap on the crest, drifting to the left side of the ridge and aiming for a beech-wood beyond **Bocca di Rapari** at 1614m (5295ft). If it is a hot day, enjoy the shade in the wood.

Follow the path uphill through the beech-wood, crossing a gap and slicing down across the slopes of **Punta di Campolongo**. The path leads into another beech-wood to reach a junction of paths on **Bocca di Laparo** at an altitude of 1525m (5003ft). There are abundant signposts for destinations such as Usciolu, Prati, Catastaghju and Cozzano. The Mare a Mare Centre crosses the gap on its coast-to-coast route between Ghisonaccia and Porticcio. ◀

*A basic unstaffed refuge lies off route.*

A painted instruction states that there is a water source ten minutes further along the GR20. Follow a path with beech trees to the left and mossy rock walls to the right. The path rises and falls, sometimes crossing bare rock, but mostly confined to the woods. Watch for arrows and the word 'Source' if water is needed. The arrows point off-route to the left, down to a wooden **hut** where water runs from a pipe into a sink further downhill. However, don't rely on this source, as it is sometimes dry. The hut isn't a refuge, and over the years signs have both forbidden and permitted camping!

The path zigzags uphill, crossing rocky slopes in the shade of beech trees. It is a well-engineered route, with a stretch that runs more or less level, then another climb leads to a bouldery hollow where the trees thin out a bit.

The higher slopes of **Punta Mozza** look like cliffs, but follow the markers and another series of stony zigzags climb even further up the steep slopes. Walk into and out of a patch of beech, then zigzag up the path to cross rocky slopes covered in juniper and spiny broom. Walk through a patch of alder and gain the crest of the ridge again. Keep following the stony path uphill, enjoying the views while negotiating areas of boulders and patches of alder.

The path levels out at the top then dips gently as it crosses a slope and rises ruggedly to the crest of the ridge not far from the summit of **Monte Furmicula**. Cross the crest at an altitude of 1950m (6400ft), about 2hrs after leaving Bocca di Laparo. The summit of Monte Furmicula is all bare rock, but it is close to hand and rises only another 30m (100ft), so some trekkers might like to make a summit bid. Others may be happy simply to look back to Monte Renosu and ahead to Monte Alcudina.

Follow the path gently downhill across the slopes of **Monte Furmicula**, but watch carefully for markers, as there are a couple of places where other paths drop too far to the left, leading into awkward terrain. The course of the GR20 swings around a hollow in the mountainside, and even climbs a little before finally descending. The descent crosses bare, sloping rock, then gradually steepens until a final series of awkward, eroded, stony paths lead down to the **Refuge d'Usciolu**, at an altitude of 1750m (5740ft). It takes about 45mins to reach the refuge from the gap near Monte Furmicula.

189

The PNRC **Refuge d'Usciolu** is built in the bergerie style and can often be heard before it is seen, if the gardien is playing loud 'mood music' to trekkers! The refuge has 31 beds in two dormitories, a kitchen/dining room and the gardien's quarters. A terrace looks out across a steep-sided valley towards Monte Alcudina. Meals are available, while a nearby hut is filled with an astonishing abundance of provisions, which has to be seen to be believed, if stocks need replenishing. Tables and chairs spread from the refuge, complete with parasols, giving the place the air of a street bar! A toilet and shower are located below the refuge, as well as hire tents and spaces for camping. The gardien is in the habit of riding his horses to Cozzano early in the morning for fresh supplies, and he also takes postcards, offering a unique 'pony express' service!

## LINK ROUTE

*Refuge d'Usciolu to Cozzano*

| | |
|---|---|
| **Start** | Refuge d'Usciolu |
| **Finish** | Cozzano |
| **Distance** | 5km (3 miles) |
| **Total ascent** | 55m (180ft) |
| **Total descent** | 1075m (3525ft) |
| **Time** | 3hrs |
| **Terrain** | A steep and stony path for the most part, needing care at times. The path is mostly confined to woodland but has some open stretches. |
| **Maps** | IGN 4253 ET and IGN 4253 OT |
| **Food and drink** | Water is available from the Fontaine du Pantanellu on the descent. Cozzano has a couple of snack bars and restaurants and local produce can also be bought. |
| **Shelter** | Woodlands offer good shade and shelter throughout the descent. |

There can be compelling reasons to descend from the Refuge d'Usciolu to Cozzano. Severe weather or thunderstorms could make any continuation along exposed ridges unwise. Trekkers who are running out of stamina, or who don't have enough time left to continue, can leave the route easily at this point. The descent to Cozzano links with a bus service to Ajaccio, for onward connections around Corsica. It would be a pity to have to leave when the end is so close, but trekkers with plenty of time to spare might consider a detour to the village well worthwhile.

Leave the **Refuge d'Usciolu** as signposted for Bocca di l'Agnonu and Refuge d'Asinau. A rough and stony path slices up a steep slope to reach a ridge, where there is a signpost indicating a way down to the village of Cozzano. The path is flashed with yellow paint, and the upper parts are rather badly eroded stony zigzags, which have taken a pounding by the horses used to supply the refuge. Walk down past a rocky pinnacle and follow the path into beech-woods.

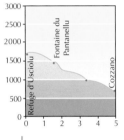

A more open stretch of path runs gently across a slope, then passes through a notch between two towers of rock. Continue down through the beech-woods, gradually losing height. The path actually runs parallel to the main GR20, which is on the rocky ridge above, but the ridge is only glimpsed from time to time. Later, swing right and drop more steeply, winding between huge, smooth outcrops of granite.

Descend further and cross a streambed above a water source at the **Fontaine du Pantaneddu**. The path pulls away from the stream and descends among tall beeches. If fallen leaves and broken branches obscure the path, keep an eye open for yellow paint marks. Emerge in a clearing where there is a stone-walled enclosure on the Crête du Miratoju. A yellow arrow points right, but after a few paces turn left to follow a narrow path down a slope of spiny broom.

Head back into beech-woods further downhill, and follow the paint marks to land on a broad turning space at the end of a forest track, at the foot of a prominent granite dome with fluted sides. There may be pigs in a nearby pen, often turned loose to forage in the woods.

Turn left down an awkward slope of bracken, broom and boulders, heading back into beech-woods as marked. Cross the **Ruisseau de Carpa** and walk roughly downstream, crossing it again as marked. Walk out of the woods to cross a tangled slope of thorny scrub, then back into the woods again. Drop down a steep and rugged slope dotted with boulders, and watch for the markers while passing some giant chestnut trees. After briefly contouring across the slope, head further downhill, then

*The village of Cozzano is seen huddled on a rounded hilltop, apparently surrounded by woodlands*

contour roughly alongside a tumbled wall and wire fence. Arbutus and heather begin to feature among the trees, and the path suddenly lands on a forest track where a signpost points back uphill for Usciolu.

Cross the track and look out for short, steep, gritty paths marked with orange paint. These cut out sweeping bends from the track, and there is a brief glimpse of Cozzano perched on a rounded hilltop. The path runs close to the Ruisseau de Mezzanu, passing a gateway, to land on the D69 at a bridge. Either turn right to reach the **Gîte d'Étape Bella Vista**, or left to pass the U Mezzanu restaurant and walk into **Cozzano**.

## COZZANO

The first glimpse of Cozzano reveals the village as a huddle of stone houses on a rounded hill, dominated by its church tower. On closer acquaintance, the village spreads out along the main D69, and this is where accommodation is found, on either side of the village. Services are sparse, but adequate for an overnight stop.

**Accommodation** The Gîte d'Étape Bella Vista, tel 04 95 24 41 59 or 06 72 92 89 46, has 30 beds in small dormitories, as well as a few private rooms and spaces for tents. It is on the D69 just northeast of Cozzano. The Auberge A Filetta, tel 04 95 24 45 61, has 8 rooms and is on the D69 just southwest of Cozzano.

**Food and drink** The U Mezzanu restaurant is beside the bridge on the D69 outside Cozzano. The Gîte d'Étape Bella Vista and the Auberge A Filetta have bar restaurants. The Snack Bar Terminus is at a crossroads in the middle of Cozzano. All these places offer good Corsican food and drink.

**Transport** A bus service from Cozzano to Zicavo and Ajaccio is operated by Autocars Santoni, tel 04 95 22 64 44. It runs daily through July and August, but not on Sundays for the rest of the year.

## STAGE 13
### Refuge d'Usciolu to
### Refuge de Matalza

| | |
|---|---|
| **Start** | Refuge d'Usciolu |
| **Finish** | Refuge de Matalza |
| **Distance** | 12km (7½ miles) |
| **Total ascent** | 340m (1115ft) |
| **Total descent** | 640m (2100ft) |
| **Time** | 4hrs 30mins |
| **Terrain** | There is a long, rocky ridge at the start of this stage, requiring scrambling in places. Patchy woodlands and open spaces occur on the descent to forested valleys, where progress is much quicker. |
| **Maps** | 4253 ET and 4253 OT |
| **Food and drink** | Water is available from a source near Monte Occhiatu, and from streams on the descent. The Bergerie de Bassetta serves meals and sells cheese. There is a water source near San Petru. The Refuge de Matalza serves meals and sells provisions. |
| **Shelter** | There is little shade at first, where the rocky ridge is exposed to sun, wind and rain. Further downhill, patchy beech-woods offer good shade. The Refuge San Petru offers basic overnight shelter. |

The first part of this stage is rough and rocky, weaving from side to side along a ridge featuring rock towers and buttresses. Be aware that there are significant route choices to be pondered later. First, on the Bocca di l'Agnonu, keep right to follow the GR20, which is flashed red/white for the Bergerie de Bassetta, Refuge de Matalza and Refuge d' I Croci. Trekkers taking this route are later presented with a further option to divert off-route down to the village of Zicavo. (See the 'Link from Tignosellu to Zicavo' below.) However, the original course of the GR20 turns left at Bocca di l'Agnonu, runs straight to Monte Alcudina, then descends to the Refuge d'Asinau. This route is flashed with double-yellow paint marks and saves a whole day on the trail. (See the 'Alternative Stage 13/14' below.) Route choices should be made depending on whether enough stamina is available for a long stage, and whether there is likely to be an afternoon thunderstorm on Monte Alcudina, in which case an ascent would be most unwise.

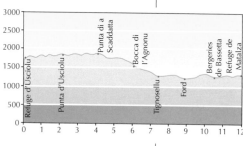

Leave the **Refuge d'Usciolu** as signposted for Bocca di l'Agnonu and Refuge d'Asinau. A rough and stony path slices up a steep slope to reach a ridge, where there is a signpost indicating a way down to the village of Cozzano. (See the previous section for a descent to the village.)

Turn left to follow the GR20 along the rugged crest of the ridge known as the **Arête a Monda**. There is a lot of bare rock at first, so follow the red and white flashes of the GR20 faithfully across sloping slabs and bulbous masses of rock. Painted arrows indicate points where particular care is needed. Trekkers need to squeeze through some gullies and between boulders. Take the time to look through notches in the ridge down to the village of Cozzano.

Although the route rises and falls, trekkers looking back always seem to be on a level

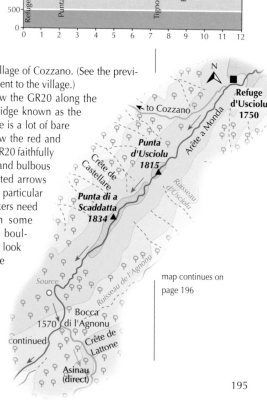

map continues on page 196

195

with the Refuge d'Usciolu. After following an easy stretch of path and passing a small, shady patch of beech trees, bare rock is again crossed on the side overlooking Cozzano. The route passes **Punta di l'Usciolu**, crossing another summit, and there is quite a variety of vegetation along the way.

Watch carefully while following the route further along the ridge, crossing rocky slopes, then scrambling over a couple of entertaining rocky notches as it switches from one side of the ridge to the other. The route passes **Punta di a Scaddatta**, and plants might be noticed such as thrift and campion, more commonly associated with low-lying coasts than high mountains. The path becomes easier for a while, then suddenly ascends to cross a very prominent rocky gap. A bouldery path leads down through beech scrub, continuing across an open slope to enter taller beech-woods. Pigs and cattle are found among the woods, as well as a signpost for a water **source** just up to the right.

Follow the path steeply down through the woods, then more gently to an open gap covered in boulders and spiny broom. This is **Bocca di l'Agnonu**, reached 2hrs 30mins after leaving the Refuge d'Usciolu, at an altitude of 1570m (5150ft). Take careful note of the signposts bolted to rocks, as there are two options for continuing the GR20. However, bear in mind that these signs are occasionally vandalised, apparently to 'encourage' trekkers to turn right! ◄

If turning left as signposted 'Rge Asinau par U Furcinchese', refer to the 'Alternative Stage 13/14' below.

Turn right, roughly southwest, as signposted 'Rge Asinau par Bassetta Matalza Croce', and follow red and white paint flashes downhill. The path can be rather vague at times, down through the valley. Cross the **Ruisseau de Padulelli** just below a point where its bed is choked with boulders. This stream may be dry, but there may be water further downhill.

A steep slope is covered in beech trees and boulders, and trekkers need to keep looking for markers to follow the path further downhill. As it drifts away from the stream, watch very carefully to spot the route rising across a slope of spiny broom, juniper scrub and boulders to cross a rugged crest at **Tignosellu**. The path rises to 1380m (4530ft), reaching a junction where there is an option to turn right for Zicavo. ▶

See 'Link from Tignosellu to Zicavo' below.

Keep straight ahead and pass a boulder bearing red and white paint flashes, an orange circle and faded blue paint reading 'Basseta'. The path runs at a gentle gradient, undulating across a slope of spiny broom. It runs roughly southwest, then swings more to the south to drop towards the **Ruisseau de Partuso**. Cross this at a point where the channel is narrow and rocky, but bear in mind that this charming spot could be a dangerous place after heavy rain, where the river flows vigorously through rock pools and over waterfalls.

Climb gently and follow the marked path, passing fallen beech trees to enter a beech-wood. Walk upstream beside the **Ruisseau de Veracolongu**. Later, the path climbs from the river and reaches a track on top of a scrubby slope. ▶ Cross the track to continue as marked, following a narrow grassy path through bracken. This becomes a track as it approaches buildings at the **Bergeries de Bassetta**, at 1310m (4300ft). Keep left of the fence surrounding the property to reach a tarmac road, about 1hr 15mins after leaving Bocca di l'Agnonu.

A direct route, flashed with abundant orange paint, is marked on the map and leads straight through the valley to the Refuge de Matalza.

The **Bergeries de Bassetta**, tel 06 27 25 95 33, offer a range of accommodation from four wooden cabins to a 30-bed dormitory, with toilets and showers. Camping is available in a fenced enclosure safe from foraging animals. The main building features a bar restaurant with good Corsican food and drink. Cheese and other food supplies can be bought. A tarmac road allows the bergerie to be re-stocked easily with supplies, and it also makes it easy for trekkers to leave the route if they need to.

Cross the road and continue as marked up a wooded slope, then cross an open hillside around 1350m (4430ft). The path descends gently through bracken into another wooded area. Keep straight ahead at a path junction, and reach a road-end, where there is a broken concrete picnic site and a water **source**. Walk to the little **Refuge San Petru** and Chapelle San Petru – a lovely granite chapel in a wooded bower at 1370m (4495ft).

The lintel stone of the **Chapelle San Petru** carries a date of 1871, although another stone around the corner is inscribed 1623. At the beginning of August it is customary for livestock to be blessed as part of a shepherd's festival. For centuries livestock have grazed the grasslands of the plateau each summer.

The very basic **Refuge San Petru** alongside consists only of two rooms and has no facilities whatsoever, apart from a nearby water source. It's a useful place to bear in mind if nearby accommodation is full.

To continue from the Chapelle San Petru, walk as marked up a short, bouldery slope covered in tall beech trees. Step down onto a dirt road and follow it gently uphill from a signpost on a bend. A large rounded boulder confirms that walkers are on the GR20. Pass a barrier gate and follow the track over a rise, to find the **Refuge de Matalza** off to the left, around 1410m (4625ft). This should be reached 45mins after leaving the Bergerie de Bassetta. ◄

Trekkers could easily continue another 3km (2 miles) to the Bergerie d' I Croci and get closer to Monte Alcudina.

The **Refuge de Matalza**, tel 06 89 30 90 43 or 09 88 77 47 97, was developed from a simple two-roomed building by adding extensions, so that it now offers 20 beds, showers and toilets. Two or three large tents alongside each contain 12 beds. The refuge and fixed tents are inside a flat, fenced, grassy area used as a

campsite, safe from foraging animals. Hot meals, food supplies and drinks are on sale. The dirt road quickly links with a tarmac road, passing the neighbouring Bergerie de Bassetta before descending through forest to Zicavo. The road allows the refuge to be re-stocked easily with supplies, and it also makes it easy for trekkers to leave the route if they need to.

*The Refuge de Matalza and its fenced-off camping ground*

## LINK ROUTE

*Tignosellu to Zicavo*

| | |
|---|---|
| **Start** | Tignosellu |
| **Finish** | Zicavo |
| **Distance** | 5km (3 miles) |
| **Total ascent** | 40m (130ft) |
| **Total descent** | 700m (2295ft) |
| **Time** | 1hr 45mins |
| **Terrain** | A path branching winds and undulates gently across a slope of maquis, descending into increasingly dense woodland. Watch carefully as the route switches between forest tracks and paths. |
| **Maps** | 4253 ET |
| **Food and drink** | Zicavo has bars restaurants and a well-stocked shop. |
| **Shelter** | Most of the descent is confined to well-wooded slopes that offer good shade and shelter. |

The trek along the GR20 is coming to an end. Those who feel that they haven't had much contact with Corsican people, or stayed in a true Corsican village, now have a chance to put that right by visiting Zicavo. After leaving the Refuge d'Usciolu, scramble along the Arête a Monda to reach Bocca di l'Agnonu. Keep right to follow the GR20 down to the crest of Tignosellu, then turn right to follow yellow paint flashes to link with forest paths and tracks for the descent to Zicavo. Links between the GR20 and Zicavo form a loop, so it is possible to spend a night in the village, then climb on the following day to the Refuge de Matalza, or continue to the higher Bergerie d' I Croci.

The GR20 passes a path junction at **Tignosellu**, around 1380m (4530ft), where a boulder bears red and white paint flashes, an orange circle and faded blue paint reading 'Basseta'. Turn right here to walk roughly northwest, watching for yellow paint flashes.

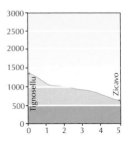

*Tignosellu, where the boulder in the centre marks the start of the descent to Zicavo*

Continue to be alert while walking down into another valley and back into beech-woods, as losing the path could lead to difficulties. The path wanders down through the woods, zigzagging quite steeply at times. Cross over a rocky lip in the stream called Ruisseau de Monte Occhiatu, then follow the path across an open slope. There are fine views of mountains far across the Taravo valley beyond Zicavo, but no sight of the village itself. The path links with a track. Walk straight ahead,

201

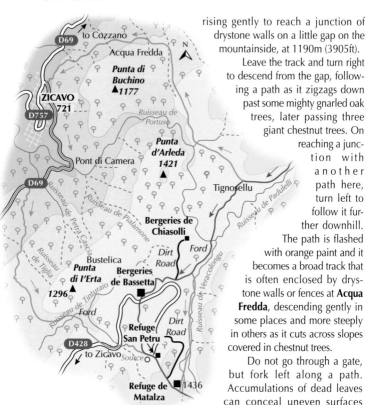

rising gently to reach a junction of drystone walls on a little gap on the mountainside, at 1190m (3905ft).

Leave the track and turn right to descend from the gap, following a path as it zigzags down past some mighty gnarled oak trees, later passing three giant chestnut trees. On reaching a junction with another path here, turn left to follow it further downhill. The path is flashed with orange paint and it becomes a broad track that is often enclosed by drystone walls or fences at **Acqua Fredda**, descending gently in some places and more steeply in others as it cuts across slopes covered in chestnut trees.

Do not go through a gate, but fork left along a path. Accumulations of dead leaves can conceal uneven surfaces beneath, so tread with care. When there are fallen boughs and tree trunks it can be like an obstacle course, but the way ahead is always clear. The track runs through an eroded groove later, and narrows as it approaches Zicavo, running down bare granite to a signboard beside a road at **Zicavo**, at 721m (2365ft).

## ZICAVO

The road at the top of the village is the D69, or Promenade Jacques-Pierre Fiamma. This road is virtually level and most of the facilities in Zicavo are arranged along it. However, by walking downhill, the steep zigzag D757 passes a post office and bar. Make the most of a break in Zicavo, where blocky three- and four-storey granite houses bear faded names and dates, and fine Corsican food and drink can be enjoyed in bars and restaurants.

**Accommodation** The Hôtel du Tourisme, tel 04 95 24 40 06, has 14 rooms and is directly below the point where the path reaches the road in Zicavo. L'Auberge A Funtana across the road has 5 rooms. The Gîte d'Étape le Paradis, tel 04 94 24 41 20, is just along the D69 in the direction of Cozzano, offering 20 beds arranged in 6 rooms, and a space for camping. The Hôtel le Florida, tel 04 95 24 43 11 or 04 95 24 40 24, has 10 rooms, is a little further along the D69, and also manages L'Auberge A Funtana.

**Food and drink** The hotels and gîte d'étape offer meals. There is also the A Funtana bar restaurant and the Pacific Sud bar restaurant, both of which serve pizzas. A small but exceptionally well-stocked alimentation is located between both bars on the D69. Anyone walking down through the village will find another bar.

**Transport** A bus service from Cozzano to Zicavo and Ajaccio is operated by Autocars Santoni, tel 04 95 22 64 44. It runs daily through July and August, but not on Sundays for the rest of the year. It passes all the accommodation options in Zicavo.

# LINK ROUTE
*Zicavo to Refuge de Matalza*

| | |
|---|---|
| **Start** | Zicavo |
| **Finish** | Refuge de Matalza |
| **Distance** | 6km (3¾ miles) |
| **Total ascent** | 730m (2395ft) |
| **Total descent** | 40m (130ft) |
| **Time** | 2hrs 30mins |
| **Terrain** | Generally easy paths and tracks on wooded slopes, but occasionally steep and rugged. |
| **Maps** | 4253 OT |
| **Food and drink** | The Bergerie de Bassetta serves meals and sells cheese. There is a water source near San Petru. The Refuge de Matalza serves meals and sells provisions. |
| **Shelter** | Shade is available in woodlands on the ascent. The Refuge San Petru offers basic overnight shelter. |

Most trekkers who leave the GR20 at Tignosellu to visit Zicavo would be happy to follow another route back uphill, even if it meant missing over 3km (2 miles) of the main route. The climb from Zicavo towards the Plateau du Cuscione is largely on well-wooded slopes, with the gradient easing around the Chapelle San Petru and the Refuge de Matalza. This link to the GR20 could easily be completed in a morning, and some trekkers might prefer to continue beyond Matalza. It is well worth walking another 3km (2 miles) to the Bergerie d' I Croci, easing the ascent of Monte Alcudina the following day.

See map in previous Link Route

Leave **Zicavo** by walking along the D69 road as signposted 'Aullene/Audde'. The road passes an alimentation and the Pacific Sud bar. Blocky three- and four-storey granite houses bear faded names and dates. There are views down to the church and the Taravo valley, as well as of the surrounding mountains. After passing the Pacific Sud bar, the road is called the Cours Abbaticci. The road

*A rugged stone stairway on a densely wooded slope above Zicavo*

rises gently, passing a small family burial plot beside a pig-pen.

As the road curves around the head of a steep-sided wooded valley, cross a bridge called the **Pont di Camera** and enjoy a view of a fine waterfall in a granite chute. The woods are holm oak and chestnut, with a rampant, tangled understorey. Cross a smaller bridge over the **Ruisseau de Petra Cascia** and look back to see the village of Zicavo spilling down its steep hillside. Watch out on the left for a

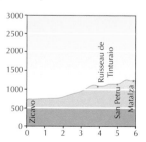

signposted path marked with yellow paint flashes rising from the road.

The path climbs uphill through a groove in the granite bedrock on a wooded slope. At a higher level the path is flanked by drystone walls and has plenty of shade. When the path levels out for a while notice the huge charred chestnut trunks, whose roots continue to sprout new boughs. Pig-pens are tucked away in the woods, explaining any grunting and squealing that might be heard.

When the wire and wooden fencing alongside runs out, the path zigzags up a sort of rugged stairway, where holm oaks give way to beech trees. At a higher level, the path runs through a rocky, stony groove and the tree cover thins out, giving good views of distant mountain ranges. There are tufts of broom and thorny scrub, then the path emerges quite suddenly into more open terrain, although there are drystone walls to one side or the other.

Keep an eye on the yellow flashes, which lead over an outcrop of granite at 1163m (3816ft), where there are walls on both sides. There is a short descent, then a left turn along a path following an old terrace. Bracken, brambles and other scrub cover former cultivated slopes. Another short descent leads into a beech-wood to ford the bouldery **Ruisseau de Tinturaio**. Follow a bouldery path zigzagging up onto a slope covered in broom, then follow a fence into an area sparsely covered in beech trees to reach a track.

Turn left along the track, then when it loops to the right, turn left again and continue uphill as marked by yellow flashes to reach a road close to a monument. The monument was raised to Pierre Kemp, who died while employed on the construction of the road. Turn left to follow the road gently uphill as it makes a loop to cross a small bridge and a larger bridge. Turn right uphill on a bouldery slope covered in tall beech trees, following signposts. A junction is reached where a left turn is signposted for the Bergerie de Bassetta. However, turn right along the 'Sentier de l'Aconit', now flashed red and white as the GR20. Turn right to reach a road-end, where there is a broken concrete picnic site and a water **source**. Walk to the little **Refuge San Petru** and Chapelle San Petru – a lovely granite chapel in a wooded bower at 1370m (4495ft).

> The lintel stone of the **Chapelle San Petru** carries a date of 1871, although another stone around the corner is inscribed 1623. At the beginning of August it is customary for livestock to be blessed as part of a shepherd's festival. For centuries livestock have grazed the grasslands of the plateau each summer.
>
> The very basic **Refuge San Petru** alongside consists only of two rooms and has no facilities whatsoever, apart from a nearby water source. It's a useful place to bear in mind if nearby accommodation is full.

To continue from the Chapelle San Petru, walk as marked up a short, bouldery slope covered in tall beech trees. Step down onto a dirt road and follow it gently uphill from a signpost on a bend. A large rounded boulder confirms that walkers are on the GR20. Pass a barrier gate and follow the track over a rise, to find the **Refuge de Matalza** off to the left, around 1410m (4625ft). This should be reached 45mins after leaving the Bergerie de Bassetta. ▶

Trekkers could easily continue another 3km (2 miles) to the Bergerie d' I Croci and get closer to Monte Alcudina.

*Following a level, open path halfway between Zicavo and the Refuge de Matalza*

The **Refuge de Matalza**, tel 06 89 30 90 43 or 09 88 77 47 97, was developed from a simple two-roomed building by adding extensions, so that it now offers 20 beds, showers and toilets. Two or three large tents alongside each contain 12 beds. The refuge and fixed tents are inside a flat, fenced, grassy area used as a campsite, safe from foraging animals. Hot meals, food supplies and drinks are on sale. The dirt road quickly links with a tarmac road, passing the neighbouring Bergerie de Bassetta before descending through forest to Zicavo. The road allows the refuge to be re-stocked easily with supplies, and it also makes it easy for trekkers to leave the route if they need to.

# STAGE 14
*Refuge to Matalza to Refuge d'Asinau*

| | |
|---|---|
| **Start** | Refuge to Matalza |
| **Finish** | Refuge d'Asinau |
| **Distance** | 11km (7 miles) |
| **Total ascent** | 665m (2180ft) |
| **Total descent** | 545m (1790ft) |
| **Time** | 4hrs 15mins |
| **Terrain** | Fairly easy walking along a dirt road, tracks and paths, gradually gaining height from valleys with patchy woodlands to open and increasingly rocky mountainsides. A detour to climb the rocky Monte Alcudina is recommended in good weather. The descent is steep and rocky. |
| **Maps** | 4253 OT and 4253 ET |
| **Food and drink** | The Bergerie d' I Croci serves meals and sells provisions. It is the last place to obtain water, as streams on Monte Alcudina usually dry up in summer. |
| **Shelter** | The lower, wooded valleys have patchy woodlands and are sheltered from the sun, wind and rain. Beyond the Bergerie d' I Croci the higher open mountainsides are exposed, with little shade or shelter. |

This stage starts remarkably easy, simply following a dirt road, tracks and paths, gradually climbing to the Bergerie d' I Croci and Monte Alcudina. Given an early start, or even better, a start from Croci, walkers should be able to reach Monte Alcudina before clouds start to gather in the afternoon. Sometimes, walkers crossing the mountain late in the afternoon run into thunderstorms. Although the climb towards the mountain is relatively straightforward, it does get quite boulder-strewn and rocky as height is gained. Note that the route doesn't actually reach the summit, but descends steep and rocky from a shoulder to the Refuge d'Asinau. However, the summit can be included with a rocky there-and-back detour, and this is well worth the effort in clear weather.

Follow the dirt road away from the **Refuge de Matalza**, crossing a ford. The dirt road climbs and bends right. ▶ Cross a rugged vehicle bridge over a river, where there is a notice about an indigenous species of trout. The dirt road later swings left round a rock outcrop. At this point keep right, in effect straight ahead, along a lesser track signposted 'Croci XX'.

The track runs parallel to the river, **Ruisseau de Croce**, dwindling to become a path on short-cropped grass. Beech trees are dotted around in small clumps, with woodlands nearby. The path climbs from the river and swings left. Watch for a prominent boulder on the right, where red and white flashes indicate a right turn. A path undulates through beech-woods, crossing a couple of streams. Apart from the red and white flashes, there are also wooden arrows nailed to tree trunks pointing

Keeping straight ahead allows a link with the 'Alternative Stage 13/14'.

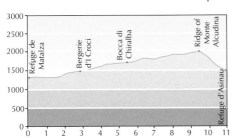

209

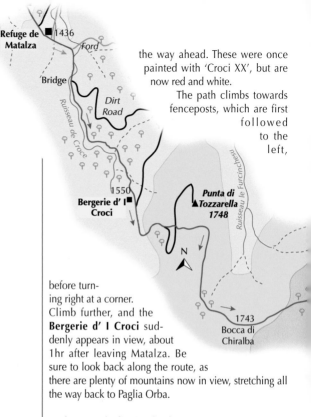

the way ahead. These were once painted with 'Croci XX', but are now red and white.

The path climbs towards fenceposts, which are first followed to the left, before turning right at a corner. Climb further, and the **Bergerie d' I Croci** suddenly appears in view, about 1hr after leaving Matalza. Be sure to look back along the route, as there are plenty of mountains now in view, stretching all the way back to Paglia Orba.

> The **Bergerie d' I Croci**, tel 06 75 49 60 59 or 09 82 12 33 10, was formerly a small building, which was extended to offer three dormitories and 46 beds, along with a dining room, berger's quarters, toilets and showers. Camping is available on a level area alongside, with exceptional views back to Paglia Orba. Hot meals, food supplies and 'GR vins' are on sale. Transport is offered off-route to Zicavo if it is needed.

Pass to the left of the building, straight up a narrow path as marked, linking with a very rough and boulder-strewn track. Although this is awkward to walk along, its course is very obvious and it climbs gradually, bending left into a higher side-valley. When a sudden right turn is reached, watch for red and white paint marks on the left, revealing a rugged, winding path that simply climbs to a higher point on the track.

Turn right to walk a short way down the track, then turn left as marked up another path. This rises and falls a little, then passes a few big boulders. There is a pleasant strip of short grass, followed by a stony path rising gently past spiny broom and juniper. A crest is reached around 1720m (5645ft), on the shoulder of **Punta di Tozzarella**. Turn right as marked and simply follow the broad, rounded crest, which is covered in stones and low spiny broom. The path gently rises, falls and rises again, before bending left to pass through a patch of alder bushes on a slope. After a gentle descent followed by a short climb, the path bends left again, rising gently, then dropping more ruggedly to pass below the gap of **Bocca**

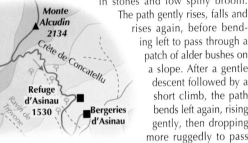

*A gentle path approaches Bocca di Chiralba on the way to Monte Alcudina*

211

**di Chiralba**, at 1743m (5719ft). This should be reached about 1hr from the Bergerie d' I Croci.

Continue along the path, rising and falling easily across a scrubby slope that becomes more rugged and rocky. Watch for a sudden right turn, which is marked by cairns and red and white paint, up a slope of bare rock. The path soon drifts left, climbing across a rugged slope covered in stones, boulders and low scrub. Drop a little to cross a dry streambed, climb steeply a short way, then continue more gently across a scrub-covered slope dotted with boulders.

Cross another small, dry streambed, then climb across a slope covered in boulders, alder bushes and juniper scrub. Keep an eye on markers, as there are some twists and turns, but the general direction is towards the summit seen ahead. As bare rock stretches in all directions, the marked route reaches a rocky ridge, about 1hr 15mins from Bocca di Chiralba. It is important to watch carefully for markers and signposts before making the next move.

At this point, at 2025m (6645ft), the direct variant route is joined. One signpost points back for 'Rge Usciolu

*The GR20 at the point where it starts descending to Refuge d'Asinau*

par Croce Matalza Bassetta'. Another signpost points ahead up the ridge for 'Rge Usciolu par U Furcinchese'. To continue, however, look to the right over a steep edge for a signpost reading 'Asinau'. ▶

Step over the rocky edge signposted for Asinau. Walk downhill and swing to the left, then pick a way across the rocky face of the mountain. Watch carefully for markers, as the route zigzags down more rocky slopes and weaves in and out of patches of alder scrub. Although the refuge is often plainly in view below and looks quite close, getting down to it is slow and difficult. Take your time and tread carefully, especially if the rock underfoot is wet.

A few slender sycamore trees rise above the alder scrub, and the path continues zigzagging downhill on rock, boulders or loose stones. Eventually, and with some relief, trekkers reach the **Refuge d'Asinau**, at an altitude of 1530m (5020ft), about 1hr after leaving the rocky ridge. The nearby **Bergeries d' Asinau** also offer accommodation, food and drink.

The PNRC **Refuge d'Asinau** was discovered as a burnt-out shell towards the end of March 2016. It had been earmarked for demolition and rebuilding, but its sudden loss does make things awkward for trekkers. The PNRC erects a large tent on the site in the summer, and ensures that meals and food supplies are available. However, this is removed for the winter, leaving nothing but camping spaces and a water source. When a new refuge becomes available, details will be posted at **www.cicerone.co.uk/852/updates**.

The **Bergeries d'Asinau**, also known as Chez Aline, tel 06 17 53 98 92, are a huddle of little stone buildings located downhill from the Refuge d'Asinau. A demi pension deal is offered, which includes a bed in a small dormitory, access to a toilet and shower, with hot meals and drinks provided.

It is possible to climb further along the rocky ridge to the 2134m (7001ft) summit of Monte Alcudina, which is well worth the effort on a clear day if time can be spared. It takes about 1hr there-and-back.

# ALTERNATIVE STAGE 13/14

*Refuge d'Usciolu to*
*Refuge d'Asinau (variant)*

| | |
|---|---|
| **Start** | Refuge d'Usciolu |
| **Finish** | Refuge d'Asinau |
| **Distance** | 17km (10½ miles) |
| **Total ascent** | 1010m (3315ft) |
| **Total descent** | 1225m (4020ft) |
| **Time** | 7hrs 15mins |
| **Terrain** | There is a long, rocky ridge at the start of this stage, requiring scrambling in places. There are patchy woodlands and open spaces on the Plateau du Cuscione, where progress is much quicker. The ascent of Monte Alcudina is easy in good weather, but should be avoided in bad weather. The final descent is steep and rocky. |
| **Maps** | IGN 4253 ET |
| **Food and drink** | Water is available from a source near Monte Occhiatu, from streams on the Plateau du Cuscione, and from a source above I Pedinieddi. Food and drink are available at the Refuge d'Asinau. |
| **Shelter** | Apart from patchy beech-woods on either side of the Plateau du Cuscione, there is very little shade. The mountains, especially Monte Alcudina, are very exposed to sun, wind and rain. |

Originally, the GR20 ran direct from the Refuge d'Usciolu to the Refuge d'Asinau, across the Plateau du Cuscione and over Monte Alcudina. There was an intermediate refuge at I Pedinieddi, but it was destroyed by lightning in 1981. This left walkers facing a long stage, with the ascent of Monte Alcudina occurring in the afternoon. Summer days often start clear, but clouds may cover the mountains in the afternoon, sometimes leading to thunderstorms. If planning to walk this direct variant, be sure to have a good weather forecast. If thunderstorms are forecast, alter plans and follow Stage 13 and Stage 14 instead. This would make it easier to cross Monte Alcudina by avoiding afternoon thunderstorms, although it costs an extra day on the trail. Bear in mind that this route is flashed with double-yellow paint marks between Bocca di l'Agnonu and Monte Alcudina, re-joining the red and white flashed GR20 for the final steep descent to Refuge d'Asinau.

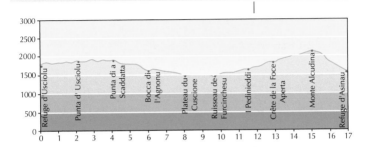

Leave the **Refuge d'Usciolu** as signposted for Bocca di l'Agnonu and Refuge d'Asinau. A rough and stony path slices up a steep slope to reach a ridge, where there is a signpost indicating a way down to the village of Cozzano. (See the 'Link from Refuge d'Usciolu to Cozzano' for a descent to the village.)

Turn left to follow the GR20 along the rugged crest of the ridge known as the **Arête a Monda**. There is a lot

*After following the Arête a Monda away from the Refuge d'Usciolu, the GR20 passes Punta di a Scaddatta*

**N**

**Refuge d'Usciolu**
**1750**

← to Cozzano

*Arête a Monda*

*Punta d'Usciolu*
**1815** ▲

*Crête de Castellare*

*Ruisseau d'Usciolu*

*Punta di a Scaddatta*
**1834** ▲

*Source* ○

*Ruisseau de l'Agnonu*

**Bocca di l'Agnonu**

to 1570
**Bassetta and Matalza**

*Crête de Lattone*

*Ruisseau de Serra di Lucianu*

*Crête de Cracella*

**Plateau du Cuscione**

continued

map continues on page 218

of bare rock at first, so follow the red and white flashes of the GR20 faithfully across sloping slabs and bulbous masses of rock. Painted arrows indicate points where particular care is needed. Trekkers need to squeeze through some gullies and between boulders. Take the time to look through notches in the ridge down to the village of Cozzano.

Although the route rises and falls, trekkers looking back always seem to be on a level with the Refuge d'Usciolu. After following an easy stretch of path and passing a small, shady patch of beech trees, bare rock is again crossed on the side overlooking Cozzano. The route passes **Punta di l'Usciolu**, crossing another summit, and there is quite a variety of vegetation along the way.

Watch carefully while following the route further along the ridge, crossing rocky slopes, then scrambling over a couple of entertaining rocky notches as it switches from one side of the ridge to the other. The route passes **Punta di a Scaddatta**, and plants might be noticed such as thrift and campion, more commonly associated with low-lying coasts than high mountains. The path becomes easier for a while, then suddenly ascends to cross a very prominent rocky gap. A bouldery path leads down through beech scrub, continuing across an open slope to enter taller beech-woods. Pigs and cattle are found among the woods, as well as a signpost for a water **source** just up to the right.

Follow the path steeply down through the woods, then more gently to an open gap covered in boulders and spiny broom. This is **Bocca di l'Agnonu**, reached 2hrs 30mins after leaving the Refuge d'Usciolu, at an altitude of 1570m (5150ft). Take careful note of the signposts bolted to rocks, as there are two options for continuing the GR20. For the direct variant route, turn left as sign-posted 'Rge Asinau par U Furcinchese'. However, bear in mind that the sign is occasionally vandalised, apparently to 'encourage' trekkers to turn right instead!

So, turn left and ensure that double-yellow paint flashes are being followed. The variant route undulates through the beech-woods, often following a track, but sometimes departing from it for short stretches. Later, a path heads left from the track, leaving the beech-woods to descend gently onto the **Plateau du Cuscione**. The plateau is generally between 1450 and 1500m (4760 and 4920ft), with Monte Alcudina rising beyond. The narrow path is flanked by spiny broom, and the surface is stony or sandy. A couple of streams are crossed and there is a bit of shade in an area of beech trees.

Follow the path over a slope of juniper and spiny broom, noting the large, rounded boulders of granite dotted around and the array of flowers among the scrub. Cross a wide expanse of spiny broom, then cross a couple more streams, the latter being the **Ruisseau d'Allucia**, before climbing up a slope of ancient beech trees. Some of the trees have toppled and are rotting on the ground.

Walk over another broad rise of spiny broom, passing more rounded boulders, then walk down into a wildly vegetated area to cross the Ruisseau de Cavallare. Climb a slope bearing a few beech trees to reach a clear track. There are signposts here, where is is possible to leave the variant route and return to the GR20 near the Refuge de Matalza. (Be suspicious of signs and waymarks, which might have been tampered with.) The track should be reached about 1hr after leaving Bocca di l'Agnonu, and the altitude is 1480m (4855ft).

Cross over the track, just to cut a loop out of it, then turn right and follow it as marked. Turn left after a short while and walk down to a river, the **Ruisseau de Furcinchesu**, which is well wooded with beech. Walk upstream to reach a footbridge and cross it. The path doubles back downstream a little, then rises up a bouldery slope covered in beech trees. There are some open areas, then the path reaches a much wider expanse of spiny broom and juniper scrub. There are signs for **I Pedinieddi Aire de Bivouac** off to the right.

The PNRC **Refuge d' I Pedinieddi** was destroyed by a lightning strike in 1981 and was never rebuilt. Bear this in mind if thunderstorms are forecast, as the summit of Monte Alcudina is more than 500m (1640ft) higher! Masonry from the ruin has been used to mark out camping spaces, and this is one of the few places where trekkers can legally pitch a tent for the night away from a refuge. A water source is signposted just uphill and this is the only facility available. If planning to camp here, remember to carry in all food supplies, take away waste, and dig toilet holes well away from the area. Also beware of predatory foxes and consider stowing food supplies at height.

Continue following the path, which rises from the bivouac area onto a slope of beech trees. A water **source** is located just to the left of the path. As it climbs higher on the slope and crosses a flowery scrub, the path is either on bare rock or has a stony surface. There is plenty of juniper scrub

Plateau du Cuscione

N

Ruisseau d'Allucia

to Matalza

Ruisseau de Cavallere

Ruisseau de Furcinchesu

Ruisseau de Cavallareccia

Footbridge

**I Pedinieddi Bivouac Site 1623**

Source

Crête de la Force Aperta

Ruisseau de Valle Tremoli

**Monte Alcudina 2134**

Crête de Concatellu

Ravin de Trevone

**Refuge d'Asinau 1530**

**Bergeries d' Asinau**

on the way to a broad, gently sloping gap on **Créte de la Foce Aperta**, at an altitude of 1805m (5920ft). This gap should be reached 1hr 15mins after leaving the track on the Plateau du Cuscione.

Look up to the summit of Monte Alcudina from the gap and follow the path steadily as it rises along the crest. The ascent poses no problems, although the path drifts away from the crest to cross a rugged slope to the right, then after turning a corner the summit is much closer to hand. The path keeps away from the rocky crest, yet still crosses plenty of bare rock and weaves between boulders

*A path climbs gently along the Crête de la Foce Aperta towards the sprawling summit of Monte Alcudina*

and alder scrub. Be sure to include the summit of **Monte Alcudina** on a clear day, visiting the monumental cross that stands on a bare dome of granite at 2134m (7001ft). Trekkers should reach the summit within 1hr of leaving Crête de la Foce Aperta, and can spend a while enjoying the view, looking back as far as Paglia Orba and ahead to the exciting rocky spires and towers of the Aiguilles de Bavella.

Follow the rocky ridge southwest to commence the descent. Cross bare rock and scramble around immense boulders to reach a gap at 2025m (6645ft). At this point, Stage 14 of the GR20 is joined. One signpost points back up the ridge for 'Rge Usciolu par U Furcinchese', while another points ahead for 'Rge Usciolu par Croce Matalza Bassetta'. However, be sure to turn left as signposted for 'Asinau'.

Step over the rocky edge, walk downhill and swing to the left, then pick a way across the rocky face of the mountain. Watch carefully for markers, as the route zig-zags down more rocky slopes and weaves in and out of patches of alder scrub. Although the refuge is often plainly in view below and looks quite close, getting down to it is slow and difficult. Take your time and tread carefully, especially if the rock underfoot is wet.

A few slender sycamore trees rise above the alder scrub, and the path continues zigzagging downhill on rock, boulders or loose stones. Eventually, and with some relief, trekkers reach the **Refuge d'Asinau**, at an altitude of 1530m (5020ft), about 1hr after leaving the rocky ridge. The nearby **Bergeries d' Asinau** also offer accommodation, food and drink.

The PNRC **Refuge d'Asinau** was discovered as a burnt-out shell towards the end of March 2016. It had been earmarked for demolition and rebuilding, but its sudden loss does make things awkward for trekkers. The PNRC erects a large tent on the site in the summer, and ensures that meals and food supplies are available. However, this is removed for the winter, leaving nothing but camping spaces and a water source. When a

new refuge becomes available, details will be posted at
**www.cicerone.co.uk/852/updates**.

The **Bergeries d'Asinau**, also known as Chez Aline,
tel 06 17 53 98 92, are a huddle of little stone buildings
located downhill from the Refuge d'Asinau. A demi
pensión deal is offered, which includes a bed in a small
dormitory, access to a toilet and shower, with hot meals
and drinks provided.

# STAGE 15A

*Refuge d'Asinau to
Village de Bavella (low-level)*

| | |
|---|---|
| **Start** | Refuge d'Asinau |
| **Finish** | Village de Bavella |
| **Distance** | 11km (6¾ miles) |
| **Total ascent** | 380m (1250ft) |
| **Total descent** | 695m (2280ft) |
| **Time** | 4hrs 45mins |
| **Terrain** | Mostly forest and woodland, although there are plenty of open areas along the way. The route is mostly along narrow paths clinging to steep slopes. Some parts can be rocky, especially towards the end. |
| **Maps** | IGN 4253 ET |
| **Food and drink** | Water is available from streams and signposted sources. There are bar restaurants and a shop at the Village de Bavella. |
| **Shelter** | Trees on the valley sides provide good shade and shelter. |

There are two routes from the Refuge d'Asinau to the Village de Bavella.
The low-level route is described here, but trekkers interested in the Alpine
Variant should refer to Stage 15B. The low-level route is the main route,
clinging to the well-wooded slopes of the Asinau valley, running round
the mountainside to the Village de Bavella. On the map it looks relatively
easy, and indeed many parts are easy, but sometimes the path is rough

and narrow, and there is more ascent and descent than might be imagined. The final climb to the Village de Bavella is rocky. Those with an interest in flowers should take this route, as there is a wealth of species not noted on the route so far. Trekkers looking for excitement and superb scenery should take the Alpine Variant.

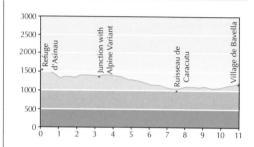

Leave the **Refuge d'Asinau** as signposted for Paliri, following a rugged path across a well-vegetated and well-watered bouldery slope. Continue across a slope of spiny broom and boulders, noting a spur path to the left leading only to the **Bergeries d'Asinau**. Continue downhill to reach a stand of pines. There are signposts here for the Refuge d' I Paliri, as well as a waymarked link with the village of Quenza.

The route goes down among the pines and fords the bouldery bed of the **Ruisseau d'Asinau**. A bouldery path rises above the river and wanders across a slope covered in pines. It passes some big boulders and continues through a couple of clearings of spiny broom and juniper scrub. While in the clearings, look up at the rocky pinnacles of the Aiguilles de Bavella.

The route climbs to a signpost for a water **source** in an area of pines and slender birch trees. An easy stretch of well-engineered path contours across a slope, touching 1400m (4590ft), although it becomes narrower and rougher later. The path descends and is quite rugged in places, crossing a couple of streambeds. Again, there are clearings and views of the Aiguilles de Bavella high above.

Reach a signpost where the Alpine Variant is marked uphill to the left, marked with yellow paint flashes. This point is reached about 1hr 15mins after leaving the Refuge d'Asinau, at 1320m (4330ft). (If suddenly deciding to take the Alpine Variant, refer to the next section for a route description.)

The main course of the GR20 stays low and continues round the slope, as signposted for Col de Bavella. The path descends to cross the open, rocky slopes of the **Ravin du Pargulu**, then continues through the forest. Watch out for a rocky viewpoint off to the right, which overlooks the valley, allows a view back to Monte Alcudina, and takes in some of the rocky pinnacles of the Aiguilles de Bavella. The path contours across the slope, then climbs, with tall heather becoming more noticeable. Reach another prominent rocky outcrop and again study the pinnacles high above.

The path starts to descend, and as the pines thin out, tall heather dominates the steep and rocky slopes. Shrubs include holm oak, wild rose, hawthorn, arbutus, and a bewildering array of flowering plants

*Massive buttresses and towers of rock are a feature of the amazing crest of the Aiguilles de Bavella*

with wonderful aromas. Yellow 'everlastings' are abundant at one point. Views down the valley from **Arbosa** lead the eye to distant hills. As the path swings gradually round to the left, a water **source** is signposted and there is a splendid view of the Aiguilles de Bavella, around 1050m (3445ft).

Bracken and brambles begin to press in as the path passes another signposted water source, then crosses a stream, the Ruisseau d'Aja Murata, where hollyoaks grow. As the route swings round a ridge and enters the next little valley, holm oak, arbutus and heather grow densely and obscure the sun and views. The path descends, then climbs, and water can be heard in the **Ruisseau de Caracutu** long before it is seen. Cross the bouldery stream, taking care if the boulders are greasy.

The path is again among tall laricio pines at this point. Follow it up another slope and the pines thin out, so that the heather and holm oak dominate again. After a bouldery stretch the path descends to cross a rocky slope and reaches the bed of the Ruisseau de Donicelli. Rocky pinnacles again tower high above.

The path is narrow as it leaves the streambed, and is flanked by scrub and pines. Watch carefully for small cairns that mark the route as it climbs up and around a rocky corner at 1055m (3460ft). There are good views up towards the Col de Bavella as it makes the turn, but the path becomes quite rough and rocky in its final stages. There are a few pines on the slope, as well as more heather scrub. Some parts of the path are easy, while others are stony or cross bare rock, picking out lines of weakness that require some short scrambles. It is almost like climbing an uneven rocky stairway.

A bouldery path passes a couple of solitary pines, aiming for the denser cover of laricio pines on the Col de Bavella. There is a steep slope of grass, and the voices of climbers might be heard high above, negotiating some of the pitches on the rock walls. It is possible to pick out some of the climbing routes by looking for signs bolted to the rock.

*The white statue of Notre Dame des Neiges is perched on a large cairn on top of the Col de Bavella*

When the D268 is reached on the **Col de Bavella**, there is a cross and a statue of Notre Dame des Neiges, as well as plenty of parked cars. Walkers should reach this point, at an altitude of 1218m (3996ft), about 3hrs 30mins after leaving the junction with the Alpine Variant route. Turn left to enter the **Village de Bavella** and choose a place to stay for the night, otherwise continue to the Refuge d' I Paliri, referring to Stage 16.

## VILLAGE DE BAVELLA

The Village de Bavella is a ramshackle collection of wooden and stone huts, mostly with corrugated iron roofs, in various states of repair. Some are ruined, while others have been rebuilt. Traditionally, the Village de Bavella is the 'summer village' for distant Conca – a name that suggests the end is drawing very close at this stage. Some trekkers actually prefer to finish at this point, while some commercial trekking companies omit the entire stretch from Bavella to Conca from their itineraries.

**Accommodation** The first building reached is Les Aiguilles de Bavella, tel 09 88 77 35 23, which has 25 beds in its gîte d'étape. The road runs downhill to reach a hairpin bend where the Auberge du Col de Bavella, tel 04 95 72 09 87, has 30 beds in 4- to 8-bed rooms. Camping is not permitted in the area, so those wishing to camp should continue to the Refuge d' I Paliri.

**Food and drink** Les Aiguilles de Bavella and Auberge du Col de Bavella have bar restaurants. Just a short way further downhill is Le Refuge, which is a bar and pizzeria. Despite its name it does not operate as a refuge. Trekkers can buy food at a little épicerie at the Auberge du Col de Bavella.

**Transport** A bus service is operated by Autocars Balesi Evasion, tel 04 95 70 15 55, **www.balesievasion.com**, to Ajaccio and Porto Vecchio, daily through July and August, then only on Monday and Friday through the rest of the year. Ricci Marcel Transports, tel 04 95 78 86 30, **www.transports-voyageurs-ajaccio.fr**, links Bavella with Ajaccio daily through July and August. Taxi services are operated by Jean Francois Crispi, tel 04 95 78 41 26 or 06 07 58 17 98.

# STAGE 15B

*Refuge d'Asinau to*
*Village de Bavella (high-level)*

| | |
|---|---|
| **Start** | Refuge d'Asinau |
| **Finish** | Village de Bavella |
| **Distance** | 8km (5 miles) |
| **Total ascent** | 550m (1805ft) |
| **Total descent** | 865m (2840ft) |
| **Time** | 4hrs 15mins |
| **Terrain** | Mostly forest and woodland at first, then a steep climb to the Aiguilles de Bavella. Paths can be steep and stony, but aren't too difficult, although one short stretch up a slab has a chain for protection. The descent is steep and rocky. Clear weather is an advantage. |
| **Maps** | IGN 4253 ET |
| **Food and drink** | Use a water source before starting the Alpine Variant, as none are available afterwards. There are bar restaurants and a shop at the Village de Bavella. |
| **Shelter** | There is shade and shelter in the trees at first, but the higher parts are more exposed to sun, wind and rain. |

The main route of the GR20 between the Refuge d'Asinau and Col de Bavella is essentially a low-level route. However, a high-level alternative called the Alpine Variant is available. It branches from the main route and climbs towards the pinnacles and towers of the Aiguilles de Bavella. It is highly recommended for those who want excitement and exceptional views, and in terms of overall effort it is probably only a little more difficult than the low-level route. Although it involves a higher climb, the route to the Village de Bavella is shorter, so the two probably balance out. The Alpine Variant requires clear weather in order to make the most of the views, which are quite remarkable. It is also helpful if the rock is dry, especially where trekkers have to climb up a slab of rock with the aid of a chain. Those reaching the Col de Bavella early in the day may wish to continue to the Refuge d' I Paliri and so shorten the final day's walk.

Leave the **Refuge d'Asinau** as signposted for Paliri, following a rugged path across a well-vegetated and well-watered bouldery slope. Continue across a slope of spiny broom and boulders, noting a spur path to the left leading only to the **Bergeries d'Asinau**. Continue downhill to reach a stand of pines. There are signposts here for the Refuge d' I Paliri, as well as a waymarked link with the village of Quenza.

The route goes down among the pines and fords the bouldery bed of the **Ruisseau d'Asinau**. A bouldery path rises above the river and wanders across a slope covered in pines. It passes some big boulders and continues through a couple of clearings of spiny broom and juniper scrub. While in the clearings, look up at the rocky pinnacles of the Aiguilles de Bavella.

The route climbs to a signpost for a water **source** in an area of pines and slender birch trees. An easy stretch of well-engineered path contours across a slope, touching 1400m (4590ft), although it becomes narrower and rougher later. The path descends and is quite rugged in places, crossing a couple of streambeds. Again, there are clearings and views of the Aiguilles de Bavella high above.

Reach a signpost where the Alpine Variant is marked uphill to the left, marked with yellow paint flashes. This point is reached about 1hr 15mins after leaving the Refuge d'Asinau, at 1320m (4330ft). (If suddenly deciding against the Alpine Variant, refer to the previous section for the low-level route description.)

Zigzag steeply uphill on a stony forest path. This swings to the right as the trees thin out on a slope littered with boulders, where the ground is clothed in juniper scrub. The yellow paint flashes and small cairns lead faultlessly uphill. Towers and sheer walls of rock rise above and it all looks quite intimidating, but around 1690m

(5545ft) the path swings right and levels out, then drops down a short way to reach an easy crest at the foot of an immense tower of rock. This tower is **Punta di u Pargulu**, also known as Tour IV. Take a break at this point and gaze in awe and wonder at the surrounding scenery. Apart from the towers and pinnacles clustered along the ridge, there is also a view down the Ravin du Pargulu to the low-level route of the GR20, and a fine view up the valley to Monte Alcudina.

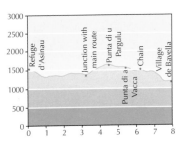

The path running down from the crest is broad and stony, but not too steep, and it is flanked by spiny broom and juniper scrub. Follow the path down to a gap where **Punta di a Vacca**, also known as Tour III, rises as a conical mass of rock. The summit can be reached by scrambling, for those who fancy a short diversion, otherwise head left across a bouldery slope, passing a few pines to reach another rocky gap on the side of the mountain.

Looking ahead, two tall and rather intimidating rock towers are visible. These are Punta di l'Ariettu, or Tour II,

*The Alpine Variant passes Punta di u Pargulu, or Tour IV, as it crosses the crest of the Aiguilles de Bavella*

and Punta di l'Acellu, or Tour I. There is obviously no way to trek over these two towers, but people might be seen picking their way along a rugged path on their eastern flanks. You will soon be walking along that same path.

Follow a stony, bouldery path down towards the gap between Punta di a Vacca and Punta di l'Ariettu. The path doesn't actually reach this gap, but drifts away to the left and keeps below it. Pass a few pines and walk beneath the rocky face of **Punta di l'Ariettu**, basically outflanking this monstrous obstacle. The path then leads up to a sloping slab of rock surmounted by an enormous jammed boulder, forcing walkers out onto the exposed, tilted slope. Fortunately, there is a chain for protection. Most walkers are happy to heave-ho their way up, hand over hand on the chain, shuffling their feet up the slab. Take care in wet weather as the rock can be slippery.

At the top, squeeze between the rocks, then walk down a rocky stairway and along a rugged path towards **Punta di l'Acellu**. Again, keep well to the left of the tower, picking a way along a rocky terrace with a slight overhang above. Follow the yellow flashes carefully beyond, across a bouldery slope and up through a stand of pines to reach a rocky little gap on the crest.

Descend through a rock-walled gully, which is grassy and bouldery at first, with a zigzag path overlooked by a tower of rock. There are plenty of laricio pines further down the slope, and tall heather too, but not enough to obscure the view towards the Bavella road and the mountains beyond. The path in the gully is rather more rugged for a while, then the markers direct walkers off to the left, more directly towards the Col de Bavella.

Cut across a more open, rocky slope, then descend again on a rough and bouldery slope where pines and heather grow. Plaques are bolted to rockfaces off to the left, giving the names of popular climbs, and there may well be several climbers picking their way up the faces. Entering a denser stand of laricio pines, pass a sign announcing the end of the Alpine Variant, and the path joins the main course of the GR20 again. Keep left to follow the GR20 a short way up the slope of grass and pines.

When the D268 is reached on the **Col de Bavella**, there is a cross and a statue of Notre Dame des Neiges, as well as plenty of parked cars. Walkers should reach this point, at an altitude of 1218m (3996ft), about 3hrs after leaving the junction with the low-level route. Turn left to enter the **Village de Bavella** and choose a place to stay for the night, otherwise continue to the Refuge d' I Paliri, referring to Stage 16.

## VILLAGE DE BAVELLA

The Village de Bavella is a ramshackle collection of wooden and stone huts, mostly with corrugated iron roofs, in various states of repair. Some are ruined, while others have been rebuilt. Traditionally, the Village de Bavella is the 'summer village' for distant Conca – a name that suggests the end is drawing very close at this stage. Some trekkers actually prefer to finish at this point, while some commercial trekking companies omit the entire stretch from Bavella to Conca from their itineraries.

**Accommodation** The first building reached is Les Aiguilles de Bavella, tel 09 88 77 35 23, which has 25 beds in its gîte d'étape. The road runs downhill to reach a hairpin bend where the Auberge du Col de Bavella, tel 04 95 72 09 87, has 30 beds in 4- to 8-bed rooms. Camping is not permitted in the area, so those wishing to camp should continue to the Refuge d' I Paliri.

**Food and drink** Les Aiguilles de Bavella and Auberge du Col de Bavella have bar restaurants. Just a short way further downhill is Le Refuge, which is a bar and pizzeria. Despite its name it does not operate as a refuge. Trekkers can buy food at a little épicerie at the Auberge du Col de Bavella.

**Transport** A bus service is operated by Autocars Balesi Evasion, tel 04 95 70 15 55, **www.balesievasion.com**, to Ajaccio and Porto Vecchio, daily through July and August, then only on Monday and Friday through the rest of the year. Ricci Marcel Transports, tel 04 95 78 86 30, **www.transports-voyageurs-ajaccio.fr**, links Bavella with Ajaccio daily through July and August. Taxi services are operated by Jean Francois Crispi, tel 04 95 78 41 26 or 06 07 58 17 98.

# STAGE 16
## Village de Bavella to Conca

| | |
|---|---|
| **Start** | Village de Bavella |
| **Finish** | Conca |
| **Distance** | 19km (12 miles) |
| **Total ascent** | 700m (2295ft) |
| **Total descent** | 1670m (5480ft) |
| **Time** | 7hrs |
| **Terrain** | Well forested at the start, but thinning out later. There are some steep and rugged slopes, but these are limited, although much of the terrain is rough and rocky. There is good woodland cover on the final descent to Conca. On the whole, it is mostly downhill to the end. |
| **Maps** | IGN 4253 ET |
| **Food and drink** | Water can be obtained before the Refuge d' I Paliri, before the Bocca di u Sordu, near the ruins of the Bergeries de Capeddu, and from the Ruisseau de Punta Pinzuta, if treated. There are a couple of bars and restaurants in Conca. |
| **Shelter** | Trees provide some shade and shelter. Beyond the Refuge d' I Paliri, most areas are open, and it can get hot on the lower slopes. |

The final stage of the GR20 looks quite long on the map, even for those who spend a night at the Refuge d' I Paliri. Apart from a few steep and rugged climbs, it is mostly an easy walk, and some paths are level and pose no problems. The mountain scenery is remarkably good throughout the first half of the walk, and the surroundings remain quite rugged even to the end. However, there is a definite feeling that height is being lost – the vegetation becomes more exotic, the temperature rises, and ultimately walkers see the little village of Conca beckoning, with the sea beyond. You can reflect on your journey through the mountains of Corsica, unravelling the path in your mind, but you also need to think about how you are going to leave Conca and return home.

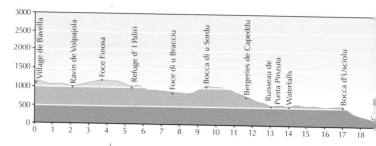

Leave the **Village de Bavella** by following the D268 downhill from Les Aiguilles de Bavella to the Auberge du Col de Bavella. Turn right off the hairpin bend in the road and walk along a clear track signposted for the GR20 and Paliri. Turn right again at another signpost reading the same, and follow a broad dirt road across a slope of laricio pines. There are a couple of signs erected by businesses

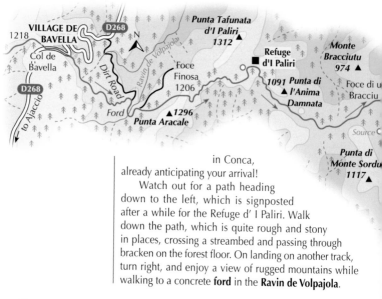

in Conca, already anticipating your arrival!

Watch out for a path heading down to the left, which is signposted after a while for the Refuge d' I Paliri. Walk down the path, which is quite rough and stony in places, crossing a streambed and passing through bracken on the forest floor. On landing on another track, turn right, and enjoy a view of rugged mountains while walking to a concrete **ford** in the **Ravin de Volpajola**.

Walk a little further along the track among tall pines, then a sign on the right indicates a narrow path climbing uphill. Follow the path as it slices up across the slope, passing pines and tall heather, before zigzagging more steeply over rockier terrain to reach a gap called **Foce Finosa** at 1206m (3957ft). Climb a little higher on the rocks behind a sign for a fine view back to the Aiguilles de Bavella, unobscured by pines. In the other direction, note the prominent peak of Punta di l'Anima Damnata.

Follow the path downhill from from the gap, zigzagging on a steep and rocky slope. This is an old mule path that has been pitched in places with carefully laid stonework. Go up through a rocky notch beside a tower of rock, noting holm oak and arbutus growing among the laricio and maritime pines. Continue walking down the path, then an easier stretch leads across a slope covered in pines, where there are views through the trees towards remarkably jagged mountains.

There is a fairly easy ascent for a short way, passing a water source and a sign for a shower before reaching the **Refuge d' I Paliri**. The refuge is situated at 1055m (3460ft), and is reached about 2hrs after leaving the Village de Bavella.

The PNRC **Refuge d' I Paliri** is built in the bergerie style and features a small dormitory and an even smaller dormitory, with 22 beds altogether. There is a kitchen/dining room in-between, and the gardien lives in a small building nearby. The toilet is out at the back of the refuge, while the shower and water source are signposted off the GR20 nearby. Camping spaces are located in the forest in the direction signposted for Conca. Hot meals, food supplies and drinks are on sale, but it's worth noting, especially if trekking south to north, that some people unburden themselves and deposit excess food and fuel at the refuge for anyone else to

continued

235

*Looking southwards from the Refuge d' I Paliri, where the mountains may be lower, but remain impressive*

use. The refuge sits at the foot of the Punta Tafunata d' I Paliri, which has a hole known as the Trou de la Bombe pierced through the rock near the top – it often looks like a huge blue eye. Heart-shaped stones marked with poetry and prose can be spotted in the forest around the refuge.

Leave the campsite and descend along a rather rocky path, enjoying the variety of flowers and shrubs alongside. The path enters a pine forest where a number of trees have toppled, but it becomes easier later, and is quite level as it passes through a denser part of the

*The striking rock tower of the Punta di l'Anima Damnata, or the Point of the Damned Soul*

forest where bracken grows quite densely. Trekkers pass the prominent peak of **Punta di l'Anima Damnata** without really seeing it. Emerging into the open, however, it becomes more clearly visible. The path climbs towards a gap, and there is plenty of evidence that the forest suffered a severe burning in the past. The scrub contains arbutus, tall heather, rock rose and other flowering plants.

As the path contours easily across the slope, notice the blue eye on Punta Tafunata d' I Paliri, watching the progress of trekkers, and the pinnacles of nearby Monte Bracchiutu. The path eventually crosses the broad gap of **Foce di u Bracciu**, where it is important to keep an eye on the paint flashes, as other paths converge on this point, around 915m (3000ft).

The path descends through pines, arbutus and tall heather as it swings to the right into the next valley. Cross a bouldery slab of granite, look out for a tiny water **source**, enjoy views across the valley, and continue descending with more tree cover.

All of a sudden the route starts climbing, sometimes on bare rock or on a rugged, stony path. There is still good shade from the trees, but the ascent, although fairly short, can be tiring. There are steep zigzags towards the top, where the route passes through a gap of bare granite and boulders. This is **Bocca di u Sordu**, around 1040m (3410ft). Look up to the right while crossing the gap to see a lone olive tree leaning out from the rock. Olive trees might not have been spotted since leaving Calenzana!

The GR20 heads off to the left, clambering over rocks and boulders, going through a small stand of pines and down a grooved channel on a slope of granite. The path leading onwards is almost level, quite narrow and sandy, passing through

pines and tall heather scrub. There is a descent on bulbous masses of bare granite, and plenty of evidence of a severe fire in the past. However, some of the trees grow from the bare rock, and have doubtless survived because there was no ground vegetation to carry the fire towards them.

Cross a fairly level area of boulders, rocky outcrops, sparse pines and heather scrub, taking care to look for the paint flashes marking the route. There is a gritty channel and a stony descent through pines to reach the ruined **Bergeries de Capeddu**. This point should be reached about 2hrs 15mins after leaving the Refuge d' I Paliri. Trekkers might take a break in the shade here, at 850m (2790ft), and note the signpost pointing the way to a handy little water **source**. There is also a skip full of rubbish nearby that seems incongruous in this sylvan setting.

There are signposts pointing back to the Refuge d' I Paliri and Col de Bavella, ahead to Conca, and off-route to the Village de Sari. Sticky leaved cistus grows under the tree cover – a plant of the maquis not really seen since leaving Calenzana. All the signs indicate that the end of the walk is close.

Follow the path out of the shade near the ruins and walk down a slope of tall maquis and scrub. The area used to be tall forest, but it was devastated by fire in 1985. A few tall laricio pines have survived, their bark scorched black, while the scrub has taken advantage of the light and grown into remarkably dense thickets. The narrow path is awkward and stony for a while, with the scrub pressing on both sides. Later it is wider, more gently graded and easier to follow. Swing to the right through arbutus and heather scrub, passing a tower of rock, with a good view of Punta Batarchione at the head of the valley.

Swing left down to the **Ruisseau de Punta Pinzuta**. The tall pines near the river survived forest fires in the past due to their higher water content, but they are still scorched along their trunks. **Ford** the river and turn right to walk between the pines as the route heads downstream. An excellent mule path develops, which has been well engineered on a steep and rugged slope, but trekkers have to leave it to continue down a more rugged path and **ford** the river again. A couple of inviting pools demand a break, and at 550m (1805ft) the water will be lukewarm on a hot day. It is advisable to treat the water if it is used for drinking, as it is popular with bathers.

Turn left after crossing the river and follow the path uphill. A series of steep zigzags climb alongside a rock wall in the shade of a stand of pine trees. The path reaches a notch in a little ridge and continues onwards. It climbs more gently to cross another notch, then rises even more gently across a scrubby slope high on the side of a valley. The stony path reaches a few pines, then there is a gradual descent until it reaches a rocky ravine. Drop down into the ravine to cross it, then climb uphill a short way through some thorny scrub.

The path descends a little, contours across the slope, then a rocky stairway leads uphill a short way to reach the **Bocca d'Usciolu**. This is a curious, narrow, crooked cleft in a rocky rib, reached at 587m (1926ft). The cleft is reached about 2hrs after leaving the ruined Bergeries de Capeddu. Turn around and take one last long look back at the mountains before they pass from sight.

You are finally leaving the mountains, and after starting the descent the village of Conca comes into view, nestling at the foot of the slope. The bells in the church tower will strike the quarter hours on the descent – it should take 45mins, so three strikes and you're out!

The narrow path is quite stony, so tread carefully where heather, broom and cistus scrub press on both sides. On the descent, the arbutus grows taller and taller, with a few pines and gnarled cork oak trees offering more and more shade. There is a water **source** at the bottom for trekkers who can't wait to reach the village to quench their thirst, and it could be quite hot now that the route has left the mountains.

The path quickly leads to a minor road, where a left turn leads down in loops to the village of **Conca** at 250m (820ft). Note the cork oak trees stripped of their bark along the way. On reaching a road junction, decide whether to hit the Bar Le Soleil Levant, just to the right, for a celebratory drink, or go directly in search of accommodation. Whatever choice is made, the trek is over and you have completed the GR20!

## CONCA

You made it – well done!

No one in Conca seems impressed that you've just trekked all the way through the mountains of Corsica to reach their little village, but all the same, they'll be happy to provide you with food, drink and accommodation. If you want to share a few tales of the trail, then do that with other trekkers. Local folk have heard it all before, many times over!

Some trekkers will want to dash away and catch a bus, but it is probably better to take a break and spend at least one night in Conca. It is a quiet, unassuming little village, where you can savour the feeling of satisfaction at completing the GR20. Think ahead about how best to to leave Conca and make your way home.

**Accommodation** The Hôtel San Pasquale, tel 04 95 10 47 30, offers 15-rooms and a lovely garden on the northern edge of the village. Alternatively, walk down past the church, passing a monument to an ancient chapel and a cemetery, then as the road leaves the village, turn left for the Gîte d'Étape La Tonnelle, tel 04 95 71 46 55. There is a choice of small rooms or small dormitories with a total of 30 beds, as well as a campsite with toilets and showers. Laundry services are available, for trekkers who want everything to be fresh before they set off home. A navette service is provided, linking with buses on the main N198 at Sainte Lucie de Porto Vecchio, but be sure to organise a transfer immediately on arrival at the gîte.

At Bastia and Ajaccio it is possible to link with bus services to other parts of Corsica, or use trains to reach Vizzavona, Corte and Calvi. Railway timetables can be picked up at the stations, or tel 04 95 32 80 61 or 04 95 23 11 03, **www. cf-corse.fr**.

Travellers hoping to link with a particular ferry or flight to leave Corsica should check and double-check all timetable details carefully. The website **www. corsicabus.org** is a useful resource. Transport can be slow and delays are normal. It is a good idea to allow a whole day to make a long transfer around Corsica. If bus and train timetables don't fit your schedule, and you need to call for a long-distance taxi, it will be very expensive.

**Food and drink** On entering Conca, the Bar Le Soleil Levant is on the right, offering food and drink, and they can organise a taxi down to the main road. The Restaurant Bar U Chjosu is off to the left and also provides food and drink. The Hôtel San Pasquale and Gîte d'Étape La Tonnelle have their own bar restaurants. There is a basic alimentation opposite the post office, for those who wish to buy food and cook their own food. The choice is limited, but the nearest supermarket is at Ste Lucie de Porto Vecchio.

**Transport** After leaving Conca to link with bus services on the main road at Ste Lucie de Porto Vecchio, there is a choice of two main destinations – Bastia and Ajaccio. To reach Bastia, use Les Rapides Bleus Corsicatours, tel 04 95 31 03 79, **www.rapides-bleus.com**. Buses run daily from mid-June to mid-September, but not on Sundays for the rest of the year. In July and August the bus also serves Bastia airport. To reach Ajaccio, use Les Rapides Bleus Corsicatours to reach Porto Vecchio, then switch to Eurocorse Voyages, tel 04 95 21 06 30, **www.eurocorse. com**. Buses run Monday to Saturday from July to mid-September. Alternatively, use Autocars Balesi Evasion, tel 04 95 70 15 55, **www.balesievasion.com**, to reach Ajaccio via the Village de Bavella, daily through July and August, but only on Monday and Friday through the rest of the year.

At Bastia and Ajaccio it is possible to link with bus services to other parts of Corsica, or use trains to reach Vizzavona, Corte and Calvi. Railway timetables can be picked up at the stations, or tel 04 95 32 80 61 or 04 95 23 11 03, **www. cf-corse.fr**.

Travellers hoping to link with a particular ferry or flight to leave Corsica should check and double-check all timetable details carefully. The website www.corsi-cabus.org is a useful resource. Transport can be slow and delays are normal. It is a good idea to allow a whole day to make a long transfer around Corsica. If bus and train timetables don't fit your schedule, and you need to call for a long-distance taxi, it will be very expensive.

Public Health England released a statement in 2014 concerning a parasitic infection in the Cavu river in Corsica. This river occurs off-route at the very end of the GR20, between Conca and Ste Lucie de Porto Vecchio. Please do not bathe or swim in this river, as it contains the parasite Schistosoma haematobium, also known as Bilharzia. Further details are on the government website... **www.gov.uk/government/news/ travellers-to-southern-corsica-warned-about-parasitic-infection**.

# APPENDIX A

*Facilities along the route (Calenzana to Conca)*

The timings below are the ones generally quoted for the sections of the route given in this table. Trekkers should adapt them to suit their own performance, and plan ahead on that basis. The timings do not take into account any breaks whatsoever for lunch, rests, taking photographs, and so on.

The facilities listed are all available in July and August. Some are available from June to September. Few are available through the winter. Note that the refuges have gardiens in residence from June to September, but they are left open, unstaffed and unsupplied through the rest of the year. Camping is available only at the refuges and at a few other designated sites.

Shops where trekkers can stock up on food and drink are few, but basic supplies of food and drink can be obtained at nearly all the refuges. Many of the bergeries also sell basic food and drink supplies. Transport links with the route are limited, and some bus services operate only through July and August. Road access for back-up vehicles is available at Calenzana, Ascu Stagnu, Hôtel Castel di Vergio, Vizzavona, Bergeries d' E Capanelle, Bocca di Verdi, Refuge de Matalza, Village de Bavella and Conca.

| Place | Time | Facilities |
|---|---|---|
| Calenzana (start of GR20) | 0hr00min | Hotel, chambres d'hôte, gîte, camping, restaurants, bars, shops, bus, taxi |
| GR20/TMM junction | 1hr 00min | |
| Arghioa | 1hr 30min | |
| Bocca a u Saltu | 1hr 30min | |
| Bocca a u Bassiguellu | 1hr 30min | |
| Refuge d'Ortu di u Piobbu | 1hr 30min | Refuge, camping, meals, supplies |
| Ruisseau de la Mandriaccia | 1hr 00min | |

| Place | Time | Facilities |
|---|---|---|
| Bocca Piccaia | 2hr 30min | |
| Bocca d'Avartol | 1hr 00min | |
| Bocca Carozzu | 0hr 45min | |
| Refuge de Carozzu | 1hr 15min | Refuge, camping, meals, supplies |
| Lac de la Muvrella | 3hr 00min | |
| Bocca a i Stagni | 1hr 00min | |
| Ascu Stagnu | 1hr 30min | Hotel, gîte, refuge, camping, restaurant, bar, supplies, bus |
| Pointe des Éboulis | 4hr 00min | |
| Bocca Crucetta | 1hr 00min | |
| Refuge de Tighjettu | 2hr 30min | Refuge, camping, meals, supplies |
| Auberge U Vallone | 0hr 30min | Camping, meals, supplies |
| Refuge de Ciottulu di I Mori | 3hr 15min | Refuge, camping, meals, supplies |
| Bergeries de Radule | 1hr 30min | Camping, meals |
| Hôtel Castel di Vergio | 1hr 15min | Hotel, gîte, camping, restaurant, bar, supplies, bus |
| Bocca San Petru | 1hr 30min | |
| Bergerie de l'Inzecche | 2hr 30min | Snacks |
| Bergeries de Vaccaghja | 1hr 00min | Camping, meals, supplies |
| Refuge de Manganu | 0hr 45min | Refuge, camping, meals, supplies |

| Place | Time | Facilities |
|---|---|---|
| Bocca a e Porte | 3hr 00min | |
| Bocca a Soglia | 1hr 15min | |
| Bocca Muzella | 1hr 45min | |
| Refuge de Petra Piana | 1hr 00min | Refuge, camping, meals, supplies |
| Bergeries de Gialgo | 0hr 30min | Cheese |
| Bergeries de Tolla | 2hr 30min | Meals, supplies |
| Passerelle de Tolla | 0hr 15min | |
| Refuge de l'Onda | 1hr 45min | Refuge, camping, meals, supplies |
| Punta Muratello | 2hr 30min | |
| Cascade des Anglais | 2hr 30min | Bar-restaurant |
| Vizzavona (midpoint of GR20) | 1hr 00min | Hotel, chambres d'hôte, refuge, camping, restaurants, bars, shop, train |
| Bocca Palmento | 2hr 45min | |
| Bergeries d' E Capanelle | 2hr 45min | Gîtes, refuge, camping, bar-restaurant, supplies |
| Pont de Casacchie | 0hr 30min | |
| Plateau de Gialgone | 3hr 00min | Camping, meals, supplies |
| Bocca di Verdi | 1hr 30min | Refuge, camping, bar-restaurant, supplies |
| Bocca d'Oru | 1hr 45min min | |
| Refuge de Prati | 0hr 15min | Refuge, camping, meals, supplies |

| Place | Time | Facilities |
|---|---|---|
| Punta Capella | 1hr 00min | |
| Bocca di Laparo | 1hr 30min | Basic refuge nearby |
| Refuge d'Usciolu | 2hr 45min | Refuge, camping, meals, supplies |
| Bocca di l'Agnonu | 2hr 30min | |
| Bergeries de Bassetta | 1hr 15min | Refuge, camping, meals, supplies |
| Refuge de Matalza | 0hr 45min | Refuge, camping, meals, supplies |
| Bergerie d'I Croci | 1hr 00min | Refuge, camping, meals, supplies |
| Ridge–Monte Alcudina | 2hr 15min | |
| Refuge d'Asinau | 1hr 00min | Refuge to be constructed, camping, meals, supplies |
| GR20/Alpine Variant junction | 1hr 15min | |
| Village de Bavella | 3hr 30min | Gîtes, bar-restaurants, shop, bus, taxi |
| Refuge d'I Paliri | 2hr 00min | Refuge, camping, meals, supplies |
| Bergeries de Capeddu | 2hr 15min | |
| Bocca d'Usciolu | 2hr 00min | |
| Conca (end of GR20) | 0hr 45min | Hotel, gîte, camping, bar-restaurants, shop, navette |

# APPENDIX B

*Facilities along the route (Conca to Calenzana)*

There are some who prefer to trek the GR20 from south to north. The route descriptions in this guidebook can be reversed without difficulty, but it can become tedious changing all the starts and finishes, lefts and rights, ascents and descents. The red and white flashes that mark the route are just as easy to follow one way as the other, and most trekkers are happy to rely on the waymarking, no matter what maps and guides they carry.

Below is a reverse route summary, which indicates the approximate length of time it takes to walk between short stages. Those walking south to north should not simply reverse each and every stage as described in this book. The first day's walk, from Conca, would be best concluded at the Refuge d' I Paliri, rather than the Village de Bavella. The last stage, down to Calenzana, proves remarkably easy when compared with the ascent from Calenzana. Adapt and amend the route to suit your own individual requirements.

| Place | Time | Facilities |
|---|---|---|
| Bocca d'Usciolu | 1hr 15min | |
| Bergeries de Capeddu | 2hr 30min | |
| Refuge d' I Paliri | 2hr 45min | Refuge, camping, meals, supplies |
| Conca (start of GR20) | 0hr 00min | Hotel, gîte, camping, bar-restaurants, shop, navette |
| Village de Bavella | 2hr 15min | Gîtes, bar-restaurants, shop, bus, taxi |
| GR20/Alpine Variant junction | 3hr 30min | |
| Refuge d'Asinau | 1hr 30min | Refuge to be constructed, camping, meals, supplies |
| Ridge–Monte Alcudina | 1hr 30min | |
| Bergerie d' I Croci | 2hr 00min | Refuge, camping, meals, supplies |

THE GR20 CORSICA

| Place | Time | Facilities |
| --- | --- | --- |
| Refuge de Matalza | 0hr 30min | Refuge, camping, meals, supplies |
| Bergeries de Bassetta | 0hr 45min | Refuge, camping, meals, supplies |
| Bocca di l'Agnonu | 1hr 30min | |
| Refuge d'Usciolu | 3hr 00min | Refuge, camping, meals, supplies |
| Bocca di Laparo | 2hr 30min | Basic refuge nearby |
| Punta Capella | 2hr 30min | |
| Refuge de Prati | 1hr 00min | Refuge, camping, meals, supplies |
| Bocca d'Oru | 0hr 15 min | |
| Bocca di Verdi | 1hr 15min | Refuge, camping, bar-restaurant, supplies |
| Plateau de Gialgone | 1hr 45min | Camping, meals, supplies |
| Pont de Casacchie | 2hr 15min | |
| Bergeries d' E Capanelle | 0hr 45min | Gîtes, refuge, camping, bar-restaurant, supplies |
| Bocca Palmento | 2hr 45min | |
| Vizzavona (midpoint of GR20) | 2hr 00min | Hotel, chambres d'hôte, refuge, camping, restaurants, bars, shop, train |
| Cascade des Anglais | 1hr 00min | Bar-restaurant |
| Punta Muratello | 3hr 15min | |
| Refuge de l'Onda | 2hr 00min | Refuge, camping, meals, supplies |
| Passerelle de Tolla | 1hr 30min | |

| Place | Time | Facilities |
|---|---|---|
| Bergeries de Tolla | 0hr 15min | Meals, supplies |
| Bergeries de Gialgo | 2hr 45min | Cheese |
| Refuge de Petra Piana | 0hr 45min | Refuge, camping, meals, supplies |
| Bocca Muzella | 1hr 30min | |
| Bocca a Soglia | 1hr 30min | |
| Bocca a e Porte | 1hr 45min | |
| Refuge de Manganu | 2hr 00min | Refuge, camping, meals, supplies |
| Bergeries de Vaccaghja | 0hr 45min | Camping, meals, supplies |
| Bergerie de L' Inzecche | 1hr 15min | Snacks |
| Bocca San Petru | 2hr 15min | |
| Hôtel Castel di Vergio | 1hr 15min | Hotel, gîte, camping, restaurant, bar, supplies, bus |
| Bergeries de Radule | 1hr 00min | Camping, meals |
| Refuge de Ciottulu di i Mori | 2hr 00min | Refuge, camping, meals, supplies |
| Auberge U Vallone | 2hr 45min | Camping, meals, supplies |
| Refuge de Tighjettu | 0hr 45min | Refuge, camping, meals, supplies |
| Bocca Crucetta | 3hr 15min | |
| Pointe des Éboulis | 1hr 00min | |
| Ascu Stagnu | 3hr 00min | Hotel, gîte, camping, restaurant, bar, supplies, bus |

| Place | Time | Facilities |
|---|---|---|
| Bocca a i Stagni | 2hr 15min | |
| Lac de la Muvrella | 1hr 00min | |
| Refuge de Carozzu | 2hr 15min | Refuge, camping, meals, supplies |
| Bocca Carozzu | 1hr 45min | |
| Bocca d'Avartoli | 0hr 45min | |
| Bocca Piccaia | 1hr 15min | |
| Ruisseau de la Mandriaccia | 1hr 45min | |
| Refuge d'Ortu di u Piobbu | 1hr 00min | Refuge, camping, meals, supplies |
| Bocca a u Bassiguellu | 1hr 15min | |
| Bocca a u Saltu | 1hr 00min | |
| Arghioa | 1hr 00min | |
| GR20/TMM junction | 1hr 00min | |
| Calenzana (end of GR20) | 0hr 45min | Hotel, chambres d'hôte, gîte, camping, restaurants, bars, shops, bus, taxi |

# APPENDIX C
*Accommodation list*

The telephone numbers of accommodation options on or close to the GR20 are listed, as well as lodgings on variant and link routes. These places range from expensive hotels and chambres d'hôte to budget gîtes d'étape and refuges, as well as campsites, including those with little or no facilities. While telephone numbers are available for many places, not all of them take advance bookings.

Beds in PNRC refuges, and hire tents outside, can only be reserved by using the online booking facility at www.parc-corse.org. Camping at PNRC refuges can be booked, but it isn't essential. Note that the online booking system doesn't work in the autumn and winter. Once it becomes live, early in the year, follow the instructions and note that full payment has to be made before the booking is confirmed. Remember to print out booking confirmations and show them to each refuge guardian. If plans change and you are unable to reach a booked refuge, the confirmation includes a telephone number to call to make other arrangements, as it isn't possible to phone the refuges directly.

**Calenzana**
Hôtel Bel Horizon
tel 04 95 62 71 72

Chambres d'Hôte L' Ombre du Clocher
tel 04 95 31 17 12 or 06 20 18 80 08

Gîte d'Étape Communal and camping
tel 04 95 62 77 13 or 04 95 62 70 08

**Stage 1 (high-level)**
Refuge d'Ortu di u Piobbu
and camping
PNRC online booking

**Stage 1 (low-level)**
Auberge de la Forêt
gîte d'étape and camping
tel 04 95 65 09 98

**Stage 2**
Refuge de Carozzu and camping
PNRC online booking

**Stage 3**
Hôtel le Chalet and gîte d'étape
tel 04 95 47 81 08

Refuge Ascu Stagnu and camping
PNRC online booking

**Stage 4**
Refuge de Tighjettu and camping
PNRC online booking

Auberge U Vallone
camping only
tel 06 12 03 44 65

**Albertacce (off-route)**
Hôtel a Sant Anna
tel 06 26 83 22 09

**Stage 5**
Refuge de Ciottulu di I Mori and camping
PNRC online booking

Bergerie de Radule
camping only
tel 06 14 39 41 87

Hôtel Castel di Vergio
hotel, gîte d'étape and camping
tel 04 95 48 00 01

**Stage 6**
Bergeries de Vaccaghja
camping only
tel 06 24 73 63 67

Refuge de Manganu and camping
PNRC online booking

**Corte (off-route)**
Refuge a Sega and camping
halfway to Corte
tel 09 88 99 35 57 or 06 10 71 77 26

Hôtel de la Paix
tel 04 95 46 06 72

Hôtel Sampiero Corso
tel 04 95 46 09 76

Hôtel du Nord
tel 04 95 46 00 68

Hôtel Duc de Padoue
tel 04 95 46 01 37

Hôtel Si Mea
tel 04 95 65 08 23

Jardins de la Glacière
tel 04 95 45 27 00

Hôtel Dominique Colonna
tel 04 95 45 25 65

Hôtel Arena Le Refuge
tel 04 95 46 09 13

Gîte d'Étape U Tavignanu and camping
tel 04 95 46 16 85

Camping Restonica
tel 04 95 46 11 59

Camping Alivetu
tel 04 95 46 11 09

Camping U Sognu
tel 04 95 46 09 07

Camping Tuani
tel 04 95 46 11 65

**Soccia (off-route)**
Hôtel U Paese
tel 04 95 28 31 92

**Stage 7**
Refuge de Petra Piana and camping
PNRC online booking

**Stage 8**
Refuge de l'Onda and camping
PNRC online booking

**Tattone (off-route)**
Camping Savaggio and gîte d'étape
tel 04 95 47 22 14 or 06 81 96 08 98

Camping Le Soleil
tel 04 95 47 21 16

Refuge Chez Pierrot and camping
tel 04 95 31 12 7706 70 90 21 14 or
06 24 69 29 85

**Stage 9
(variant) – La Foce**
Hôtel Monte d'Oro and gîte d'étape
tel 04 95 47 21 06

La Halte du Prince
chalets and camping
tel 04 95 46 31 02 or 06 09 95 63 06

**Vizzavona**
L'Alzarella
camping only
tel 04 95 31 13 19

Bar Restaurant de la Gare
refuge
tel 04 95 47 22 20

Hôtel I Laricci and dormitory
tel 04 95 47 21 12

Casa Alta Chambres d'Hôte
tel 04 95 47 21 09

Hôtel U Castellu
tel 04 95 30 53 00

**Stage 10**
Refuge d' E Capanelle
PNRC but no advance booking
apply at U Fugone

Gîte d'Étape U Fugone/Gîte de
Capanelle
chalets and camping
tel 04 95 57 01 81

**Stage 11**
Casetta di Ghjalcone
camping only
tel 06 16 56 10 81

Refuge di Verdi and camping
tel 04 95 24 46 82

**Stage 12**
Refuge de Prati and camping
PNRC online booking

Refuge d'Usciolu and camping
PNRC online booking

**Cozzano (off-route)**
Gîte d'Étape Bella Vista and camping
tel 04 95 24 41 59 or 06 72 92 89 46

Auberge A Filetta
tel 04 95 24 45 61

**Stage 13**
Bergeries de Bassetta
chalets, dormitory and camping
tel 06 27 25 95 33

Refuge de Matalza and camping
tel 06 89 30 90 43 or 09 88 77 47 97

**Zicavo (off-route)**
Hôtel du Tourisme
tel 04 95 24 40 06

Hôtel le Florida
tel 04 95 24 43 11 or 04 95 24 40 24

L'Auberge A Funtana
managed by Hôtel le Florida

Gîte d'Étape le Paradis and camping
tel 04 94 24 41 20

**Stage 14**
Bergerie d' I Croci and camping
tel 06 75 49 60 59 or 09 82 12 33 10

Refuge d'Asinau (to be constructed) and
camping
PNRC online booking

Bergeries d'Asinau/Chez Aline
dormitory
tel 06 17 53 98 92

**Alternative Stage 13/14**
Refuge d'I Pedinieddi ruins
camping only
no facilities apart from water

**Stage 15**
Les Aiguilles de Bavella
gîte d'étape
tel 09 88 77 35 23

Auberge du Col de Bavella
tel 04 95 72 09 87

**Stage 16**
Refuge d'I Paliri
PNRC online booking

**Conca**
Hôtel San Pasquale
tel 04 95 10 47 30

Gîte d'Étape La Tonnelle and camping
tel 04 95 71 46 55

# APPENDIX D
*Basic language notes*

**Arrival in Corsica**

| | |
|---|---|
| Hello!/good evening/how are you? | *Bonjour!/bonsoir/ça va?* |
| Where can I get a taxi? | *Où puis-je trouver un taxi?* |
| Take me to … | *Conduisez-moi à …* |
| … the railway station/the hotel/this address … | *la gare/l'hôtel/cette adresse* |
| How much is it? | *C'est combien?* |
| Where is the bus stop/train station? | *Où se-trouve l'arrêt de bus/la gare?* |
| Tourist information office | *L'office de tourisme* |
| Post office/grocery | *La poste/alimentation* |
| I'd like a single/return ticket to … | *Je voudrais un billet aller simple/aller-retour à …* |
| Can I have a timetable? | *Puis-je avoir un horaire?* |
| Information/open/closed | *Reseignements/ouvert/fermé* |

**Staying the night**

| | |
|---|---|
| Rooms available/no vacancies | *Chambres libres/complet* |
| I'd like a single/double room | *Je voudrais une chambre pour une personne/deux personnes* |
| How much does it cost per night? | *Quel est le prix par nuit?* |
| How much does it cost for bed and breakfast/half board? | *Quel est le prix avec petit déjeuner/demi pension?* |
| Is there hot water/a toilet/a shower? | *Y-a-t-il l'eau chaude/une toilette/un douche?* |
| Where is the dining room/bar? | *Où est la salle à manger/bar?* |

**Walking the GR20**

| | |
|---|---|
| Where is the GR20? | *Où est le GR20?* (pronounced 'jairvan') |
| The path/the waymarks/rucksack | *Le sentier/les balisés/sac à dos* |
| Where are you going? | *Vous allez où* |

| | |
|---|---|
| I'm going to … | *Je vais à …* |
| Right/left/straight ahead | *À droit/à gauche/tout droit* |
| Can you show me on the map? | *Est-ce-que vous pouver me le montrer sur la carte?* |
| Camping/fire prohibited | *Camping/feu interdit* |

**At the refuge**

| | |
|---|---|
| Male/female guardian | *Gardien/Gardienne* |
| Can I stay in the refuge? | *Puis-je reste dans le refuge?* |
| Dormitory/bed/sleeping bag | *Dortoir/lit/sac à couchage* |
| Can I camp here? | *Puis-je camper ici?* |
| Tent/camping space/campsite | *Tente/emplacement/aire de bivouac* |
| Where are the toilets/showers? | *Où sont les toilettes/douches?* |
| Can I have a meal/a beer/breakfast? | *Puis-je avoir un repas/une bièra/petit déjeuner?* |
| What is the weather forecast for tomorrow? | *Quel est le météo demain?* |
| Hot/cold/rain/snow/storm | *Chaud/froid/pluie/neige/orage* |

**When it all goes wrong**

| | |
|---|---|
| Help me! | *Aidez-moi!* |
| I feel sick | *Je suis malade* |
| There has been an accident | *Il y a eu un accident* |

**Last resort**

| | |
|---|---|
| I don't understand | *Je ne comprends pas* |
| Do you speak English? | *Parlez-vous anglais?* |

**Common food and drink terms**

| | |
|---|---|
| *Ail* | Garlic |
| *Beurre* | Butter |
| *Bièra* | Beer |
| *Boissons(froid/chaud)* | Drinks (cold/hot) |
| *Brocciu* | Fresh goats' or sheeps' cheese |

| | |
|---|---|
| *Café/café au lait* | Black/white coffee |
| *Champignons* | Mushrooms |
| *Charcuterie* | Cold cured sliced pork meats |
| *Châtaigne* | Chestnut, used in main courses, desserts and even beer |
| *Chocolat* | Chocolate |
| *Confiture* | Jam |
| *Coppa* | Smoked pork shoulder |
| *Crudités* | Chopped raw vegetables or salad |
| *Figatellu* | Pork liver sausage |
| *Flan* | An egg custard dessert |
| *Fromage* | Cheese |
| *Gâteau* | Cake |
| *Haricots* | Beans |
| *Huile* | Oil |
| *Jambon* | Ham |
| *Jus d'orange* | Orange juice |
| *Légumes* | Vegetables |
| *Lentilles* | Lentils |
| *Miel* | Honey |
| *Oeufs* | Eggs |
| *Omelette* | Omelette |
| *Pain (chaud)* | Bread (hot) |
| *Panini* | Filled bread rolls, often toasted |
| *Pâtes* | Pasta |
| *Picnic* | Packed lunch |
| *Poivre* | Pepper |
| *Pomme de terre* | Potato |
| *Ravitaillement* | Food store |
| *Riz* | Rice |

| | |
|---|---|
| *Sanglier* | Wild boar |
| *Saucisson* | Sausage |
| *Sel* | Salt |
| *Soup Corse* | Thick or thin soup, with or without meat, anything goes! |
| *Sucre* | Sugar |
| *Thé/thé au lait* | Black/white tea |
| *Thon* | Tuna |
| *Vin blanc/rouge* | White/red wine |

**Lazy trekker's French**

*'Bonjour', 'merci'* and *'s'il vous plaît'* will get you a long way!

Hello *Bonjour*! (A standard greeting, which is useful everywhere you go. For instance, on entering a refuge or bar, greet all present with this.)

Please, a bed/a meal/a beer *S'il vous plaît, un lit/un repas/une bièra* (the simplest and politest way of dealing with requests and needs)

How much? Thank you! *Combien? Merci!* (keep it polite and simple!)

Goodbye *Au revoir*

See you later *À tout à l'heure* (as English 'toodleloo'!)

The bigger the word is in English, the more likely the French word is to be similar! And, whatever you say, be polite...

| PRICE LIST SEEN OUTSIDE THE CAFÉ LA PETIT SYRAH IN NICE | |
|---|---|
| 'Un café' | €7 |
| 'Un café, s'il vous plaît' | €4.25 |
| 'Bonjour, un café, s'il vous plaît' | €1.40 |

## Topographical glossary

| Corsican | French | English |
|---|---|---|
| *Bocca/foce* | *col* | gap/saddle |
| *Caminu* | *sentier* | path |
| *Capu* | *sommet* | summit |
| *Furesta* | *forêt* | forest |
| *Funtana* | *source* | spring |
| *Lavu* | *lac* | lake |

| Corsican | French | English |
|----------|--------|---------|
| *Monte* | *mont/montagne* | mountain |
| *Pianu* | *plateau* | plateau |
| *Pozzi* | *puits* | pools |
| *Punta* | *pointe* | peak |
| *Serra* | *crête* | ridge/crest |
| *Valdu* | *vallée* | valley |

# APPENDIX E
*Useful contacts*

**Government**
Corsica is a 'Collectivité Territoriale' of France, and is divided into two 'Départements', with the northern half of the island being Haute-Corse and the southern half Corse-du-Sud:

Collectivité Territoriale de Corse
www.corse.fr

Département de la Haute-Corse
www.haute-corse.fr

Département de la Corse-du-Sud
www.corsedusud.fr

**Tourist information**
For general information about the island, check Visit Corsica, www.visit-corsica.com. For specific enquiries, contact tourist information offices in the following towns:

**Bastia**
tel 04 95 54 20 40
www.bastia-tourisme.com

**Ajaccio**
tel 04 95 51 53 03
www.ajaccio-tourisme.com

**Calvi**
tel 04 95 65 16 67
www.portail-corse-balagne.fr

**Porto Vecchio**
tel 04 95 70 09 58
www.ot-portovecchio.com

**Corte**
tel 04 95 46 26 70
www.corte-tourisme.com

**Ponte Leccia**
tel 04 95 47 70 97

**GR20 and Parc Natural Régional de Corse (PNRC)**
For PNRC information and online booking of PNRC refuges

www.pnr.corsica

For up-to-date information about the GR20 and important notices, see the PNRC blog
randoblogpnrc.blogspot.co.uk

To discuss the GR20, compare notes with trekkers, or find a trekking partner, see Corsica for Hikers
http://corsica.forhikers.com/forum

To study detailed online IGN mapping of the GR20 at a variety of scales, see Géoportail
www.geoportail.gouv.fr

## Getting to Corsica

### Overland and ferries
Eurolines
www.eurolines.com

Eurostar
www.eurostar.com

Corsica Linea
www.corsicalinea.com

La Méridionale
www.lameridionale.fr

Corsica Ferries
www.corsica-ferries.fr

Moby Lines
www.mobylines.fr

### Airports, bus and taxi transfers
### Bastia
Airport
www.bastia.aeroport.fr

Airport bus, Société des Autobus Bastiais
tel 04 95 31 06 65
www.bastiabus.com

Airport taxis,
Les Taxis de l'Aéroport
tel 04 95 36 04 65
www.corsica-taxis.com

### Calvi
Airport
www.calvi.aeroport.fr

Airport taxis
Radio Taxis Calvais
tel 04 95 65 30 36

### Ajaccio
Airport
www.2a.cci.fr/Aeroport-Napoleon-Bonaparte-Ajaccio.html

Airport bus
TCA Bus
tel 04 95 23 29 41
http://capa-bus-tca.locbus.fr

(Also airport taxis by several operators)

### Figari
Airport
www.2a.cci.fr/Aeroport-Figari-Sud-Corse.html

Airport bus
Transports Rossi
tel 04 95 71 00 11

Airport taxi
tel 06 17 77 37 96

### Selected airlines
Air France
www.airfrance.com

Air Corsica
www.aircorsica.com

Easyjet
www.easyjet.com

Flybe
www.flybe.com

Ryanair
www.ryanair.com

Lufthansa
www.lufthansa.com

Eurowings
www.eurowings.com

## Getting around Corsica

### Railway
The railway, operated by Chemins de Fer de La Corse, www.cf-corse.fr, could prove particularly useful at Vizzavona, roughly halfway along the GR20, especially as the village no longer has bus services. Information from stations at:

**Ajaccio**
tel 04 95 23 11 03

**Bastia**
tel 04 95 32 80 61

**Calvi**
tel 04 95 65 00 61

**Corte**
tel 04 95 46 00 97

**Île Rousse**
tel 04 95 60 00 50

### Buses serving the GR20
For general 'unofficial' information and timetables:

Corsicabus
www.corsicabus.org

For specific information about bus services relevant to the GR20:

**Bastia-Calvi and Calvi-Calenzana**
Beaux Voyages
tel 04 95 65 11 35 or 04 95 65 08 26
www.corsicar.com

**Ascu Stagnu-Ponte Leccia**
Corsica Giru
tel 07 60 65 03 02 or 06 03 61 40 14
(and also Ascu Stagnu-Calasima if the Cirque de la Solitude is closed)

**Castel di Verghio-Albertacce-Corte**
Autocars Cortenais
tel 04 95 46 02 12
tel 04 95 46 22 89 or 06 22 66 52 39
www.autocars-cortenais-corse.fr
(and also the Corte-Bergeries de Grotelle navette service)

**Cozzano-Zicavo-Ajaccio**
Autocars Santoni
tel 04 95 22 64 44 or 04 95 24 51 56

**Bavella-Ajaccio/Porto Vecchio**
Autocars Balesi Evasion
tel 04 95 70 15 55
www.balesievasion.com

**Bavella-Ajaccio**
Ricci Marcel Transports
tel 04 95 78 86 30
www.transports-voyageurs-ajaccio.fr

**Conca-Ste Lucie de Porto Vecchio**
Navette service
tel 04 95 71 46 55

**Ste Lucie de Porto Vecchio-Porto Vecchio/Bastia**
Les Rapides Bleus Corsicatours
tel 04 95 31 03 79 or 04 95 20 20 20
www.rapides-bleus.com

**Porto Vecchio-Ajaccio**
Eurocorse Voyages
tel 04 95 21 06 30
www.eurocorse.com

### Taxis
One taxi company specifically offers GR20 pick-ups and drop-offs, as well as baggage transfers, operating from Ponte Leccia: Taxi Corse
tel 04 95 48 24 74 or 06 33 09 82 07
www.taxi-corse.fr

Other taxi operators are available from the following places on or near the GR20:

**Calenzana**
Calenzana Taxis
tel 04 95 62 77 80 or 06 08 16 53 65

**Pietra**
Jean-Charles Antolini
tel 04 95 48 01 97

**Albertacce**
Francois Luciani
tel 04 95 48 08 17 or Françoise Luciani
tel 04 95 48 04 07

**Corte**
Michel Salviani
tel 06 03 49 15 24 or Thérèse Feracci
tel 04 95 61 01 17

**Sagone/Soccia**
Luc Canale
tel 06 07 49 71 09 or 06 07 25 90 19

**Vivario/Tattone**
Taxi Alain
tel 04 95 47 23 17

**Bavella**
Jean Francois Crispi
tel 04 95 78 41 26 or 06 07 58 17 98

**Conca**
Navette service from Gîte d'Étape La Tonnelle
tel 04 95 71 46 55

**Weather forecast**
Weather forecasts (météos) can also be obtained from the gardiens at the PNRC refuges.

Météo France
tel 08 99 71 02 20
www.meteofrance.com

**Organisations offering mountain insurance**
British Mountaineering Council (BMC)
www.thebmc.co.uk/insurance

Austrian Alpine Club (AAC)
www.aacuk.org.uk and click on Benefits

**Emergencies**
There are separate telephone numbers for each of the emergency services, and it is possible to call direct for mountain rescue (PGHM), but if in doubt about which service to call, use the standard European emergency number 112.

Police (*Gendarmerie*), tel 17

Ambulance (*Samu*), tel 15

Fire Service (*Pompiers*), tel 18

European emergency number, tel 112

PGHM (*Peleton de Gendarmerie de Haute Montagne*), tel 04 95 61 13 95

VHF Emergency Canal E, 161.300 MHz

# APPENDIX F
*The Cirque de la Solitude*

**The Glory Days**

When the GR20 was initially planned, back in the 1970s, one of the biggest problems was how to get past Monte Cinto, the highest mountain in Corsica. It took several attempts before a route was pieced together through the Cirque de la Solitude, also known as e Cascettoni. Boulder-choked gullies and steep, bare rock lay on the western flank of Punta Minuta, between the Col Perdu and Bocca Minuta.

Even when a route had been finalised, it needed careful marking in order to keep trekkers on course through remarkably complex terrain. It was less of a trodden path, and more of a series of choreographed manoeuvres, requiring the use of arms and legs, strength, agility and a head for heights. It quickly became apparent that safety aids needed to be installed, including an 8-rung iron ladder to avoid having to climb overhanging rock, and a series of chains to provide security on steep slopes of rock. Even with the safety aids, it was common for some trekkers to lose their nerve and refuse to move in some places, causing long tailbacks of irate trekkers to form.

In time, the reputation of the Cirque became formidable. Descriptions of it were enough to cause some trekkers to believe they would never be able to complete the GR20. Others were keen to rise to the challenge, but there were always a few who quietly abandoned the trek when fear of what lay ahead got the better of them. Of those who traversed the Cirque, a few would vow never to return, but most would emerge from its rocky confines with a feeling of elation and pride. Those were the glory days of the Cirque de la Solitude, when it was an integral part of the GR20. It was a classic mountain day and regarded as a rite of passage.

**Disaster Strikes**

On 10 June 2015, despite a bad weather forecast having been announced, several trekkers set off to traverse the Cirque de la Solitude. By all accounts, the severity of the rainfall during the day was worse than most people could recall in the mountains. As the trekkers made their way through the Cirque, gullies that were normally dry became furious torrents of water, but there was a greater danger lurking above.

High on the slopes of Punta Minuta, a large patch of snow lay on top of a compacted mass of boulders and rubble, which itself lay on top of very steep rock. The torrential rain, streaming down the cliffs and gullies of the Cirque, made the snow become sodden, heavy and unstable, as well as lubricating the rock and rubble beneath it. Without any warning, the snow and rubble suddenly tore loose and came down as an unstoppable landslide. At this point, several trekkers were making their way up towards Bocca Minuta, hanging on safety chains on bare rock, with nowhere to run or hide. Seven were killed and many more were injured. It was the worst accident ever to occur on the GR20.

Word quickly got out that there had been a disaster, and rescuers were rapidly deployed to the scene, with helicopter relays flying back and forth. The emergency services and PNRC authorities, in consultation with Corsica's government officials, declared the Cirque de la Solitude closed the following day. It took days to establish how many had been killed, and weeks before the last body was dug from the rubble. The Cirque, which had been an adventure playground for decades, was now being regarded as a graveyard.

A geologist was commissioned to enter the Cirque and report on its future safety. He concluded that several more tons of rock and rubble remained poised in an unstable state above the Cirque, and recommended another inspection in 2016. The closure notice remained in force, and to date, the rock and rubble remains ready to fall.

### The Variant Route

In order to keep trekkers moving, a series of daily shuttle buses were quickly put in place, carrying passengers between Ascu Stagnu and Calasima. The village of Calasima is within easy walking distance of the Auberge U Vallone, on the GR20. It was an expensive bus service, but throughout the summer of 2015, hundreds of trekkers were willing to pay the price in order to keep their trek on track.

By the middle of June, PNRC staff looked at the possibility of re-routing the GR20 to avoid the Cirque de la Solitude altogether. There was only one practical route, which involved crossing the shoulder of Monte Cinto, taking the route much higher than it had ever been in the past. It was quickly waymarked as a 'variant', no doubt in the hope that the Cirque would re-open in the future. Big noticeboards were installed explaining the new arrangement. Rocky parts were later secured with a number of safety chains. The route was walked and checked for this edition of the guide, and previously vague paths were suddenly becoming much more well-trodden.

The first trekkers on the variant route gave mixed reports. Some found it very difficult, while others really enjoyed the experience of a high mountain traverse. It didn't take long before hundreds of trekkers were following the route, including individuals and large groups. Several trekkers were keen to take the opportunity to include the summit of Monte Cinto, which is commendable, so the summit is now much busier than it used to be. It goes without saying that clear weather was essential for a safe and enjoyable trek, and the shuttle buses remained in operation throughout the summer of 2015. As the season drew to a close, a big question mark remained over the future of the Cirque de la Solitude.

### Re-routing the GR20

By the end of February 2016, announcements began to be made about the future course of the GR20. It was declared that the Cirque de la Solitude was no longer to be part of the route, and furthermore all safety aids would be removed, along with all the intricate waymarking. The 'variant' route that had been marked over the shoulder of Monte Cinto was declared to be the 'main' route. In fact, it is now the only route for the GR20 between Ascu Stagnu and the Refuge de Tighjettu.

Hardy mountain walkers have climbed Monte Cinto from Ascu Stagnu for decades, and a route up the mountain and back the same way was included for many years in previous editions of this guide. The descent in the opposite direction, to the Refuge de Tighjettu and Auberge U Vallone, is a splendid route with exceptional views in clear weather. However, because of its height and exposure, it is definitely not a route to follow in bad weather, and especially if there is snow and ice on the ground.

### The Cirque Today

Anyone tempted to make their own way through the Cirque de la Solitude should bear a number of things in mind. First and foremost, there remains an unstable mass of rock and rubble, poised above a slope where it would be impossible to escape in the event of a landslide. Even a single falling rock could kill instantly.

Without its safety chains, and especially without the 8-rung ladder to negotiate an overhanging rock, any traverse of the Cirque should be regarded more as rock-climbing, rather than trekking. Without any waymarking, anyone unfamiliar with the place would experience great difficulty finding a way through. When the Cirque was traversed on a daily basis each summer, the rock slabs were generally kept free of debris. Without frequent traffic, those slabs are already covered in stony debris that acts like ball-bearings underfoot. Helmets, ropes and climbing equipment would need to be used, but there is absolutely no way to protect against landslides or rock-falls. Every so often, a trekker has disregarded advice and attempted to pass through the Cirque de la Solitude. Some have become hopelessly lost, even for several days, before being rescued.

It should be added that the author does not recommend that anyone should traverse the Cirque de la Solitude, without first being a competent climber, being aware of the many risks, and thinking very carefully about whether it would be fair to expect someone else to risk their life if it all went wrong and a rescue was required. Using the route description from previous editions of this guidebook is most unwise, because the description relied on the safety aids and spotting the clear waymarking. With these now gone, the route description is worthless and should not be used.

The Cirque de la Solitude is no longer part of the GR20. There are many trekkers who would be relieved to hear that. Others might be disappointed, but the new route is an excellent mountain traverse. Those who have already completed a traverse of the Cirque in the past may relish the memories, but now it is time to bid it farewell.

# NOTES

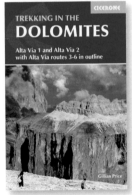
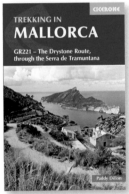

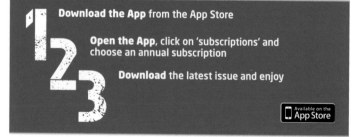

# LISTING OF CICERONE GUIDES

## SCOTLAND
Backpacker's Britain:
    Northern Scotland
Ben Nevis and Glen Coe
Cycling in the Hebrides
Great Mountain Days in
    Scotland
Mountain Biking in Southern
    and Central Scotland
Mountain Biking in West and
    North West Scotland
Not the West Highland Way
    Scotland
Scotland's Best Small Mountains
Scotland's Far West
Scotland's Mountain Ridges
Scrambles in Lochaber
The Ayrshire and Arran
    Coastal Paths
The Border Country
The Cape Wrath Trail
The Great Glen Way
The Great Glen Way Map
    Booklet
The Hebridean Way
The Hebrides
The Isle of Mull
The Isle of Skye
The Skye Trail
The Southern Upland Way
The Speyside Way
The Speyside Way Map Booklet
The West Highland Way
Walking Highland Perthshire
Walking in Scotland's Far North
Walking in the Angus Glens
Walking in the Cairngorms
Walking in the Ochils, Campsie
    Fells and Lomond Hills
Walking in the Pentland Hills
Walking in the Southern
    Uplands
Walking in Torridon
Walking Loch Lomond and
    the Trossachs
Walking on Arran
Walking on Harris and Lewis
Walking on Jura, Islay
    and Colonsay
Walking on Rum and the
    Small Isles
Walking on the Orkney and
    Shetland Isles
Walking on Uist and Barra
Walking the Corbetts Vol 1
Walking the Corbetts Vol 2
Walking the Galloway Hills
Walking the Munros Vol 1
Walking the Munros Vol 2
West Highland Way Map
    Booklet

Winter Climbs Ben Nevis and
    Glen Coe
Winter Climbs in the Cairngorms

## NORTHERN ENGLAND TRAILS
Hadrian's Wall Path
Hadrian's Wall Path Map Booklet
Pennine Way Map Booklet
The Coast to Coast Walk
The Coast to Coast Map Booklet
The Dales Way
The Pennine Way

## LAKE DISTRICT
Cycling in the Lake District
Great Mountain Days in the
    Lake District
Lake District Winter Climbs
Lake District:
    High Level and Fell Walks
Lake District:
    Low Level and Lake Walks
Lakeland Fellranger
Mountain Biking in the
    Lake District
Scafell Pike
Scrambles in the Lake District
    – North
Scrambles in the Lake District
    – South
Short Walks in Lakeland
    Book 1: South Lakeland
Short Walks in Lakeland
    Book 2: North Lakeland
Short Walks in Lakeland
    Book 3: West Lakeland
Tour of the Lake District
Trail and Fell Running in the
    Lake District

## NORTH WEST ENGLAND
## AND THE ISLE OF MAN
Cycling the Pennine Bridleway
Isle of Man Coastal Path
The Lancashire Cycleway
The Lune Valley and Howgills
The Ribble Way
Walking in Cumbria's Eden
    Valley
Walking in Lancashire
Walking in the Forest of Bowland
    and Pendle
Walking on the Isle of Man
Walking on the West
    Pennine Moors
Walks in Lancashire
    Witch Country
Walks in Ribble Country
Walks in Silverdale and Arnside

## NORTH EAST ENGLAND,
## YORKSHIRE DALES
## AND PENNINES

Cycling in the Yorkshire Dales
Great Mountain Days in
    the Pennines
Historic Walks in North Yorkshire
Mountain Biking in the
    Yorkshire Dales
South Pennine Walks
St Oswald's Way and
    St Cuthbert's Way
The Cleveland Way and the
    Yorkshire Wolds Way
The Cleveland Way Map Booklet
The North York Moors
The Reivers Way
The Teesdale Way
Walking in County Durham
Walking in Northumberland
Walking in the North Pennines
Walking in the Yorkshire Dales:
    North and East
Walking in the Yorkshire Dales:
    South and West
Walks in Dales Country
Walks in the Yorkshire Dales

## WALES AND WELSH BORDERS
Glyndwr's Way
Great Mountain Days
    in Snowdonia
Hillwalking in Shropshire
Hillwalking in Wales – Vol 1
Hillwalking in Wales – Vol 2
Mountain Walking in Snowdonia
Offa's Dyke Path
Offa's Dyke Map Booklet
Pembrokeshire Coast Path
    Map Booklet
Ridges of Snowdonia
Scrambles in Snowdonia
The Ascent of Snowdon
The Ceredigion and Snowdonia
    Coast Paths
The Pembrokeshire Coast Path
The Severn Way
The Snowdonia Way
The Wales Coast Path
The Wye Valley Walk
Walking in Carmarthenshire
Walking in Pembrokeshire
Walking in the Forest of Dean
Walking in the South
    Wales Valleys
Walking in the Wye Valley
Walking on the Brecon Beacons
Walking on the Gower
Welsh Winter Climbs

## DERBYSHIRE, PEAK DISTRICT
## AND MIDLANDS
Cycling in the Peak District
Dark Peak Walks
Scrambles in the Dark Peak

Walking in Derbyshire
White Peak Walks:
    The Northern Dales
White Peak Walks:
    The Southern Dales

## SOUTHERN ENGLAND

20 Classic Sportive Rides
    in South East England
20 Classic Sportive Rides
    in South West England
Cycling in the Cotswolds
Mountain Biking on the
    North Downs
Mountain Biking on the
    South Downs
North Downs Way Map Booklet
South West Coast Path Map
    Booklet – Minehead to St Ives
South West Coast Path Map
    Booklet – Plymouth to Poole
South West Coast Path Map
    Booklet – St Ives to Plymouth
Suffolk Coast and Heath Walks
The Cotswold Way
The Cotswold Way Map Booklet
The Great Stones Way
The Kennet and Avon Canal
The Lea Valley Walk
The North Downs Way
The Peddars Way and Norfolk
    Coast Path
The Pilgrims' Way
The Ridgeway Map Booklet
The Ridgeway National Trail
The South Downs Way
The South Downs Way
    Map Booklet
The South West Coast Path
The Thames Path
The Thames Path Map Booklet
The Two Moors Way
Walking in Cornwall
Walking in Essex
Walking in Kent
Walking in London
Walking in Norfolk
Walking in Sussex
Walking in the Chilterns
Walking in the Cotswolds
Walking in the Isles of Scilly
Walking in the New Forest
Walking in the North
    Wessex Downs
Walking in the Thames Valley
Walking on Dartmoor
Walking on Guernsey
Walking on Jersey
Walking on the Isle of Wight
Walking the Jurassic Coast
Walks in the South Downs
    National Park

For full information on all our
guides, books and eBooks,
visit our website:
**www.cicerone.co.uk**.

## Walking – Trekking – Mountaineering – Climbing – Cycling

**Over 40 years, Cicerone have built up an outstanding collection of over 300 guides, inspiring all sorts of amazing adventures.**

Every guide comes from extensive exploration and research by our expert authors, all with a passion for their subjects. They are frequently praised, endorsed and used by clubs, instructors and outdoor organisations.

All our titles can now be bought as **e-books**, **ePubs** and **Kindle** files and we also have an online magazine – **Cicerone Extra** – with features to help cyclists, climbers, walkers and trekkers choose their next adventure, at home or abroad.

Our website shows any **new information** we've had in since a book was published. Please do let us know if you find anything has changed, so that we can publish the latest details. On our **website** you'll also find great ideas and lots of detailed information about what's inside every guide and you can buy **individual routes** from many of them online.

It's easy to keep in touch with what's going on at Cicerone by getting our monthly **free e-newsletter**, which is full of offers, competitions, up-to-date information and topical articles. You can subscribe on our home page and also follow us on **Facebook** and **Twitter** or dip into our **blog**.

**Cicerone – the very best guides for exploring the world.**

## CICERONE

Juniper House, Murley Moss, Oxenholme Road, Kendal, Cumbria LA9 7RL
Tel: 015395 62069  info@cicerone.co.uk
**www.cicerone.co.uk** and **www.cicerone-extra.com**